A guide to TV's Wonder Woman and Isis

Book 4 in the BRBTV fact book series

Billie Rae Bates

BRBglobal

Copyright © 2012 by Billie Rae Bates. All rights reserved.

ISBN-13: 978-1480250468
ISBN-10: 1480250465
First print edition, evolved in part from BRBTV material originally released to Amazon's Kindle platform in 2011.

No part of this work may be reproduced or transmitted in any form or by any means, electronic or mechanical, including photocopying, recording or by any information storage or retrieval system without written permission from the author, except for inclusion of brief quotations in a review.

This work has not been approved, licensed or sponsored by any entity involved in creating or producing the "Wonder Woman" or "The Secrets of Isis" TV series.

"Wonder Woman" the TV series is a property of Warner Bros. Television (a division of Warner Bros. Inc.). The Wonder Woman character and related indicia are trademarks of DC Comics. "The Secrets of Isis" TV show is a property of Entertainment Rights, PLC / Classic Media. The artwork of the comic books depicted here is copyrighted by DC Comics and Bluewater Productions. All rights reserved. BRBTV makes no claims, expressed or otherwise, on the trademarks / properties of "Wonder Woman" and "The Secrets of Isis" or any related trademarks / properties discussed in this book.

Wonder Woman created by William Moulton Marston.

Cover art by Dale Cuthbertson.

Where not otherwise noted, photography / screenshots by Billie Rae Bates. Author photo on the back cover courtesy of ComicsContinuum.com.

Dedicated to my cousin Markita, a true superchick with the power to earn a bachelor's degree, build a successful career serving humanity as a schoolteacher, sustain a longterm marriage, stay beautiful, *and* shoot a seven-point buck.

Well, OK, that was the case up to presstime of this book, which was the second day of deer season 2012. Make that — *ahem* — nine-point buck.

Seriously.

To see other books and reports available from BRBTV,
check out the home page at
BRBTV.com

To contact Billie Rae Bates, email
BillieRaeBates@yahoo.com
or visit
BillieRae.com

SUPERCHICKS: A GUIDE TO TV'S WONDER WOMAN AND ISIS

Contents

Foreword

Wonder Woman

Background: *As cultural icons go, she's wondrous* 13
Cast 39
Characters 57
Episodes 61
Credits 149
A Comic Comparison 153
Fun & Useless Information 159
And Now a Word From ...
   - S. Pearl Sharp: *Death by sliding door? Not when he's around!* 163
   - Anne Collins-Ludwick: *Scripting an Amazon princess* 168
   - Jeannie Epper: *Daughter of a stunt dynasty carves her own niche.* . 173
Birthdays 187
Merchandise 189

THE SECRETS OF ISIS

Background: *Blazing a trail for little girls everywhere* 205
Cast 233
Characters 237
Episodes 241
Credits 275
A Comic Comparison 277
And Now a Word From ...
   - Brian Cutler: *Nowadays, this teacher ... well, teaches!.* 283
   - Joanna Pang Atkins: *For this positive gal, life dances on.* 289
   - Andy Mangels: *Bringing it all together for future generations.* 293
Birthdays 301
Merchandise 303

Acknowledgments 309

SUPERCHICKS: A GUIDE TO TV'S WONDER WOMAN AND ISIS

Foreword

It was a changing world.

Women had just gotten the right to vote. Hemlines were creeping farther above the ankle. The men had been called to war, and it was time for Rosie the Riveter. And so much more.

From the brain of an accomplished Harvard grad — a well-known psychologist and author — came a new vision. He was a little older than many of the others working in comics, a learned scholar very familiar with Greek and Roman mythology. He saw the modern women around him, intelligent women like his law-degree-holding wife, and he saw the limited options they still faced, even as they were stepping into new societal roles.

So he gave them a new inspiration.

This is the story of one of the superchicks of this book, the one who really paved the way for the other. Because even though Isis made it to the live-action TV screen for her own show a couple months earlier, Wonder Woman was really where it began.

Now feminists, please don't be offended by my use of the term superchick. Because it's all about power. And it's in our femininity that we hold so much of our power.

William Moulton Marston knew this when he created the first real female superhero. She was powerful, yet she wore bracelets. She was iron-willed, yet she wore a skirt. She was rock-solid, yet she had the beauty of Aphrodite.

And — *gasp!* — she had no use for a boyfriend.

By the time these two television shows were rolling into my little-girl field of vision in the 1970s, women's lib was old news. Not everybody at school had a mom who stayed at home; some "worked out," as my grandma used to call it (and she briefly worked out, too, in the '20s). But as a female species, we still had a ways to go.

Cue the white tennis dress.

And the eagle-clad corset.

It may seem crazy, but it's the way we wanted it back then. It was the very message we were hungry for. The smart chick who was also sexy. The brains … the legs, the breasts. Because really, therein lay the power! Sorry, Gloria Steinem, but it was like we could have it both ways. It was like the sex kitten got smart. Or the bra-burner shook her tail a little.

Both Wonder Woman and Isis had everything. This was not Jennifer Marlowe on "WKRP in Cincinnati." This was not the prim and brainy Miss Beadle on "Little House on the Prairie." This was not sensible, modest June Cleaver or loopy Lucy Ricardo. This was *clearly* a hybrid.

And speaking of Ms. Steinem, it is said that she was almost laughed out of the boardroom when she proposed Wonder Woman for the cover of the very first issue of Ms. Magazine. She knew exactly what she was doing, now didn't she?

So did all of us little girls of the '70s.

"William Moulton Marston was giving us permission to believe in real goddesses," says artist and writer Trina Robbins on the DVD extras for the 2010 "Wonder Woman" animated movie. "Do you know how empowering that is?"

Gloria Steinem might have gotten laughed at, but she won! The very first issue of Ms. Magazine, July 1972, iconic to this day.

Dan DiDio of DC Comics says, "She is constantly a trailblazer. Wonder Woman is just as relevant today as when she was created. ... Even though so much progress has been made on the rights issues since the time of the '40s, she still stands as the ultimate symbol of equality."

Lauren Montgomery, director of the "Wonder Woman" animated feature, has this take: "Wonder Woman's always been the strongest of the female DC characters, and so her popularity definitely helped pave the way for other female characters."

Artist Paul Davison's tribute to Lynda Carter's Wonder Woman. Image courtesy of Paul Davison.

The story behind the scenes of these two TV shows has already been told well in other books, magazine articles and web features. What BRBTV offers you here is a fun reference guide — a place where you can look up the actor who played that obscure character in that one episode, or who's the long-lost child of whom, and other assorted little facts and such. The BRBTV fact book series follows a formula — cast list, character guide, episode guide and so on, in an easy-to-page-through format that you can have at your side while you're watching the show.

So grab that golden lasso, and let's get started ...

BRB

October 2012

Our Superchicks, nowadays: Lynda Carter backstage at the 2009 The Heart Truth's Red Dress Collection Fashion Show (photo from Wikimedia Commons), and Joanna Cameron in Hawaii in 2009 (photo by Kendale Photography, courtesy of Joanna Cameron).

Wonder Woman

> **❝** I think that what is unique about Wonder Woman is her combination of strength and beauty and brains. **❞**
> — Hugh Hefner

> **❝** That hit the cultural American zeitgeist like a ton of bricks. **❞**
> — Gregory Noveck, executive producer of the 2010 animated "Wonder Woman" feature, on the casting of Lynda Carter in the '70s TV show

Wonder Woman

As cultural icons go, she's wondrous

She certainly was no stranger to tiaras.

Beauty queen Lynda Carter, crowned Miss World USA in 1972. Did she have any idea that just three years later she would trade the jeweled tiara for simple gold — albeit with a ruby star — as the world's most famous female superhero?

Well, actually, Carter believes she was destined to play Wonder Woman.

Created in 1941 by William Moulton Marston, the red-white-and-blue-clad DC Comics superhero — first appearing in All Star Comics No. 8 in December 1941 — seemed the ideal chick role. ABC had attempted to bring Wonder Woman to the small screen with March 1974's pilot starring Cathy Lee Crosby. Carter, more than familiar with the character, had auditioned for that pilot but didn't get a call back.

It was probably a good thing. The ill-fated Warner Bros. production is not remembered fondly among fans. The pilot was a departure from the hero's comic book roots, depicting this blond female in more of a secret

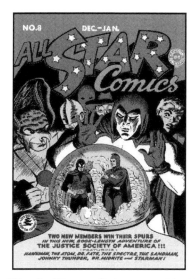 

Wonder Woman first appeared in All Star Comics No. 8 in December 1941, then a month later she got her first cover in Sensation No. 1.

agent drama than a superhero story. She was skilled — she could toss a guy around a room and perform a few acrobatics. But she was hollow and terminally serene, and she had no real powers.

Plus, many fans saw her costume as a big fat zero: red collared minidress with starry blue sleeves, blue spandex tights and matching blue boots. She wore a golden belt and bracelets, and she did retrieve a golden lasso from her belt, but by and large, the traditional elements of the true Wonder Woman of the comics were sorely missing. She mentioned the invisible plane, though it was not shown (and no, that's not a joke).

And she actually wasn't the first attempt to bring Wonder Woman to the small screen. Linda Harrison of "Planet of the Apes" portrayed our hero in an unaired 1967 screen test before the Cathy Lee Crosby TV movie aired. It was a promotional short produced by Batman's William Dozier as a prospective series for Warner Bros.

Angie Bowie (whose modeling name was Jipp Jones) also did a photo shoot for the second attempt at a Wonder Woman show. WonderWomanMuseum.com elaborates: Bowie's audition was mentioned in the February 11, 1974 issue of Newsweek, in which it was reported that Bowie had been considered for the role of Wonder

Woman for an upcoming ABC-TV movie but lost the part for her refusal to wear a bra.

At any rate, it was back to the drawing board. This time they got it right.

"The problem is, when you're creating myth, everyone has their own vision of that myth," explains Douglas S. Cramer, executive producer, in the DVD extras. "So to sit with a director, myself as a producer, with Warner Bros. executives, and then the network executives, and come close to everyone's feeling about Wonder Woman was a very difficult task."

It was a challenge not just in the construction of the character, but also in the casting, he says.

"Whoever we found seemed to have part of the whole equation. They looked good in clothes, or they were a wonderful actress. But usually if they looked good in clothes, they couldn't act. Or if they were a good actress, they approached the job like a lady truck driver."

Carter is forthright in admitting she was green at the time, at this tender age of 24. Cramer had to fight to cast her.

"Everyone wanted the Wonder Woman — the ideal Wonder Woman — to have a certain resemblance obviously to the cartoon character," Cramer says. "That we needed a large woman, statuesque woman, a buxom woman, and an angelic face. And beyond all that, we needed someone that could play it, could act and sustain a television movie and a series hopefully that would run for a long time."

So with a great sigh of relief, Carter got the gig.

"You cast me against all odds in this," she tells Cramer in her commentary with him on the pilot episode in the DVD extras. "I think it's a great story. I had 25 dollars left in my bank account when I got the call from my agent that I got 'Wonder Woman.' ... I called my parents. I really just called some people and walked around this apartment where I was barely paying my rent just happy, just so excited that I was fulfilling my dreams."

It was the beginning of a legacy Carter probably couldn't have imagined at the time, and it was certainly a whirlwind tour.

"I immediately went in to Donfeld for fittings," Carter continues in the commentary, "and immediately started in talking with you and meeting people. ... From the screen test to the call seemed like it was a year. I called my agent every day — 'have you heard, have you heard, have you heard.' At the time there were really no parts for women my age."

And almost as important as the choice of actress was the choice of costume. This is one of the most recognizable comic book costumes ever, after all.

"Wonder Woman was that outfit, to begin with, and it had to be perfect," Cramer says. "I can't tell you how many times we looked at fabrics, looked at different cuts, how they looked on Lynda, how they moved and operated. But we were there every day, getting it right."

Carter still owns one of her Wonder Woman costumes and says she's on the lookout for another so she can give one to each of her two children. "The way I felt the first time I wore this was actually pretty darn good. I was a little uncomfortable with the bullet breasts, you know? That was a little odd to me. But I remember in the very beginning they put in a slant board, because there were bones in the front and when I sat down these whale bones would crimp, so they had a slat board for me, but later on they took those bones out so I could just sit normally."

Carter, who jokes that she did that "bullet breast" thing long before Madonna did, comments in her DVD interviews on how the costume evolved.

"When Donfeld redid the costume after the first season, they weren't quite as pronounced," she says of those much-noticed eagle wings. "Don't forget this was the ban-the-bra time, this was sexual freedom time, this was bikinis and midriffs. And I wasn't really thinking about being sexy."

Thus, ABC's reworked "Wonder Woman" debuted on November 7, 1975 with the 90-minute pilot "The New Original Wonder Woman." After the pilot, the next two episodes (sometimes called "specials" but considered to be a continuation of the show's first season) aired in April

1976, then continued with the fourth episode the following October. The show aired new episodes a couple months into 1977 to complete the 13-part first season.

This first season on ABC really returned Wonder Woman to her 1940s roots, not only setting her in the Nazi era in which she debuted on the printed page, but also utilizing various comic book touches, such as the colorful panels of the musical intro, all awash in reds and blues, as well as the comic placecards giving time and location context throughout the story, and the flurry of cartoon star icons between scenes. Black-and-white newsreel footage in the pilot episode lent an authentic touch.

A little backstory in the pilot episode set the scene: Queen Hippolyta (only referred to as the Queen and initially played by Cloris Leachman) has set up the Amazons on Paradise Island to flee the enslavement and corruption of evil men. Women, she explains, were once slaves of men in ancient Rome and Greece, and she refuses to let that happen again. It's

The first season of the series returned our hero to her 1940s roots, as shown in the art from the first-season DVD set, released in 2004.

clear there's a little immortality going on here with these females. But, the Queen explains to her daughter Diana, if she leaves the island she could revert to a mortal human being. The golden belt, however, allows Diana to retain her "cunning and strength" away from the island of the Amazons. Her bracelets fend off bullets, and her lasso commands truth from those it encircles. Some powerful stuff she has, as she returns the recuperating Steve Trevor, shot down over Paradise Island, to his native U.S.

Though Diana's mission in the pilot episode was clearly outlined, what wasn't clearly explained was why she was allowed to stay in the United States, becoming Steve's new secretary, rather than returning to Paradise Island. That didn't come until several episodes later, when the action returned to Paradise Island (this time with Carolyn Jones of "The Addams Family" in the role of the Queen).

Lyle Waggoner, known at that point for his work on the '60s "Carol Burnett Show," seemed the perfect fit for Steven Leonard Trevor, Major, U.S. Air Corps. Not only was the handsome actor well over six feet tall to take on Carter's formidable height, his carriage and gentlemanly mannerisms resonated.

"Once Lyle read, we all knew he was our first choice," Cramer says.

The series in its first season was true to other elements of the original Wonder Woman lore. Take those bullet-repelling bracelets, for instance. They presented their own challenges.

"We had a really wonderful special effects man and property man, and after Donfeld designed the actual cuffs or the bracelets, they had to come up with how they could fire," Carter says. "So he came to me with the apparatus almost complete, and he wired almost like matchsticks in the front where the stars were, these stars on the bracelets, and within those stars there were some wires. And those wires went up the back of my wrist and into the palm of my hand. So I had to have my hands closed in order to fire. There were three different buttons. They perfected it over the years, but there was not much that they had to do. ... Occasionally we had a misfire and we had to redo it, and of course we had to change the bracelets out. We put the special effects bracelets on just before the stunt. ... It was pretty ingenious."

Also brought in for the series was the invisible plane (which had previously been seen, so to speak, on the small screen in 1973's animated "Super Friends" series, though referred to on that show as her "transparent plane"). But there is one element of the character's identity that was created on the show first and then crossed over.

The spin. *Oh*, the spin …

Carter explains in the special features for the first-season DVD set that the famous spin was her suggestion when the producers were looking for some way for Diana to change into her alter ego.

The spin evolved over the course of the show. At first, it was in slow motion, with the images of Diana Prince and Wonder Woman superimposing on each other during the transition. Wonder Woman would stop, now holding her Diana Prince attire in her arm, and check her belt and tiara before running off to save the day. Later, the spin sped up considerably, our heroine was no longer holding her Diana clothes at its completion, and a starburst was flashed over the transition (much easier, from a special-effects perspective!).

To everything a time … and a season!

During the first season, DC moved the Wonder Woman comics from the '70s to the '40s to match the series. Then the show moved from ABC to CBS, and from the Nazi era to a modern '70s setting. The comics again followed.

Whereas the comics originally had the character simply changing her clothes into Wonder Woman, in the '70s, she spun her lasso around her to transition. The comics then matched her TV full spin.

The second season with its modern setting launched on CBS in September 1977. For Carter, it was a welcome change.

"For me, I think I liked it better when we moved it up from the '40s into present-day, because I never wanted her to be sort of — for it to be tongue-in-cheek," the actress says.

Others seemed to agree.

"As I recall, the first season of 'Wonder Woman' was very tongue-in-cheek and cartoonish and probably, because of its WWII background, hard for the show's young, Friday night audience to relate to," series writer Anne Collins-Ludwick tells BRBTV.

Collins-Ludwick, who served as the executive story consultant for 24 episodes and story editor for 14 episodes, came along in this second season and tells us she's glad for that.

"The network and/or studio hoped to boost the show's ratings by modernizing the stories and changing the tone to be more fun and adventure/fantasy-oriented in a 'Wild Wild West' type of way," she says, "which was right up exec producer Bruce Lansbury's alley. In short, no, I would not've liked to have written for the first iteration of 'WW' — I'm not sure I would've 'gotten' it."

The show was now titled "The New Adventures of Wonder Woman," rather than "The New Original Wonder Woman," though nowadays all seasons are really just known as "Wonder Woman." Woven through the second season's scenes is certainly a maturity of not only storyline but also lead character. Diana Prince is no longer the secretary of Steve Trevor — this Steve is the original character's son in this modern setting, and Diana is an agent out in the field for the InterAgency Defense Command (IADC), with more responsibility and respect. The wild appreciation of American citizens for the superhero Wonder Woman has

The second season sent the Amazon princess ahead 30 years to (then!) modern times, and allowed her to branch out to a few extra outfits, like the diving outfit shown on the Season 2 DVD set.

followed her through the decades, however.

"I made a very specific choice to play her absolutely for real," Carter says in her DVD interviews. "That she believed that she was who she was, and she wasn't very impressed with her own abilities, because all her sisters on Paradise Island could do the same thing. And I really just wanted to play her for real. I believed in her. ... Wonder Woman didn't take herself all that seriously. She had a sense of herself that, other people fell all over themselves, and made fools of themselves when they saw her ... but she took herself and her powers as just an everyday occurrence."

And what powers they were. The show took some pretty great pains, for that era, to display the lead character's physical prowess. Though Carter had the desire to do her own stunts, and did some of them, the show heavily utilized professional stuntwomen like Jeannie Epper to stretch Wonder Woman's skill.

Getting physical

Epper, part of a four-generation family dynasty of Hollywood stunt artists, was featured in the 2004 documentary movie, "Double Dare" for her work on the "Wonder Woman" series. In her 60s then, she was still going strong and refused to retire. Not much has changed, years later. When BRBTV chatted with her via phone, she'd just done an explosion scene on CBS' "Criminal Minds."

Carter talks about the support Epper provided on the series.

"She helped me get comfortable in Wonder Woman's skin. She taught me," the actress says. "I think Jeannie Epper really saw me grow up."

For Epper, the show was a true career-cementer, but it had an impact on a personal level, as well.

"What I got out of it most was what Lynda showed, that whatever character she played, she played it smart," Epper tells BRBTV. "She wasn't just a comic book person. She thought things out. Of course, I knew her magical lasso was magical. But for me it was a turning point in my career. I never thought the photos we took with my camera the last day of the shoot would be the things that traveled around the world and made me the most famous stuntwoman. I had fun. I was tested daily on that show with the stunts. I think it was fun for every girl to have a superhero. She didn't have to punch everyone out; she thought things through. I think, the fact that we had a great relationship and still do. We bonded a lot."

Epper says it was a challenge keeping Carter on the sidelines for the stunts, particularly the fight work.

"We had to keep her wrangled down, because she was really good at doing the fight work and wanted to do it," Epper says. "She had those beautiful long legs. When you do a fight routine, it's like a dance routine. It's complicated beyond what you would think a fight would be. She always wanted to be a part of that. So we would let her. But not too much, because we couldn't let her get smashed in the face."

So Epper did just about everything for this superheroine except the gymnastics, skateboarding and motorbiking, which required a more specialized touch. Wonder Woman's motorcycle work, for instance, was done by Debbie Evans, Epper recalls.

"Debbie Evans, she's probably among the top stunt drivers in Hollywood," she says. "She's one of those girls we kinda took a chance on, and lo and behold, she did an amazing job. She's like 5 foot 2. It was kinda a funny story. We were looking for a girl who could do anything, driving, jumping, etc., and we couldn't find anyone Lynda's height who could do all those things. My brother knew someone. We hired her even though she was so small."

The gymnastics, such as in the episodes "Going, Going, Gone" and "Screaming Javelins" were done by Sandi Gross.

"I was her (Carter's) main double," Epper says, "and anytime they needed someone who had a specialty, we searched for someone who was good in that field. Sandi was a world-class gymnast."

Though Epper tells BRBTV that neither she nor Carter were ever really injured in the series, beyond a few bruises, there was a close call with the episode "The Deadly Dolphin," where our hero must stop a dolphin

This author's own Wonder Woman comics from the '70s. When the TV show made the jump to the modern times, the comics followed suit, returning our hero to the '70s.

trained for a suicide mission, strapped down with explosives and heading toward an oil tanker.

"The funny thing about that episode is that the major camera work was done at the water park down there — I think it was Sea World or Marineland. I don't even think it's there anymore," she says. "People used to come and watch the dolphins swim and the sharks swim. But when we filmed that, I started to lose my direction underwater. I don't know anything about drowning; I'd have to read about it. I think you get kind of lethargic, and you don't know where you are. The dolphin grabbed me by the arm and pulled me to the surface. That's a true story. He or she sensed I was in danger and actually took a hold of me and pulled me up, and the crew came and got me. They found that my body temperature had dropped dramatically. So that's the lesson to be learned — listen to your body."

Horseback riding such as in the two-parter "The Boy Who Knew Her Secret" came easy for Epper, though she says having to wear hosiery provided for a more slippery ride! ("We wore panty hose in those days," she quips.) But as you can imagine, that wasn't the only peril of the costume, when it came to stunts.

"We had to figure out how to keep that costume on," she muses. "They made the costumes with satin, and those stays; it was like a bustier, so when you jumped or moved, it would fold out. So it took a while for the wardrobe department to figure that out."

Collins-Ludwick tells BRBTV that the inspiration from the comics for the character's physical feats was somewhat tempered by more practical considerations.

"The comics provided us with parameters for Wonder Woman — the lasso, tiara, bracelets, her strength, speed, etc. — but for the more physical 'feats' a great deal depended on what could actually be produced and what would look cool on camera," Collins-Ludwick says. "As I recall, I think the first time Wonder Woman saved a falling person's life by catching them was in an episode I wrote (we did that stunt to death in the episodes that followed). In any case, I don't recall ever referring to the comics to come up with stunts for show — the stories, and our imaginations, usually dictated them."

As the new season evolved, that newfangled invention of the computer came into play, as the powerful and full-of-attitude IRAC began to help Steve and Diana bring in the bad guys, along with his roving, satellite-sort of doggie, "Rover." Steve now had a new secretary at the IADC, Eve, played by Saundra Sharp, now a director, filmmaker, dancer and poet who goes by S. Pearl Sharp.

"She was gorgeous and bright!" laughs Sharp to BRBTV when asked if there was any similarity between the actress and the character. More seriously, she says of her role on "Wonder Woman," "It was an interesting time, because along with a number of my colleagues that came out here from New York, we had done a lot of theater. Because of shows like 'Good Times' and 'The Jeffersons,' we felt there was going to be a lot of work for us. There was a sort of exodus here at the time. The unique thing about Eve is that she was a black woman but it was not referenced on the show. That was important."

Sharp enjoyed her time on the show. And she alludes to something touched on by Carter in her interviews for the "Double Dare" movie, that this former beauty queen was not in a great time of her personal life for much of the series. For one thing, Carter was in an unhappy marriage.

"It was good. It was a good show to work on," Sharp tells me, but adds, "It got interesting because of the politics. There was a period when sometimes she wouldn't show up, and then they would have to figure out something else to shoot for the day. At one time I had an inkling of what that was about, but I'll censor that."

But what was the iconic Lynda Carter like to work with, overall?

"She was kinda regular, when she was there," Sharp says. "There was no drama on the set, where I was concerned, or they were concerned. People were very professional. They did their lines. They were lovely. Once in a while with her not showing up, people were getting stressed out."

Throughout her time in the second season, Sharp had a rather sharp impression of Waggoner as he displayed the altogether-dignified Steve Trevor in suits furnished by Botany 500.

"He's lovely. A gentleman," she tells me. "I did have one incident on the set when I was going through the automatic doors (in the IADC offices) one day, and I don't know whether I wasn't paying attention, or the guy operating them wasn't, but the door came right down on my head. I was still walking through, and the door came down. And when I came to, Lyle was holding me in his arms with this worried look on his face, hoping that I was OK. He was a gentleman. ... Sometimes you're on sets where people are 'on' all the time, you know, when they're always in character, but that didn't seem to be the way on that set. People were sort of doing the job, getting the show done."

Collins-Ludwick elaborates further about the spirit of work behind the scenes of the show.

"I cannot over-stress how much of a collaborative effort it was (and no doubt still is) to come up with ideas and plots for 'WW' and all the other series I worked on afterwards," she tells us. "Everyone had a say, from the producers to the stars to the studio to the network, whether it was as simple as, 'Let's do a show we can shoot at Magic Mountain,' or so-and-so is willing to do a guest spot — let's do a show that exploits his/her assets. I'm not sure there's such a thing as a totally blank slate when it comes to TV writing, but it never bothered me — I always considered collaboration to come with the territory. And on 'WW,' I was fortunate to be working with Bruce Lansbury, who had a wonderful imagination and was always full of great ideas."

She continues, "Lyle was just happy to be doing the show and rarely had any kind of feedback for the writers, either positive or negative. Lynda would have suggestions and concerns every now and then, but she was never overbearing about it and never caused any problems."

Mego released a 12" Wonder Woman doll in different variations through the run of the show. As a child, BRB had this first-season version, complete with Diana Prince outfit (shown in another photo later in the book).

How much did Collins-Ludwick feel influenced by the actors' own nuances as she was working on these scripts, and, perhaps, how many episodes did it take her to get used to the particular actors' mannerisms and ways of presenting themselves?

"The main characters weren't exactly what you would call complex and they were cast accordingly," she tells us. "Lynda, bless her heart, was extremely new to acting, and I quickly learned it was wise not to give her huge speeches to memorize or long sentences to say. She tried her best but my gosh, she was young and inexperienced and under tremendous scrutiny and pressure and the whole situation was tough for her. She and I got along fine and I liked her — she had (and no doubt still has) a very good and kind heart."

The show coasted to a stop at the end of its third season. The episode "The Man Who Could Not Die," airing in August 1979, might seem a real bummer for fans. This episode was reportedly the last one produced, though it aired before the two-part series finale, "Phantom of the Roller Coaster." In "The Man Who Could Not Die," Waggoner was gone from the show's intro (and from the show), leaving just Carter listed with the episode's guest stars. The IRAC and Rover interplay was also a thing of the past. A new guy named Dale Hawthorn was established as Diana's boss in L.A., it was implied that Bret Cassiday would have a hand in the future action, and the spunky kid-around-the-office T. Burton Phipps III seemed to have the makings of a civilian sidekick.

So what gives, with all of that? All this setup, at the end of the series? What did we miss?! We pose the question to Collins-Ludwick.

"Sorry, but I really don't recall the precise genesis of the 'Man Who Could Not Die' episode, though it was obviously an attempt to retool the show and save it from cancellation," she says. "I do remember that either Lyle Waggoner wanted off the show or the powers-that-be wanted him off, but in any case, this was an attempt (no doubt spearheaded by the studio) to show the network what the series might be like if Steve Trevor left and Diana got to interact with some new, fresh characters. But the network didn't go for it and 'WW' became history."

The future of Wonder Woman

Carter expresses an interest, in her commentary for the pilot episode on the 2004 DVD, in an update of this Wonder Woman series, where the story of the years between 1979 and the present would be told. At the time her commentary was taped, plans were still afloat for a big-screen Wonder Woman feature, but the more-concrete plans for a new TV show would only come years later.

"The only thing Wonder Woman didn't have, and maybe they'll answer this in a movie, is she didn't have love in her life," Carter says. "She didn't have children. I would hope that that story would be told. That's such a huge part of womanhood. That's something we all have over Wonder Woman."

But Carter cautions about a new take on her beloved character: "I think there's a big trap in people in the past that have played superheroes, that they play a superhero when you don't need to. The costume and the action and all the rest of it takes care of it. That's why I think 'Spider-Man' was so successful," she says. "I think people want to be her. They want to be able to identify, and if she's too perfect, and you want to either be her friend or be her. And you have to be able to identify."

Cramer tells her in the DVD commentary, "For most people, Wonder Woman is Lynda Carter. The two of you, you're so identified with her, and she with you, it would be difficult to see anyone else play her."

Indeed, as plans began to solidify for the new TV pilot in early 2011, Adrienne Palicki was cast in that essentially unenviable role. As added pressure, after a controversial, headline-grabbing new "street" outfit was unveiled for Wonder Woman in the comics in 2010, it was decided the new garb would be utilized in the TV show. Initial shots of Palicki met with much response in March 2011, and it seemed the show's producers were on a bit of a test run with this, as the Internet exploded with fan criticism and speculation. Big on the list were the thoughts that the outfit was too "shiny" with its heavily vinyl approach, along with the idea that the bright blue of the pants just didn't fit. The color of boots also varied from the new outfit in the comics. Amid the criticism, at least one fan even Photoshopped the image of Palicki in an outfit of darker, navy pants, without the sheen, a darker, richer red of bodice, and different color boots. Sure enough, Palicki's outfit was soon edited — incorporating those touches. We do live in a crowd-sourced age, for sure.

"The first one, I hated what they did, then they kinda redesigned it," Epper tells BRBTV of the 2011 costume. "I thought it was a cool costume, but it just wasn't Wonder Woman. They never changed Spider-Man. They never changed Batman. My gut feeling from the very beginning was that that costume was kinda going to bite them."

When Carter appeared on Wendy Williams' show in 2011, the new TV show idea — and the costume — inevitably came up in conversation:

"My Wonder Woman, she never really thought of herself as all that," Carter said. "I never played Wonder Woman trying to be sexy."

In a 2012 TV interview in the local area where she attended high school, she commented on the failure of the new "WW" pilot to get off the ground: "What I'd heard, they missed the boat a bit on her vulnerability and her sweetness. There's a trap in that, if you go for that, you can't play a superhero. You have to play a person."

Later in 2012, the news broke that the CW was developing another take on "Wonder Woman" for TV, this time scripted by Allan Heinberg, who has written the character for DC Comics. The project was titled "Amazon" and at the script point, as of this book's presstime.

In 2011, the character of Wonder Woman made an appearance on the popular animated series "Batman: The Brave and the Bold." The Cartoon Network show toasted the first season of this '70s series, depicting the character in her eagle corset with the show's familiar theme song playing!

But that hasn't been the only recent animated appearance for the character. Besides a full run on the 2001-launched "Justice League / Justice League Unlimited" series, Wonder Woman got her own animated direct-to-DVD feature in 2010. This "Wonder Woman" movie came from the crack team at Warner Bros. Animation: Bruce Timm, Andrea Romano and Co. Like the live-action series, it presents an origin story of Steve crashing on the island (Themyscira, in this case) and an Amazon being chosen via a contest to take him back to the U.S. But the story by Gail Simone and Michael Jelenic takes it a step further, showing Hippolyta's

Like the live-action TV series, 2010's "Wonder Woman" feature deals in issues of gender relations. Interestingly, though, sisterly relations on the island are more greatly explored, particularly where the fire-tressed warhawk Artemis is concerned. Straight from the comic book page, with her mile-high and mile-long ponytail, Artemis resents her sweet and bookish sister Alexa.

life before the island, and even the formation of baby Diana from beach clay.

This animated Wonder Woman, voiced by Keri Russell of "Felicity," bears the twin Ws on her chest rather than the golden eagle, but she still explores elements of gender relations and the power struggles therein. And of course, as with the live-action series, there are themes of war and peace, though in the animated movie there is the question of whether or not the Amazons sequestering themselves on the island is really a good thing. This idea comes up in the "Justice League" series, as well.

The legacy of Lynda

As alluded to above, once Carter stepped into those red and white boots, any other female who dared portray the Amazon princess for decades to come would be judged against her. This extends to the women who've voiced her in the more-modern animated takes: Besides Keri Russell, there was Susan Eisenberg on "Justice League" and Lucy Lawless for the 2008 "Justice League: The New Frontier" animated feature. Heck, even Shannon Farnon, who predated Carter on 1973's "Super Friends," has probably been lined up on the Lynda yardstick.

Some of those little kids so enthralled by the live-action show in the '70s grew up to work in the comics or TV industry, like Alex Ross, one of the comics artists who has immortalized Wonder Woman on the printed page.

"Lynda Carter has a near equal importance to the legend of Wonder Woman, a character that's 60 years old, as the creators," Ross says in the show's first-season DVD extras. "She personified it for the modern generation in a way that — it'll never be forgotten. She embodied a superhero, unlike where there's been multiple people who have played Superman and Batman over the years. There's really only one Wonder Woman to anybody's eyes."

He continues, "There was nothing off about her. She was perfectly that face. The beauty and sensitivity and really this quality of her looking like a heroic figure as well as her looking like the all-American girl. All these things are brought to bear in the way she is."

Phil Jimenez has been very inspired by Carter in his own drawing of Wonder Woman in the comics: "What I took from her was a sense of grace and style and dignity, which you don't often see in most female characters. Most female characters in comics today are playing sort of the sex vixens, or sort of a little more kittenish, or just sort of men in women's clothing. And what was great about Lynda was that she brought to this character this incredible femininity, this sense of style and regality, which I still use whenever I draw Wonder Woman."

Fellow comics artist Michael Netzer, a Michigan native now based in Israel, talks about his own touch with greatness in this Facebook post he gives BRBTV permission to share:

"In late 1976, I drew a couple of WW covers and one story for DC. Soon after, my roommate comes home with a lady who said she was a hairstylist who shared a home with Lynda Carter in California, visiting N.Y. Hard to believe 'til we saw her photos. She was as impressed by fate as we were and asked for a drawing of Lynda from me along with one of the comics I'd drawn. I did just that, sharpened my pencil on WW/LC, and she went back home happy.

"Soon after I was asked by Paul Levitz to contribute a cover for Amazing World of DC that was to feature Wonder Woman and Lynda Carter. Well, I'd already had a little romp with the wondrous subject and produced this piece as part of the cover.

"A few weeks later, Lynda's roommate calls the studio at 3 a.m. and finds my roommate and I there. She said that she's with Lynda, who

wants to say thanks for the drawing and comic book. I think that at that age 21, it was the closest I'd ever come to autistic shock when Lynda said, 'Hi, Mike ... wow, what a nice drawing. Thank-you so much!' She was even more beautiful on the phone at that moment."

Yes, Carter surely seems to have that effect. Take Washington, D.C., photographer James R. Green Jr., who tells BRBTV about meeting the star. (Carter lives in Montgomery County, Maryland, just northwest of D.C. This author happens to live there, too, though I haven't had the pleasure of seeing her yet!)

Images courtesy of Michael Netzer.

"I had the opportunity to meet Lynda Carter on numerous occasions," Green says. "My first time meeting Lynda was the most memorable one. When I was covering the Kennedy Center Honors for the second year in 2000, I saw this incredible vision walking toward me on the red carpet, and I recognized her immediately as Wonder Woman. And as she approached and I greeted her, words like ''70s icon,' 'sex symbol,' flashed through my mind and in that instant it felt like meeting the president, the Queen of England all rolled up into one."

He says, "After you get over the initial shock, and you see her with her multitude of fans who followed her career for over 30 years, and when you see her in this environment, you see that her demeanor is down-to-earth, easygoing, and she loves talking about the series 'Wonder Woman' and she appreciated her fans. And the fans feel this. You see nothing but smiles and laughter when she's around. If I had to describe

Lynda Carter in one word, it would be gracious. That's why she's a fan favorite and my favorite."

Green had the opportunity to see Carter again during the premiere of "Double Dare" in D.C. And he photographed her, too, as she took part in a panel discussion with others from the film. Then he saw her again in March 2012 as she returned to the Kennedy Center.

The radiant Carter, who turned 60 in July 2011 but never seems to age, has credited eating healthy organic food and staying out of the sun.

James Green with Lynda Carter. Photo courtesy of James R. Green Jr.

Still a series with a message, so many years later

"'Wonder Woman' came along at a time in the '70s that was absolutely right," Cramer says. "It was a time where the women's movement was hitting its stride, where feminism, and all that it conveyed and was about, was being listened to, was being studied, and was slowly, quietly exploding across the country."

We ask Collins-Ludwick what she thinks is the most important message of this '70s "Wonder Woman" series, years later.

"Like most '70s TV, 'Wonder Woman' was just mindless, innocent escapism, far different from the hour-long, somber, in-your-face shock fests so rampant on TV today. Maybe its message today would be, 'Hey, it's okay that tonight's episode wasn't ripped from the headlines — this is your chance to just sit back, empty your mind, and enjoy.'"

But, she says, "In the early '70s, it was pretty much unheard of for the success of an hourlong series to depend on a female lead, let alone to feature a female character that could hold her own physically against male villains ('Police Woman' was the exception that proved the rule). 'Wonder Woman' was ground-breaking in getting audiences to accept the fact that women and action are not mutually exclusive concepts, something that audiences now take totally for granted."

Sharp expresses a slightly different view to us.

"I think probably to the extent that Superman had the message of doing good and righting wrongs, Wonder Woman was the female counterpart of that. The idea that women had that power, and that authority. Again, it has to be transferred to the magical. The rest of us were sort of supporting pawns in that agenda."

Carter relates her own thoughts in her series DVD interviews:

"I found that grain of truth inside myself that I shared with that character. That part of me that would stand up for what I believed in and wanted to make things better. Those qualities that I saw in myself or felt within myself that I gave to her."

Special snapshot: Lynda Carter at the nation's capital

Before we move on and talk more about the "Wonder Woman" TV series, can we just take a moment and — *ahem* — behold the beauty that is Lynda? BRBTV profusely thanks our buddy James R. Green Jr., Washington, D.C., photographer extraordinaire who has met oodles of fine celebs over many years, for these additional photographs of our star. Carter received the Lifetime Achievement Award here from the National Museum of Women in the Arts in Washington, D.C., in November 2008, wearing a stunning sapphire blue gown and looking every inch the thoroughly un-aged superchick.

Photo courtesy of James R. Green Jr.

Photos courtesy of James R. Green Jr.

James R. Green Jr. also photographed Carter at the premiere of the 2004 documentary film "Double Dare" in Washington, D.C., where the star took part in a panel discussion with Jeannie Epper, her stunt double on "Wonder Woman." Epper was profiled in the film; see the full text of our interview with her later in this book. Photo courtesy of James R. Green Jr.

Cast

You'll certainly be seeing stars

When you look back at the cast of "Wonder Woman" a few decades later, you really appreciate what a who's-who of the classic television world it truly was. Here, we include all the cast members we could gather, even those who just made one guest appearance. Though we may compare various sources of information, as much as possible we base this cast list on what was actually displayed on screen during the episodes. It's all organized alphabetically by first name. So enjoy!

Adam Clement ("Time Bomb") ... **Ted Shackelford**
Adelle Kobler ("Amazon Hot Wax") ... **Kate Woodville**
Adler ("Light-Fingered Lady") ... **Larry Ward**
Admiral ("The Deadly Dolphin") ... **Colin Hamilton**
Admissions Clerk ("The Man Who Could Not Die") ... **Sherry Miles**
Adolf Hitler clone ("Anschluss '77") ... **Barry Dennen**
Alan Ackaroy ("The Man Who Wouldn't Tell") ... **Gary Burghoff**
Alfie ("Hot Wheels") ... **John Durren**
Alien ("The Starships Are Coming") ... **Jack Kissel**
Amazon ("The New Original Wonder Woman") ... **Jean Karlson**
Ambassador ("Diana's Disappearing Act") ... **Maurice Sherbanee**

Ambassador Kitu Yamura ("Seance of Terror") ... **John Fujioka**
Ambassador McCauley ("Formula 407") ... **Charles Macaulay**
Ambassador Orrick ("The Queen and the Thief") ... **John Colicos**
Ambulance Attendant ("The Richest Man in the World") ... **Charles Young**
Amos Hoffman ("The Pied Piper") ... **George A. Cooper**
Andros ("Judgment from Outer Space") ... **Tim O'Connor**
Andros II ("Mind Stealers from Outer Space") ... **Dack Rambo**
Angel Velasquez ("Knockout") ... **Alex Colon**
Angelique McKenna ("Disco Devil") ... **Ellen Weston**
Angie Capucci ("The Deadly Sting") ... **Scott Marlowe**
Anton ("Amazon Hot Wax") ... **Rick Springfield**
Anton Caribe ("Light-Fingered Lady") ... **Greg Morris**
Antonio Cruz ("Formula 407") ... **Armando Silvestre**
Arthur Deal III ("Wonder Woman Meets Baroness Von Gunther") ... **Bradford Dillman**
Asclepia ("The Return of Wonder Woman") ... **Bettye Ackerman**
Ashley Norman / Carl ("The New Original Wonder Woman") ... **Red Buttons**
Ashton Ripley ("My Teenage Idol Is Missing") ... **Michael Lerner**
Assassin ("Stolen Faces") ... **Jimmy Nickerson**
Atma Bakru ("Seance of Terror")... **Christine Avila**
Babette ("The Bushwhackers") ... **Christelle Pierrette Gaspart**
Bad Guy ("The New Original Wonder Woman") ... **Severn Darden**
Bank Manager ("The New Original Wonder Woman") ... **Ian Wolfe**
Barbi Gordon ("Amazon Hot Wax") ... **Sarah Purcell**
Barney ("The Richest Man in the World") ... **Barry Miller**
Baroness Paula Von Gunther ("Wonder Woman Meets Baroness Von Gunther") ... **Christine Belford**
Bartender ("The Deadly Sting") ... **Frank Downing**
Beamer ("The Deadly Sting") ... **Marvin Miller**
Beast Man ("The Boy Who Knew Her Secret") ... **Tim Rossovich**
Benjamin Springfield ("My Teenage Idol Is Missing") ... **Robert Patten**
Berghoff ("Judgment from Outer Space") ... **Ted Roter**
Berkeley Student ("The Fine Art of Crime") ... **Mitchel Young-Evans**
Betsy ("Beauty on Parade") ... **Linda Carpenter**
Betty Lou ("Beauty on Parade") ... **April Tatro**
Beverly ("The Return of Wonder Woman") ... **Brooke Bundy**
Bill Bethude ("Screaming Javelins") ... **Roger Callard**
Bill Keller ("The Boy Who Knew Her Secret") ... **John Milford**
Bill Michaels ("The Deadly Sting") ... **Ron Ely**

Billy ("The Deadly Dolphin") ... **Britt Leach**
Billy Dero ("Amazon Hot Wax") ... **Martin Speer**
Black Avenger ("Spaced Out") ... **Ken Wilson**
Bleaker ("The Girl from Ilandia") ... **Alan Arbus**
Bo Taggart ("Screaming Javelins") ... **Robert Sampson**
Bob Baker ("The Girl with a Gift for Disaster") ... **Charles Haid**
Bobbie ("The Starships Are Coming") ... **Sheryl Lee Ralph**
Bobby Jensen ("The Pluto File") ... **Sean Kelly**
Bodyguard ("My Teenage Idol Is Missing") ... **Herman Poppe**
Bonnie Murphy ("The Girl with a Gift for Disaster") ... **Jane Actman**
Boy ("Stolen Faces") ... **Harold P. Pruett**
Brad ("Spaced Out") ... **Peter Marc Jacobson**
Broadcaster ("The Deadly Sting") ... **Gil Stratton**
Bryce Candall / Bret Cassiday ("The Man Who Could Not Die") ... **Bob Seagren**
Bully ("The Girl from Ilandia") ... **Todd Hoffman**
B.W. ("The Man Who Wouldn't Tell") ... **Millie Slavin**
Cab Driver ("The Richest Man in the World") ... **Bobby Baum**
Cabbie ("Fausta: the Nazi Wonder Woman") ... **Angelo Gnazzo**
Cabbie ("My Teenage Idol Is Missing") ... **Lanny Duncan**
Cameron Michaels ("The Boy Who Knew Her Secret") ... **Michael Shannon**
Camilla Moret ("The Pluto File") ... **Mikki Jamison-Olsen**
Capt. Anne Colby ("Flight to Oblivion") ... **Corinne Michaels**
Capt. Drangel ("The New Original Wonder Woman") ... **Eric Braeden**
Capt. Grau ("Judgment from Outer Space") ... **Erik Holland**
Capt. Hal Shaver ("The Murderous Missile") ... **Hal England**
Capt. Louie ("Going, Going, Gone") ... **Milton Selzer**
Capt. Parelli ("Mind Stealers from Outer Space") ... **Sol Weiner**
Capt. Radl ("The Feminum Mystique") ... **John Saxon**
Captain ("Beauty on Parade") ... **Wayne Grace**
Captain ("The Deadly Dolphin") ... **Gregory Chase**
Carl ("Wonder Woman vs. Gargantua!") ... **Tom Reese**
Carl Schwartz ("The Pied Piper") ... **Denny Miller**
Carla Burgess ("Mind Stealers from Outer Space") ... **Pamela Mason**
Carlo Indrezzano ("Death in Disguise") ... **George Chakiris**
Carolyn Hamilton ("Knockout") ... **Jayne Kennedy**
Cassandra Loren ("Time Bomb") ... **Joan Van Ark**
Cawley ("Formicida") ... **Stan Haze**
Chaka ("Mind Stealers from Outer Space") ... **Earl Boen**
Charles Benson ("The Pluto File") ... **Albert Stratton**

Joan Van Ark shared a "Wonder Woman" episode with her on-screen husband from "Dallas" and "Knots Landing," Ted Shackelford. In "Time Bomb" she was Cassandra Loren, the ambitious historian from the future who comes to the 1970s to make a fortune, Shackelford pursuing her as Adam Clement. Van Ark joked to BRBTV when we interviewed her for our "Dallas" reference guide, that she had her doubts during the "Dallas" casting that she and Shackelford would work well together. "We had just worked together on 'Wonder Woman,'" she told us, "and I thought we were too much alike. It turned out they were 100,000 percent right, and I was 100,000 percent wrong." Photo courtesy of Joan Van Ark.

Charlie ("Pot of Gold") ... **Gary Epper**
Charlie Bright Eagle ("The Bushwhackers") ... **David Yanez**
Chemist ("Formicida") ... **Ben Young**
Chief Justice Brown ("I Do, I Do") ... **Kent Smith**
Christian Harrison ("I Do, I Do") ... **John Getz**
Chuck ("Skateboard Wiz") ... **David Cadiente**
Claudine ("A Date with Doomsday") ... **Colette Bertrand**
Cleaning Lady ("Mind Stealers from Outer Space") ... **Betty Cole**
Cocktail Waiter ("Seance of Terror") ... **Brad Savage**
Codger ("A Date with Doomsday") ... **Patrick Cranshaw**
Col. Acevo ("The Return of Wonder Woman") ... **Carlos Romero**
Col. Charlie Scott ("Fausta: the Nazi Wonder Woman") ... **Jeff Cooper**
Col. Dekker ("Seance of Terror") ... **Jean-Ivan Dorin**
Col. Flint ("Beauty on Parade") ... **William Lanteau**
Col. Hans Eichler ("Wonder Woman vs. Gargantua!") ... **Robert Loggia**
Col. Kesselman ("Fausta: the Nazi Wonder Woman") ... **Bo Brundin**
Col. Minh ("The Man Who Made Volcanoes") ... **Philip Ahn**
Col. Oberst Von Blasko ("The New Original Wonder Woman") ... **Kenneth Mars**
Col. Robert Elliot ("The Starships Are Coming") ... **Tim O'Connor**
Colonel ("Disco Devil") ... **Russell Johnson**
Connie ("Mind Stealers from Outer Space") ... **Anne Ramsey**

Conrad Steigler ("Wonder Woman vs. Gargantua!") ... **John Hillerman**
Cop ("The New Original Wonder Woman") ... **Tom Rosqui**
Cori ("IRAC Is Missing") ... **Tina Lenert**
Corporal ("Death in Disguise") ... **Katherine Charles**
Corporal ("The Murderous Missile") ... **Maurice Sneed**
Count Cagliostro ("Diana's Disappearing Act") ... **Richard Gautier**
Cpl. Jim Ames ("Wonder Woman in Hollywood") ... **Robert Hays**
Cpl. Rogers ("Wonder Woman vs. Gargantua!") ... **Curtis Credel**
CPO ("The Deadly Dolphin") ... **Paul Tuerpe**
Customs Agent ("The Pluto File") ... **Brigid O'Brien**
Dale Hawthorn ("The Man Who Could Not Die") ... **John Durren**
Dalma the Amazon ("The Feminum Mystique") ... **Erica Hagen**
Dan Fletcher ("Last of the Two-Dollar Bills") ... **Dean Harens**
Daniel Berger ("Gault's Brain") ... **Ari Sorko-Ram**
Daniel Reynolds ("Time Bomb") ... **Allan Miller**
Darrell ("The Deadly Dolphin") ... **Brian Tochi**
Dave Pruett ("The Man Who Made Volcanoes") ... **James R. Parkes**
David Allen ("I Do, I Do") ... **Henry Darrow**
David / Leon Gurney ("Phantom of the Roller Coaster") ... **Jared Martin**
Deacon Jones ("The Deadly Sting") ... **Deacon Jones**
Debbie Chambers ("Mind Stealers from Outer Space") ... **Kristin Larkin**
Dede ("A Date with Doomsday") ... **Carol Vogel**
Del Franklin ("Disco Devil") ... **Paul Sand**
Denny Lake ("I Do, I Do") ... **Brian Avery**
Dentist ("Last of the Two-Dollar Bills") ... **Don Eitner**
Deputy Minister Kell ("Seance of Terror") ... **Hanna Hertelendy**
Desk Clerk ("I Do, I Do") ... **Scott Mulhern**
Desk Clerk ("Spaced Out") ... **Lester C. Fletcher**
Desk Sergeant ("Light-Fingered Lady") ... **Stack Pierce**
Destroyer Captain ("Wonder Woman in Hollywood") ... **Alex Rodine**
Destroyer Commander ("The Feminum Mystique") ... **Newell Alexander**
Dick ("IRAC Is Missing") ... **W.T. Zacha**
Diner Customer ("Last of the Two-Dollar Bills") ... **Naomi Grumette**
Director ("IRAC Is Missing") ... **Colin Hamilton**
Director ("Wonder Woman in Hollywood") ... **Alan Bergmann**
Dirk ("IRAC Is Missing") ... **Lee Paul**
Doctor ("Stolen Faces") ... **Murray MacLeod**
Doctor ("The Deadly Toys") ... **Randy Phillips**
Doctor ("The Girl from Ilandia") ... **Buck Young**

Doctor on Paradise Island ("The New Original Wonder Woman") ... **Fannie Flagg**
Dolly Tucker ("I Do, I Do") ... **Celeste Holm**
Dr. Akers ("The Man Who Could Not Die") ... **Robert Sampson**
Dr. Andrea ("The Return of Wonder Woman") ... **Raye Sheffield**
Dr. Barnes ("The Pluto File") ... **Kenneth Tigar**
Dr. Crippin ("Gault's Brain") ... **Peter Mark Richman**
Dr. Diderich ("Last of the Two-Dollar Bills") ... **John Howard**
Dr. Douglas Emery Radcliffe ("Formicida") ... **Robert Shields**
Dr. Eli Jaffe ("The Boy Who Knew Her Secret") ... **Bert Remsen**
Dr. Heimlich Von Klemper / Dr. Stern ("Anschluss '77") ... **Leon Charles**
Dr. Hutchens ("Diana's Disappearing Act") ... **Allen Williams**
Dr. Joseph Reichman ("The Man Who Could Not Die") ... **Brian Davies**
Dr. Kenneth Wilson ("The Man Who Could Move the World") ... **Lew Ayres**
Dr. Koren ("The Girl with a Gift for Disaster") ... **Ina Balin**
Dr. Lazaar ("The Deadly Toys") ... **Ross Elliott**
Dr. Norris ("The Pluto File") ... **Peter Brandon**
Dr. Osmond ("Wonder Woman vs. Gargantua!") ... **Herb Voland**
Dr. Prescott ("The Deadly Toys") ... **James A. Watson Jr.**
Dr. Rand ("Mind Stealers from Outer Space") ... **Allan Migicovsky**
Dr. Roberts ("A Date with Doomsday") ... **John O'Leary**
Dr. Ross ("The Return of Wonder Woman") ... **Johana DeWinter**
Dr. Royce Tobias ("The Deadly Toys") ... **Donald Bishop**
Dr. Samson ("Hot Wheels") ... **Don Mitchell**
Dr. Solano ("The Return of Wonder Woman") ... **Fritz Weaver**
Dr. Sylvia Stubbs ("The Deadly Dolphin") ... **Penelope Windust**
Driver / Guard ("The Bermuda Triangle Crisis") ... **George Ranito Jordan**
Duane Morrisey ("Skateboard Wiz") ... **Ron Masak**
Dunfield ("The Richest Man in the World") ... **Roger Perry**
Dupris ("The Man Who Could Not Die") ... **John Aprea**
Eddie Allen Bell ("The Deadly Sting") ... **Eddie Allen Bell**
Edgar Percy ("Stolen Faces") ... **Joseph Maher**
Edmund Dante ("Flight to Oblivion") ... **John Van Dreelen**
Eldon Beamer ("Death in Disguise") ... **Christopher Cary**
Elena Atkinson ("The Pied Piper") ... **Eve Plumb**
Ellis ("Time Bomb") ... **Ted Hamaguchi**
Emmett Dawson ("The Bushwhackers") ... **Tony George**
Eric ("Screaming Javelins") ... **Vaughn Armstrong**
Eric Kell ("Seance of Terror") ... **John Birk**

Eric Landau ("Amazon Hot Wax") ... **Curtis Credel**
Erica Belgard ("Wonder Woman vs. Gargantua!") ... **Gretchen Corbett**
Ernie ("The Murderous Missile") ... **Sam Edwards**
Etta Candy ... **Beatrice Colen**
Evadne ("The Return of Wonder Woman") ... **Dorrie Thomson**
Evan Donalsen ("Skateboard Wiz") ... **Eric Braeden**
Evan Mallory ("Judgment from Outer Space") ... **Christopher Cary**
Evan Robley ("The Queen and the Thief") ... **David Hedison**
Eve ... **Saundra Sharp**
Falcon ("The Pluto File") ... **Robert Reed**
Fan ("Spaced Out") ... **Rex Riley**
Fausta Grables ("Fausta: the Nazi Wonder Woman") ... **Lynda Day George**
Female Dancer ("Disco Devil") ... **Linda Fernandez**
First Mate ("The Girl from Ilandia") ... **Mike Kopcha**
Flo ("The Murderous Missile") ... **Lucille Benson**
Foreman ("Formicida") ... **Frank Farmer**
Foreman ("Hot Wheels") ... **John Lawrence**
Foreman ("The Richest Man in the World") ... **Buck Young**
Foreman ("Time Bomb") ... **Ivan Naranjo**
Formicida / Dr. Irene Janus ("Formicida") ... **Lorene Yarnell**
Frank Willis ("The Pluto File") ... **Michael Twain**
Frank Wilson ("Last of the Two-Dollar Bills") ... **Richard O'Brien**
Fred Roman ("Stolen Faces") ... **Bob Seagren**
Freddie ("The Bushwhackers") ... **Justin Randi**
Freddy ("Wonder Woman in Hollywood") ... **Barry Van Dyke**
Friedman ("Skateboard Wiz") ... **Art Metrano**
Fritz Gerlich ("Anschluss '77") ... **Mel Ferrer**
Gaffer / Melvin Schultz ("The Deadly Dolphin") ... **Albert Popwell**
Gaitan ("Anschluss '77") ... **Julio Medina**
Gargantua ("Wonder Woman vs. Gargantua!") ... **Mickey Morton**
Gatekeeper ("The Pied Piper") ... **Bob Hastings**
Gen. Clewes ("Judgment from Outer Space") ... **George Cooper**
Gen. Miller ("Mind Stealers from Outer Space") ... **Barry Cahill**
Gen. Phil Blankenship ... **John Randolph / Richard Eastham**
Gen. Ulrich ("The Feminum Mystique") ... **Curt Lowens**
Gen. Zachary Kane ("Judgment from Outer Space") ... **Archie Johnson**
General ("The Starships Are Coming") ... **Ben Chandler**
General ("The Starships Are Coming") ... **David White**
George ("A Date with Doomsday") ... **Bob Hastings**
George ("The Murderous Missile") ... **James Luisi**

George ("Wonder Woman in Hollywood") ... **Danil Torppe**
George Hess ("Mind Stealers from Outer Space") ... **Del Hinkley**
George P. Turk ("Gault's Brain") ... **Erik Stern**
Gideon D. Harcourt ("Formicida") ... **Robert Alda**
Gilda ("The Deadly Sting") ... **Bobbie Bartosh**
Gino ("Pot of Gold") ... **Jaime Tirelli**
Girl 1 ("My Teenage Idol Is Missing") ... **Abbie Wolfson**
Girl 2 ("My Teenage Idol Is Missing") ... **Suzanne Crough**
Girl 3 ("My Teenage Idol Is Missing") ... **Michele Laurita**
Gloria Beverly ("Wonder Woman in Hollywood") ... **Christopher Norris**
Gloria Marquez ("The Return of Wonder Woman") ... **Jessica Walter**
Goodspeed ("The Deadly Dolphin") ... **Macon McCalman**
Gorel ("Judgment from Outer Space") ... **Vic Perrin**
Gormsby ("Judgment from Outer Space") ... **Patrick Skelton**
Grease ("Light-Fingered Lady") ... **Gary Crosby**
Greyson ("The Deadly Toys") ... **Daniel Selby**
Guard ("A Date with Doomsday") ... **John Garwood**
Guard ("IRAC Is Missing") ... **Lloyd McLinn**
Guard ("Light-Fingered Lady") ... **Thomas Hilliard**
Guard ("The Bermuda Triangle Crisis") ... **James Staley**
Guard ("The Deadly Toys") ... **Harv Selsby**
Guard ("The Deadly Toys") ... **Michael W. Kinney**
Guard ("The Starships Are Coming") ... **Walt Davis**
Guard ("Time Bomb") ... **René Levant**
Guard ("Wonder Woman in Hollywood") ... **Carmen Filpi**
Guide ("Time Bomb") ... **Gwenn Mitchell**
Hamlin Rule ("The Pied Piper") ... **Martin Mull**
Hank (Henry) Miller ("Last of the Two-Dollar Bills") ... **David Cryer**
Hanson ("Wonder Woman Meets Baroness Von Gunther") ... **Ed Griffith**
Harlow Gault ("Gault's Brain") ... **John Carradine**
Harold Farnum ("Diana's Disappearing Act") ... **Ed Begley Jr.**
Harris ("The Feminum Mystique") ... **Kurt Grayson**
Harrison Fynch ("Phantom of the Roller Coaster") ... **Joseph Sirola**
Heavy ("Going, Going, Gone") ... **Fil Formicola**
Heavy 1 ("The Fine Art of Crime") ... **George Caldwell**
Henchler ("The Feminum Mystique") ... **Kurt Kreuger**
Henry ("The Deadly Dolphin") ... **Michael Stroka**
Henry Roberts ("The Fine Art of Crime") ... **Roddy McDowall**
Henry Wilson ("The Starships Are Coming") ... **Jeffrey Byron**

Howard Ketchum ("Skateboard Wiz") ... **Neil Flanagan**
IADC Officer ("The Richest Man in the World") ... **Joe Warfield**
Infra Red ("Disco Devil") ... **Wolfman Jack**
Intruder ("The Deadly Toys") ... **Mike Kulik**
IRAC ... **Tom Kratochvil**
Jack Corbin ("The Man Who Made Volcanoes") ... **Roger Davis**
Jack Wood ("Beauty on Parade") ... **Dick Van Patten**
James Porter ("The Pluto File") ... **Jason Johnson**
Jamie O'Neill ("Skateboard Wiz") ... **Cynthia Eilbacher**
Janet ("Spaced Out") ... **Candy Ann Brown**
Jason ("Last of the Two-Dollar Bills") ... **Victor Argo**
Jazreel ("Diana's Disappearing Act") ... **J.A. Preston**
Jeff Gordon ("Amazon Hot Wax") ... **Judge Reinhold**
Jeff Hadley ("The Bushwhackers") ... **Lance Kerwin**
Jerry ("Amazon Hot Wax") ... **Danil Torppe**
Jerry (the aide) ("The Starships Are Coming") ... **James Coleman**
Jim the engineer ("Amazon Hot Wax") ... **Gene Krischer**
J.J. MacConnell ("Time Bomb") ... **Fredd Wayne**
Joan ("The Girl with a Gift for Disaster") ... **Renee Brown**
Joe ("The Fine Art of Crime") ... **Joe E. Tata**
Joe Atkinson ... **Normann Burton**
Joey ("The Feminum Mystique") ... **Brad Rearden**
John Austin ("Stolen Faces") ... **Kenneth Tigar**
John Blake ("A Date with Doomsday") ... **Michael Hoit**
John Edward Key ("Skateboard Wiz") ... **James Ray**
John Kelly ("Knockout") ... **Arch Johnson**
Johnny ("I Do, I Do") ... **Steve Eastin**
Johnny Chambers ("Mind Stealers from Outer Space") ... **Vincent Van Patten**
J.P. Hadley ("The Bushwhackers") ... **Roy Rogers**
June ("Beauty on Parade") ... **Eddie Benton**
Kalanin ("The Man Who Made Volcanoes") ... **Milt Kogan**
Kalten ("The Return of Wonder Woman") ... **William Tregoe**
Karen ("Mind Stealers from Outer Space") ... **Lana Marie Henricks**
Karen ("The Girl with a Gift for Disaster") ... **Dulcie Jordan**
Kathy Munro ("Disco Devil") ... **Kerry Sherman**
Kerwin ("Disco Devil") ... **Dennis J. Stewart**
Kevin Wendell ("Skateboard Wiz") ... **Peter Wise**
Kim ("Amazon Hot Wax") ... **Michael Botts**
Kim ("Mind Stealers from Outer Space") ... **Lori Ann Henricks**
Kimball ("Spaced Out") ... **Rene Auberjonois**

Kirk ("Phantom of the Roller Coaster") ... **Fred Lerner**
Kleist ("The Return of Wonder Woman") ... **Russ Marin**
Koenig ("Anschluss '77") ... **Kurt Kreuger**
Krug ("Death in Disguise") ... **Art Batanides**
Kurt ("Wonder Woman in Hollywood") ... **Charles Cyphers**
Lab Man ("The Richest Man in the World") ... **Joe Medalis**
Lance ("Disco Devil") ... **Victor Mohica**
Lane Curran ("Knockout") ... **Frank Parker**
Lane Kincaid / Mike ("My Teenage Idol Is Missing") ... **Leif Garrett**
Lawrence McCutcheon ("The Deadly Sting") ... **Lawrence McCutcheon**
Lawson Koslo ("Seance of Terror") ... **Rick Jason**
Leech ("Light-Fingered Lady") ... **Joseph R. Sicari**
Leslie ("Stolen Faces") ... **Catherine Campbell**
Leslie O'Neill ("Skateboard Wiz") ... **Grace Gaynor**
Lieutenant ("Beauty on Parade") ... **John David Yarbrough**
Lieutenant ("Flight to Oblivion") ... **Walt Davis**
Lieutenant ("Skateboard Wiz") ... **Abraham Alvarez**
Lieutenant ("The Murderous Missile") ... **Alan McRae**
Lin Wan ("The Man Who Made Volcanoes") ... **Richard Narita**
Linc ("The Bushwhackers") ... **Christoff St. John**
Lisa ("Pot of Gold") ... **Sherrie Wills**
Lisa Engel ("Judgment from Outer Space") ... **Christiane Schmidtmer**
Logan ("The Return of Wonder Woman") ... **Frank Killmond**
Lois Taggart ("Screaming Javelins") ... **E.J. Peaker**
Lola Flynn ("Beauty on Parade") ... **Anne Francis**
Lou Davis ("The Girl from Ilandia") ... **Fred Lerner**
Louis the Lithuanian ("The Deadly Sting") ... **Danny Dayton**
Louise ("The Pied Piper") ... **Sandy Charles**
Lt. Bill Rand ("Wonder Woman in Hollywood") ... **Ross Bickell**
Lt. Cmdr. Robert Mansfield ("The Bermuda Triangle Crisis") ... **Larry Golden**
Lt. Karl Wertz ("The Feminum Mystique") ... **Paul Shenar**
Lt. McMasters ("The Pied Piper") ... **Melvin F. Allen**
Lt. Stonehouse ("Flight to Oblivion") ... **Michael Shannon**
Lt. Weil ("The Feminum Mystique") ... **Rayford Barnes**
Lucas ("Going, Going, Gone") ... **Kaz Garas**
Lucy DeWitt ("The Richest Man in the World") ... **Marlyn Mason**
Ludwig ("My Teenage Idol Is Missing") ... **David Ellis**
Luther ("The Murderous Missile") ... **Mark Withers**
Lydia Moreno ("Formula 407") ... **Maria Grimm**
Mac MacDonald ("The Murderous Missile") ... **Steve Inwood**

Prolific actor Alan Fudge portrayed Maj. Alan Cornell in the episode "Flight to Oblivion." Here he's shown in a 1977 promo shot for NBC. Photo from Wikimedia Commons; public domain.

Magda the Amazon ("The Feminum Mystique") ... **Pamela Shoop**
Maggie Robbins ("Last of the Two-Dollar Bills") ... **Barbara Anderson**
Magician 1 ("Diana's Disappearing Act") ... **James Mark Wilson**
Magician 2 ("Diana's Disappearing Act") ... **Don W. Brockhaus**
Maitre d' ("Death in Disguise") ... **Maurice Marsac**
Maj. Alan Cornell ("Flight to Oblivion") ... **Alan Fudge**
Maj. Anita Finley ("Death in Disguise") ... **Carol Worthington**
Maj. Dexter ("The Deadly Toys") ... **John Rubinstein**
Maj. Gaines ("The Return of Wonder Woman") ... **David Knapp**
Maj. Karl Keller ("Formula 407") ... **John Devlin**
Male Secretary ("Formicida") ... **Neil Elliot**
Man ("The Bushwhackers") ... **Murray MacLeod**
Manageress ("The Return of Wonder Woman") ... **Argentina Brunetti**
Marcia / Agent M. ("The New Original Wonder Woman") ... **Stella Stevens**
Marge Douglas ("Light-Fingered Lady") ... **Judyann Elder**
Maria ("Formula 407") ... **Marisa Pavan**
Maria ("The Bushwhackers") ... **Rita Gomez**
Marion Mariposa ("Screaming Javelins") ... **Henry Gibson**
Marius Macropolis ("Death in Disguise") ... **Lee Bergere**
Mark Bremer ("Wonder Woman in Hollywood") ... **Harris Yulin**
Mark Reuben ("The Girl with a Gift for Disaster") ... **James Sloyan**
Marshall Henshaw ("The Richest Man in the World") ... **Jeremy Slate**
Marty ("Amazon Hot Wax") ... **Bob Hoy**

Mary Jane Thrip ("A Date with Doomsday") ... **Hermione Baddeley**
Mary Lou Thompkins ("The Starships Are Coming") ... **Lilibet Stern**
Masaaki ("The Man Who Could Move the World") ... **Arthur Song**
Masaaki as a boy ("The Man Who Could Move the World") ... **Peter Kwong**
Mason Steele ("The Starships Are Coming") ... **Andrew Duggan**
Matthew Koslo ("Seance of Terror") ... **Todd Lookinland**
Maxwell ("Pot of Gold") ... **Arthur Batanides**
M.C. at war bonds fundraiser ("Fausta: the Nazi Wonder Woman") ... **Larry Ellis**
Meg Kellogg ("The Man Who Wouldn't Tell") ... **Jane Actman**
Mei Ling ("The Man Who Made Volcanoes") ... **Irene Tsu**
Melanie ("The Boy Who Knew Her Secret") ... **Lenora May**
Michael Sutton ("Light-Fingered Lady") ... **Titos Vandis**
Mime 1 (male) ("Diana's Disappearing Act") ... **Peter DePaula**
Mime 2 (female) ("Diana's Disappearing Act") ... **Kathlyn**
Mitch ("Flight to Oblivion") ... **Mitch Vogel**
Mitzie ("Beauty on Parade") ... **Paulette Breen**
Monty Burns ("Beauty on Parade") ... **Bobby Van**
Moreaux ("The Fine Art of Crime") ... **Michael McGuire**
Morgana LeFay ("Diana's Disappearing Act") ... **Brenda Benet**
Morley ("My Teenage Idol Is Missing") ... **Michael Baseleon**
Morton Danzig ("Gault's Brain") ... **David Mason Daniels**
Mover ("The Man Who Could Not Die") ... **Douglas Broyles**
Mr. Brown ("Going, Going, Gone") ... **Mako**
Mr. Jones ("Going, Going, Gone") ... **Marc Lawrence**
Mr. Munn ("Spaced Out") ... **George Cheung**
Mr. Smith ("Going, Going, Gone") ... **Charlie Brill**
Mrs. Ellsworth ("The Fine Art of Crime") ... **Patti MacLeod**
Mrs. Keller ("The Boy Who Knew Her Secret") ... **Joyce Greenwood**
Mrs. Walls ("Pot of Gold") ... **Jeanne Bates**
Ms. Patrick ("Phantom of the Roller Coaster") ... **Jocelyn Sommers**
Mueller ("Fausta: the Nazi Wonder Woman") ... **Keene Curtis**
Mustapha ben-Hassan, Emir of Quiana ("Diana's Disappearing Act") ... **Aharon Ipalé**
Nadia Samarra ("Screaming Javelins") ... **Melanie Chartoff**
Nancy Clark ("Stolen Faces") ... **Diane Lander**
Narrator ("The New Original Wonder Woman") ... **Paul Frees**
Neil ("The Girl with a Gift for Disaster") ... **Dick Butkus**
Newsman ("The Starships Are Coming") ... **Frank Whiteman**
Nick ("The Deadly Sting") ... **Bob Minor**

Nick Carbone / Moreno ("Disco Devil") ... **Michael DeLano**
Nickolas ("The New Original Wonder Woman") ... **Henry Gibson**
Nordling ("Mind Stealers from Outer Space") ... **Curt Lowens**
Norman ("Disco Devil") ... **Bob Hoy**
Nurse ("Stolen Faces") ... **Daryle Ann Lindley**
Nurse Barbie Brown ("The Girl from Ilandia") ... **Pamela Toll**
Nurse Buck ("The New Original Wonder Woman") .. **Helen Verbit**
Officer ("Going, Going, Gone") ... **Jim Stein**
Officer Hernandez ("Knockout") ... **Abraham Alvarez**
Official ("IRAC Is Missing") ... **Cletus Young**
Orlich Hoffman ("The Deadly Toys") ... **Frank Gorshin**
Oshima ("The Man Who Could Move the World") ... **James Hong**
Otis Fiskle ("Hot Wheels") ... **Lance LeGault**
Otto Dietrich ("Formula 407") ... **Gary Cashdollar**
Pat O'Hanlan ("Pot of Gold") ... **Dick O'Neill**
Paul Bjornsen ("Judgment from Outer Space") ... **Scott Hylands**
Paul Rojak ("Light-Fingered Lady") ... **Bubba Smith**
Peasant Girl ("Fausta: the Nazi Wonder Woman") ... **Mary Rings**
Pete Johnson ("Knockout") ... **Ted Shackelford**
Pete Pearson ("The Boy Who Knew Her Secret") ... **Tegan West**
Peter Knight ("The Feminum Mystique") ... **Charles Frank**
Phyllis ("The Deadly Sting") ... **Luise Heath**
Pierce ("Phantom of the Roller Coaster") ... **Marc Alaimo**
Pilot ("The Return of Wonder Woman") ... **Edward Cross**
Plotkin ("Death in Disguise") ... **Jack Kissell**
Pole Vaulter ("Screaming Javelins") ... **Dennis M. Madalone**
Prime Minister ("The Richest Man in the World") ... **Carmen Zapata**
Prison Guard #1 ... **Jude Farese**
Prison Guard #2 ... **Cletus Young**
Prof. Arthur Chapman ("The Man Who Made Volcanoes") ... **Roddy McDowall**
Prof. Brubaker ("The Deadly Sting") ... **Harvey Jason**
Prof. Graebner ("Judgment from Outer Space") ... **Hank Brandt**
Prof. Moreno ("Formula 407") ... **Nehemiah Persoff**
Prof. Paul Eidleman ("Mind Stealers from Outer Space") ... **Rege Cordic**
Prof. Warren ("The Pluto File") ... **Hayden Rorke**
Prof. Zander ("A Date with Doomsday") ... **Arthur Malet**
Professor ("The Man Who Could Not Die") ... **Hal Frederick**
Queen Hippolyta ... **Cloris Leachman / Carolyn Jones / Beatrice Straight**

Queen Kathryn ("The Queen and the Thief") ... **Juliet Mills**
Radarman ("The Bermuda Triangle Crisis") ... **Barry Hamilton**
Radioman ("Fausta: the Nazi Wonder Woman") ... **Ron Lombard**
Radioman ("The Bermuda Triangle Crisis") ... **Joseph Chapman**
Raleigh Crichton ("My Teenage Idol Is Missing") ... **Albert Paulsen**
Rancher ("Pot of Gold") ... **Ric DiAngelo**
Randy ("Phantom of the Roller Coaster") ... **Ike Eisenmann**
Raymond Manta ("The Bermuda Triangle Crisis") ... **Charles Cioffi**
Receptionist ("Disco Devil") ... **Betty Bridges**
Receptionist ("Formicida") ... **Carol Carrington**
Receptionist ("Phantom of the Roller Coaster") ... **Judith Christopher**
Receptionist ("The Pied Piper") ... **Pam Rice**
Receptionist at movie studio ("Wonder Woman in Hollywood") ... **June Whitley Taylor**
Rena the Amazon ("The New Original Wonder Woman") ... **Inga Neilson**
Reporter ("The Starships Are Coming") ... **Mario Machado**
Reves ("Time Bomb") ... **Ernie Orsatti**
Rita ("Beauty on Parade") ... **Christa Helm**
Robby the Robot ("Spaced Out") ... **Robby the Robot**
Rogel ("Anschluss '77") ... **Tom Ormeny**
Roger ("Wonder Woman in Hollywood") ... **Eric Boles**
Rojak ("Fausta: the Nazi Wonder Woman") ... **Christopher George**
Roman Gabriel ("The Deadly Sting") ... **Roman Gabriel**
Rosalie ("Beauty on Parade") ... **Derna Wylde**
Ross ("Light-Fingered Lady") ... **Ric DiAngelo**
Rossman ("Mind Stealers from Outer Space") ... **Gary Bisig**
Rudolph Furst ("The Man Who Wouldn't Tell") ... **Philip M. Thomas**
Runner ("Screaming Javelins") ... **Sam Freed**
Ruth Blaine ("Mind Stealers from Outer Space") ... **Linda Ryan**
Ryan ("Light-Fingered Lady") ... **Chris Stone**
Sakri ("Judgment from Outer Space") ... **Janet MacLachlan**
Saleslady ("The New Original Wonder Woman") ... **Fritzi Burr**
Sam ("The Deadly Sting") ... **Craig T. Nelson**
Sam Tucker ("I Do, I Do") ... **Simon Scott**
Samantha ("My Teenage Idol Is Missing") ... **Michele Laurita**
Sampson ("My Teenage Idol Is Missing") ... **Tony Brubaker**
Samuels ("The Return of Wonder Woman") ... **George Ives**
Schmidt ("Formula 407") ... **Peter MacLean**
Secretary ("Phantom of the Roller Coaster") ... **Jessica Rains**
Secretary Bakru ("Seance of Terror") ... **Adam Ageli**

Security Guard ("Mind Stealers from Outer Space") ... **Walt Davis**
Security Guard ("Spaced Out") ... **J.J. Johnston**
Security Officer ("The Man Who Could Move the World") ... **Alan McRae**
Sell ("Mind Stealers from Outer Space") ... **Barbara O. Jones**
Sen ("The Bushwhackers") ... **Carey Wong**
Sen. Wainright ("Mind Stealers from Outer Space") ... **Eric Mason**
Sentry ("Beauty on Parade") ... **Bill Adler**
Sergeant ("Judgment from Outer Space") ... **Fil Formicola**
Sergeant ("Phantom of the Roller Coaster") ... **Michael Kopcha**
Sergeant ("The Bermuda Triangle Crisis") ... **Herman Poppe**
Sgt. Cline ("Stolen Faces") ... **Al White**
Sgt. Dobson ("IRAC Is Missing") ... **James Veres**
Sgt. Harry Willard ("Wonder Woman in Hollywood") ... **David Himes**
Sgt. Henderson ("Wonder Woman vs. Gargantua!") ... **Jim Driskill**
Sgt. Strassey ("Wonder Woman Meets Baroness Von Gunther") ... **John Brandon**
Shadow ("Hot Wheels") ... **Fuddle Bagley**
Sheldon Como ("Going, Going, Gone") ... **Hari Rhodes**
Sheriff Anson Bodie ("The Bushwhackers") ... **David Clarke**
Sheriff Beal ("The Murderous Missile") ... **Warren Stevens**
Shopkeeper ("Diana's Disappearing Act") ... **George Skaff**
Shubert Goring ("The Fine Art of Crime") ... **Joe Maross**
Silas Lockhart ("The Deadly Dolphin") ... **Nicolas Coster**
Simon Penrose ("The Girl from Ilandia") ... **Harry Guardino**
Simon Rohan ("Spaced Out") ... **Paul Lawrence Smith**
Skip Keller ("The Boy Who Knew Her Secret") ... **Clark Brandon**
Skye Markham ("Skateboard Wiz") ... **John Reilly**
Slim ("Hot Wheels") ... **Marc Ross**
Smitty ("I Do, I Do") ... **Thomas W. Babson**
Soldier ("Wonder Woman vs. Gargantua!") ... **John Zenda**
Soldier #1 ("Fausta: the Nazi Wonder Woman") ... **Gene Biegouloff**
Soldier #2 ("Fausta: the Nazi Wonder Woman") ... **Kenneth Smedberg**
S.S. Colonel ("Last of the Two-Dollar Bills") ... **Michael Dan Wagner**
S.S. Gen. Von Dreiberg ("Judgment from Outer Space") ... **Kurt Kaszner**
S.S. General ("Formula 407") ... **Curt Lowens**
Stagehand ("Beauty on Parade") ... **Henry Deas**
Starker ("Death in Disguise") ... **Charles Pierce**
Steve Trevor ... **Lyle Waggoner**
Steve Trevor Jr. ... **Lyle Waggoner**

Strasser ("Anschluss '77") ... **Peter Nyberg**
Stryker ("Gault's Brain") ... **Floyd Levine**
Sunny ("The Boy Who Knew Her Secret") ... **A.J. Blake**
Susan ("Beauty on Parade") ... **Jennifer Shaw**
Sylvester Grogan ("Spaced Out") ... **Steven Anderson**
T. Burton Phipps III ("The Man Who Could Not Die") ... **James Bond III**
Tad Ellsworth ("The Fine Art of Crime") ... **Gavin MacLeod**
Taft ("The Man Who Could Move the World") ... **J. Kenneth Campbell**
Takeo Ishida ("The Man Who Could Move the World") ... **Yuki Shimoda**
Takeo Ishida as a boy ("The Man Who Could Move the World") ... **Steven Ken Suehiro**
Tall Man ("Knockout") ... **Frank Marth**
Tara Landon ("Gault's Brain") ... **Cathee Shirriff**
Taylor the Foreman ("Disco Devil") ... **Frank McRae**
Taxi Driver ("The New Original Wonder Woman") ... **Anne Ramsey**
Technician ("IRAC Is Missing") ... **Mathias Reitz**
Technician ("The Man Who Made Volcanoes") ... **Grant Owens**
Ted ("The Man Who Wouldn't Tell") ... **Michael Cole**
Ted Johnson ("Knockout") ... **K.C. Martel**
Teutonic Woman ("The New Original Wonder Woman") ... **Maida Severn**
Thackery ("Pot of Gold") ... **Brian Davies**
Theodora Koslo ("Seance of Terror") ... **Kres Mersky**
Thomson ("The Girl from Ilandia") ... **Chuck Hicks**
Thorpe ("Phantom of the Roller Coaster") ... **Craig Littler**
Thug ("Formula 407") ... **John Ashton**
Thug ("Going, Going, Gone") ... **Jophery C. Brown**
Thug ("Going, Going, Gone") ... **Tim Rossovich**
Thug ("The Fine Art of Crime") ... **Tony Epper**
Thug ("The Richest Man in the World") ... **Del Monroe**
Tim Bolt ("Hot Wheels") ... **Peter Brown**
Tina ("Beauty on Parade") ... **Lindsay Bloom**
Tina / Emma-Donna ("The Girl from Ilandia") ... **Julie Anne Haddock**
Tobirov ("The Man Who Made Volcanoes") ... **Ray Young**
Todd Daniels ("Stolen Faces") ... **John O'Connell**
Tom ("The Feminum Mystique") ... **Jay Fenichel**
Tom ("The Man Who Wouldn't Tell") ... **Tony Brubacker**

Tom Baker ("Knockout") ... **Burr DeBenning**
Tom Hamilton ("Screaming Javelins") ... **Rick Springfield**
Tommy ("Wonder Woman Meets Baroness Von Gunther") ... **Christian Juttner**
Tony Borden ("Disco Devil") ... **Robert Dunlap**
Turner Circus Guard ("Wonder Woman vs. Gargantua!") ... **Jerry Fitzpatrick**
Twins ("Screaming Javelins") ... **Kearney twins**
U.N. Delegate ("Mind Stealers from Outer Space") ... **Phyllis Flax**
Val ("A Date with Doomsday") ... **Taaffe O'Connell**
Van Driver ("Hot Wheels") ... **Frank Doubleday**
Vincent Bonelli ("Pot of Gold") ... **Steve-Allie Collura**
Violet Louise Tree ("Death in Disguise") ... **Jennifer Darling**
Vladmir Zukov ("Going, Going, Gone") ... **Bo Brundin**
Walter Lampkin ("The Bushwhackers") ... **Henry Darrow**
Ward Selkirk ("A Date with Doomsday") ... **Donnelly Rhodes**
Warden ("Wonder Woman Meets Baroness Von Gunther") ... **Edmund Gilbert**
Watchman ("Formicida") ... **Jim Nola**
Whitney Springfield ("My Teenage Idol Is Missing") ... **Dawn Lyn**
William Havitol ("IRAC Is Missing") ... **Ross Martin**
William Mayfield ("The Girl with a Gift for Disaster") ... **Raymond St. Jacques**
William Ryan ("The Murderous Missile") ... **Neil Elliot**
Woman ("The Starships Are Coming") ... **Marlena Giovi**
Wonder Girl / Drusilla ... **Debra Winger**
Wonder Woman / Diana Prince ... **Lynda Carter**
Wonder Woman Impersonator ("Stolen Faces") ... **Jeannie Epper**
Woodward Nightingale ("Death in Disguise") ... **Joel Fabiani**
Wotan ("Last of the Two-Dollar Bills") ... **James Olson**
Yamura Sr. ("Seance of Terror") ... **Tad Horino**
Yuri Grovka ("Going, Going, Gone") ... **Jean Ivan Dorin**
Zambezia Delegate at U.N. ("Mind Stealers from Outer Space") ... **Dee Dee Young**

Another Wonder Woman doll, this time a Barbie from the early 2000s. This one reflects Mattel's move to make Barbie's bod a little more realistic in shape; her hips are wider and her breasts not as pronounced. She came with a cute little (doll-sized) plastic lunch box and stand. This series also featured Batgirl and Poison Ivy.

Characters

Who's who and what's what

Princess Diana / Wonder Woman / Diana Prince
Born 550 B.C.
Parent: Queen Hippolyta
Sibling: Drusilla
Cousin: Evadne

Amazon princess living on Paradise Island, somewhere within the Bermuda Triangle, until Steve Trevor lands on the island and must be escorted back to the United States. Wins a contest in disguise to be the one to escort Steve. First in Washington, D.C., in the 1940s, adopts the persona of Yeoman Diana Prince in the War Department, working as an assistant to Steve. Later returns to D.C. in the 1970s to again assume the role of Diana Prince, this time as an agent for the IADC (InterAgency Defense Command). As Wonder Woman, wears a golden tiara with a ruby that can be used to contact Paradise Island, as well as the lasso of truth, a belt bestowing super strength, and bracelets that deflect bullets. Sensible, savvy, beautiful and a strong believer in the value of women. D.C. address ('70s): 410 Spruce Building. L.A. address: 409 S. Vine.

Queen Hippolyta
Children: Princess Diana, Princess Drusilla
Niece: Evadne (no doubt others on the island, too)
Beautiful, immortal ruler of Paradise Island, where she shields the Amazons from the corruption of the outside world.

Drusilla / Wonder Girl
Parent: Queen Hippolyta
Sibling: Princess Diana
Cousin: Evadne
Precocious, athletically gifted young female Amazon on Paradise Island who is sent by her mother to check on her sister in the United States. Able to spin and don the costume of Wonder Girl, assuming similar powers to her older sister.

Steven Leonard Trevor
Child: Steve Trevor Jr.
Major in the U.S. Air Corps whose plane crashes over the Bermuda Triangle after a fight with a Nazi pilot. Lands on Paradise Island and is nursed back to health by the Amazon women there. Returned to Washington, D.C., by Wonder Woman, who continues to aid him there in the subsequent years. Falls in love with Wonder Woman, oblivious to the fact that his "plain" secretary, Yeoman Diana Prince, is secretly the same person.

Steve Trevor Jr.
Parent: Steve Trevor
Agent of the IADC (InterAgency Defense Command). Grew up hearing stories of the famous Wonder Woman from his father, then met her himself in the 1970s. Promoted within the IADC and taken out of the field. Supervised field agent Diana Prince.

Gen. Phil Blankenship
Commanding officer of Steve Trevor at the U.S. War Department in the 1940s. Played football in school with J.P. Hadley of the Diamond H Ranch in Texas.

Etta Candy
Officer at the U.S. War Department in the 1940s. Coworker of Yeoman Diana Prince. Single and generally not considered attractive.

Joe Atkinson
Child: Elena Atkinson
Supervisor to Steve Trevor Jr. and Diana Prince at the IADC in the '70s. Single parent.

Eve
Serene, level-headed assistant to Steve Trevor Jr. at the IADC in the '70s.

Harold Farnum
Parent: Sen. Farnum
Geeky neighbor of Diana Prince in D.C. who is rather enamored with her. Lives in #73. Student and aspiring magician who helps Diana in the case of Count Cagliostro and his alchemy ("Diana's Disappearing Act").

IRAC
Information Retrieval Associative Computer at the IADC that thinks pretty highly of itself and costs $100 a minute to use.

Rover
Roving computer module of IRAC patterned after a canine. Likes to play tricks. Programmed by "the boys at the lab" of the IADC and basically has free rein at the IADC offices.

Marcia
Blond secretary to Steve Trevor Sr. at the War Department and Nazi spy. Dated Steve. Address: 2809 W. 20th Street, Chevy Chase, Maryland.

Andros
Child: Andros II
Socrates-quoting alien who comes to Earth in the 1940s on a mission from a planetary council to assess Earthlings and their World War II. Becomes enthralled with Wonder Woman, who also is rather enthralled with him.

Andros II
Parent: Andros
Alien investigator / bounty hunter who visits Earth in the 1970s pursuing the evil Scrill, and meets Wonder Woman, who knew his father. Based at the planet Octaros, 29 light-years from Earth.

An adorable little Amazon princess from the DC Super Friends line by Fisher Price, on shelves in 2012.

66 We twirled around and we thought that we might become Wonder Woman. 99

— *L.S. Kim, film studies professor,*
"Wonder Women: the Untold Story of America's Superheroines," March 2012

Episodes

Here's where all the action is

Season 1

"The New Original Wonder Woman"
(90-minute pilot)
November 7, 1975
Written by Stanley Ralph Ross; directed by Leonard Horn.
Aaaaahhhhh ... BRBTV loves this first season the best, as it sets Diana Prince in the Nazi era in which she originated when she debuted on the comic page in 1941. In this inaugural story, after an intro of black-and-white newsreel footage and the clever, snazzy, comic-book-designed musical intro, the Nazis are plotting a secret mission to blow up the Brooklyn Navy Yard and a strategic Allied factory. U.S. Intelligence catches wind of it, and Maj. Steve Trevor flies to the Devil's Triangle to intercept this Nazi plane. Both planes are destroyed, and as the two pilots parachute toward land, the Nazi shoots Steve. He lands on the shores of Paradise Island, where he's discovered by two of the beautiful Amazon women living there. "It's a man!" they note with surprise. One just happens to be the Princess, the only daughter of the Queen *(though that would be contradicted later in the season)*, and that quite dewy-eyed

princess can't help but nurse the ailing Steve back to health.

When the Queen sets an athletic competition to determine which Amazon will return Maj. Trevor to his home (before his "savage" manly ways corrupt the tranquil island, you understand), the Princess, forbidden by her mother to compete, wins the contest in disguise. The Queen grants her the golden belt, tiara and lasso of truth, then Diana reveals herself. Reluctantly, the Queen accepts this, and soon Diana hops her invisible jet to the U.S. War Department, her precious cargo in tow. Back in D.C., Maj. Trevor has been assumed dead, meanwhile, and it's clear something's up with his assistant, Marcia. She's not at all happy after Wonder Woman drops off Steve — alive if not well — at the hospital, and she calls on an associate named Carl to help the situation.

Lynda Carter's star-spangled superheroine is wide-eyed and sweet as she experiences Washington, D.C., for the first time, causing a sensation strolling down a crowded street in her unique attire, and even bemusedly offering social commentary after stopping a robbery and being asked to "fill out forms." She's approached by a theatrical agent, Ashley Norman, who promptly makes some cash off her bullets-and-bracelets act but then tries to swindle her. But he's got another angle he's working, anyway.

The Nazi plot thickens, and though Wonder Woman has an innocent quality about her, she veers to the highly shrewd as she works to unravel the scheme. In a key historical moment *(and a move that was mimicked by little girls everywhere!)*, we see Diana spin around to transform from her nurse's garb into Wonder Woman for the first time.

The Paradise Island beach scenes were shot off Malibu, executive producer Douglas S. Cramer has said, and the Paradise Island stuff was shot first. In the 2004 DVD commentary for this pilot episode, Carter is surprised as she sees herself running on the beach in that first scene, evidently the first time in many years she's seen it, musing at how young and "cherubic" she looks. And to prove that the show appealed not only to little girls but to men everywhere, there's a great "Dynasty"-style catfight thrown in with Stella Stevens' character Marcia. Flashes of women's lib, however, pepper the script, reflecting the social proclivities of the '70s. Marcia remarks, for example, how Wonder Woman is described as "unfemininely pushy" in her initial appearance. By the way, BRBTV is delighted to see Stevens, whom we know as Phyllis Blake of the NBC's '80s daytime soap "Santa Barbara," and she sure gets some fab '40s fashions in this pilot. Cramer has remarked how her wardrobe came from old Warner Bros. movies and had been worn by the likes of Joan Crawford and Barbara Stanwyck. Then there's even Eric Braeden, the longtime Victor Newman of CBS' "The Young and the Restless,' as Capt. Drangel, the Nazi pilot who shoots Steve.

Cloris Leachman lays the comedy aside (for the most part) for an exotic turn as Queen Hippolyta (though she would be replaced later by Carolyn Jones). John Randolph plays Gen. Blankenship in this pilot only; he's replaced by Richard Eastham when the show returns in the spring. Lyle Waggoner has little to do in this pilot, but he's so easy in the role of Steve Trevor it's not even funny. Fannie Flagg is the doctor on Paradise Island, and adviser to the Queen, while Red Buttons is the swindling Ashley Norman.

The very first time Lynda Carter is shown in her Wonder Woman costume in these episodes is on Paradise Island in this pilot, as her mother is giving her the instruction she'll need for her journey to America. Diana wears the lovely star-spangled miniskirt — no doubt a nod to her roots and that very first appearance in Sensation Comics — though she promptly takes it off and only wears it again sparingly on the series. In the DVD commentary of this episode, Cramer tells Carter, "Once you took that skirt off, the network never wanted it to go back on again."

"Wonder Woman Meets Baroness Von Gunther"
April 21, 1976
Written by Margaret Armen; directed by Barry Crane.
It's 1942 at the U.S. War Department, and word arrives that Maj. Steve Trevor may be in danger. His assistant, Yeoman Diana Prince, kicks into her Wonder Woman spin right off the bat to track him and pull him out of danger (quite literally, with her lasso, as his Army truck goes over a ravine and bursts into flames). Steve suspects his vehicle was sabotaged, and Gen. Blankenship tells him that there will be a Senate hearing because Steve has drawn suspicion in these sabotaged weapons shipments. Steel magnate Arthur Deal III is going to preside over the hearing, he says. Then Steve gets a mysterious call to meet an informant. It's a trick to frame him in an ammunitions fire.

Clues point Steve and Diana to the imprisoned Baroness Von Gunther, who makes great effort to convince them she has no more interest in Nazi affairs. Steve is struck by the Baroness' unique pendant, which seems familiar to him. The prison warden's young son, Tommy, meanwhile, is a Sherlock Holmes aficionado and has discovered not only a secret tunnel at the prison but also lights being flashed from the watchtower. When Wonder Woman rescues him from a precarious position in the prison courtyard, she then must leave in a hurry, entrusting her golden lasso to the boy.

The Baroness pays a secret moonlight visit from the prison to the Arlington estate of Arthur Deal, with whom she's been conspiring to cast Steve in a double-agent light. She then tricks Tommy to learn where the lasso is, having a cohort, the prison guard Hanson, follow Tommy to the item's hiding place. Steve is scheduled for the special hearing on the sabotage incidents, but the night before the hearing, he disappears. He

The Season 1 DVD set includes not only the commentary by Lynda Carter and Douglas S. Cramer on the pilot, but also the documentary "Beauty, Brawn and Bulletproof Bracelets: A Wonder Woman Retrospective" and some facts and trivia.

has visited Deal and put two and two together — a very dangerous prospect. The Baroness uses the lasso to threaten him to sign a letter confessing to being a Nazi spy. When Wonder Woman finds him, she's captured with the help of some Third Reich knockout gas.

Back at the prison, the guards tell the warden that both his son Tommy and their fellow guard Hanson are gone. The warden gets clued in when he finds Tommy's casebook, especially that part about a secret hidden tunnel at the facility.

Voted favorite episode by BRBTV! There was just something about this one as this author was watching as a little girl. Creepy cool, maybe? The element of a kid solving a mystery, spying from up in a tree and carefully scribbling clues into a notebook? More than any of the others, this one just seemed to communicate the dark edge of Nazi Germany much more clearly. This first regular episode of the show's first season originally aired several months after the pilot, and there's a sense that some time has passed in the action, too, as Steve draws attention to Diana's art for intuition and her loyalty. The episode also includes a good knockout punch or two by Steve Trevor and a grassy-slope-rolling catfight between Wonder Woman and the Baroness that ends with one of them in the pool. Christine Belford, such a Jaclyn Smith look-alike, portrays the Baroness, and she shows up a few years later, ironically, as nanny Susan Farragut on "Dynasty," though she's able to avoid the catfights there!

"Fausta: The Nazi Wonder Woman"
April 28, 1976
Written by Bruce Shelly (credited as Shelley) and David Ketchum; directed by Barry Crane.
The Fuhrer has taken note of this American "Wonder Woman," so he tasks some Nazi agents with capturing her for study. The bait? Steve Trevor, of course. A pretty blond fraulein — a '36 Olympian — poses as a cleaning woman to abduct Steve at his office, then calls his office later to set the trap for Wonder Woman, telling Diana she is someone who found a mysterious SOS note from Steve. Diana responds readily (with a twirl, of course). When she follows the lead to a warehouse, she dukes it out with some Nazi guys, then uses her lasso to find out where Steve is. The observant Nazis take note. They decide they must capture the lasso and use it to compel Wonder Woman to reveal her secrets.

They stage a demonstration at a war bonds fundraiser — complete with the fraulein Fausta disguised as a second Wonder Woman — to capture her and use the lasso against her. Steve sees through Fausta's disguise and he and Etta give chase as the Nazis flee the demonstration. The Nazis manage to fly off to Germany with our hero, and Steve is unable to marshal official resources to rescue her, even after an urgent appeal to Gen. Blankenship. Steve goes on "furlough" to England to connect with an old buddy, Charlie, at the Office of Strategic Services and sneak into Nazi territory.

Wonder Woman, meanwhile, stripped of her belt and lasso, is interrogated, but the Nazis think this notion of an island of women is quite preposterous *(just wait a couple episodes!)*. The Amazon gets to prove she's still a formidable force without her belt, even while trying to appeal to Fausta's womanhood and self-esteem. She escapes — just in time for Steve to be captured. About as soon as Diana Prince reports back to work, she turns around and hops her invisible plane to fly right back to Germany to retrieve Steve, having learned the bad news about his capture from Etta and the General. In the midst of the male Nazi agents' misogynist bickering with Fausta, Wonder Woman's divide-and-conquer approach with the fraulein eventually works.

Ironic, that the two lookalikes in this episode are portrayed by actresses with the same first name, as Lynda Day George delivers the role of Fausta. Her husband Christopher George is Rojak. Steve's old buddy Charlie is played by Jeff Cooper, who would go on to portray Sue Ellen Ewing's psychiatrist, Dr. Simon Ellby, on "Dallas."

"Beauty on Parade"
October 13, 1976
Written by Ron Friedman; directed by Richard Kinon.
It's May 1942, and a top-secret assembly chain has been taking some hits, the latest being an explosion at Fort Russell, Maryland. The Miss GI Dreamgirl beauty contest has just happened to be at every stop along the sabotage chain. An agent is needed to infiltrate the contest, but this has to be a very "gorgeous" girl, as Steve says, turning down Diana's offer to help. So it's the redheaded "Diana Paradise" who enters the competition. Wearing a slinky white cotton dress *(no, that's not an oxymoron!)*, she wows 'em in her dance audition, despite the reservations of the contest

pianist, Monty Burns, and some of the other contestants. Manager Lola Flynn thinks Diana reminds her of herself many years ago.

Diana must step in as Wonder Woman to aid Steve when he's targeted by the saboteur operation. She uses her lasso on the perps, but this "cheap muscle" can't tell them everything about who's behind this. Back at the contest, Monty has done some checking around on this Diana Paradise, who then dodges not only catty contestants (particularly the insecure Rita) but also the frisky judge and emcee, Jack Wood. She follows a lead from Steve that night and discovers a masked saboteur at the site of the military's top-secret scanner project. But the evil operation goes deeper than that, all the way to an assassination target: Gen. Dwight D. Eisenhower, whose plane will soon be landing at Avery Field. After Steve and Gen. Blankenship sort through the details, Etta Candy tries to get word to Diana at the contest at the Officer's Club Theatre but can't get through. Then, during the contest, Wonder Woman must thwart Monty's attempts to do-in Diana Paradise, then scoot out to where the bad guys are opening fire on Gen. Eisenhower's entourage, which now includes Steve and Gen. Blankenship, running out of luck. "There's our luck, General," Steve says as she runs onto the scene, "and it never came in a more beautiful package."

And guess who wins the contest? Well, you're half-right! Lynda Carter revisits her former beauty-contest days as she walks the winner's row as this highly reluctant, barely smiling Amazon princess!

For the first time, the action shifts away from the Nazis. Diana certainly lays the groundwork for her "promotion" in the second season, showing her ingenuity to step out of her secretary's skirt and go undercover at the beauty contest. A pre-"Eight is Enough" Dick Van Patten guests as radio comic Jack Wood, emcee of the beauty contest. Anne Francis is the den mother of the contestants. The episode marks the first use of the starburst effect to cover Diana's spinning transition to Wonder Woman (and when she stops spinning, she's no longer clutching her other outfit!), plus the spin is no longer in slow motion. Steve Trevor continues his major Lois-Lane ways when all it takes is Diana putting her glasses back on with her red wig to keep him from realizing she's Wonder Woman — though he does note that in the slinky dress she reminds him of someone ... Joan Crawford, actually.

"The Feminum Mystique," Part 1
November 6, 1976
Written by Jimmy Sangster, Barbara Avedon and Barbara Corday; directed by Herb Wallerstein.
"Introducing Debra Winger" in the opening credits is right, because this role marked the future movie star's debut. In the story, at Aldridge Field, Virginia, in June 1942, Diana is amazed when Steve shows her the XPJ-1, a top-secret aircraft just developed by the military. Scientist Peter Knight explains that it flies by jet propulsion. But before Steve can take it for a spin, it's plane-napped right in front of their eyes. Two Nazis, Capt. Radl and Lt. Wertz, have washed up on shore and have been watching from the sidelines. Steve calls Gen. Blankenship to enact a Code Z and blow the plane out of the sky, and the Nazis buy the ruse, thinking this experimental plane is no good.

Wertz, the pilot, is fished out of the sea and taken back home, while Radl hides out at the Forestry Service in Virginia. These Nazi agents have taken note of Wonder Woman's powerful bracelets and want to know more about this amazing Amazon. *This seems to largely ignore the plot of two episodes earlier, though that's not the only continuity issue: The action takes us back to Paradise Island, and amid the Amazons' spectacular gymnastic feats we hear the Queen's praise for her young daughter Drusilla — little sis to that "only child" she'd mentioned in the pilot! (But hey, perhaps it's because the Queen is also different — Carolyn Jones rather than Cloris Leachman!)*

It seems the Queen misses her elder daughter; she sends Drusilla to the U.S. to fetch her. When Dru arrives, we see a better view of Diana's apartment as we hear a better explanation *(than was offered in the pilot episode)* as to why Diana stayed in the U.S. after dropping off the recuperating Steve Trevor. Dru picks up more cues on men that evening, when Diana hosts a quiet dinner at her place for Steve and Peter Knight.

The next day, Dru wanders off on her own and evokes the same kind of glances as she heads down the street in her nightie-looking Amazon attire as her sister once did in her Wonder Woman duds. A stop at the soda shop cures that, and soon she's adorned like the pre-'50s sock hop. Gen. Blankenship plays host to her, planning on a tour of Mount Vernon, but then he's kidnapped. It takes a couple tries, but soon Dru is doing her own spin to become ... Wonder Girl! She tries to rescue the General but gets captured. The Nazis now think they have Wonder Woman.

Longtime actor John Saxon, shown here at the Motor City Comic Con in Novi, Michigan, in May 2006, has appeared in a LOT of TV series. In "The Feminum Mystique" he's the evil Nazi captain, Radl, who for a time manages to take over Paradise Island and enjoys adversarial conversation with its queen.

"The Feminum Mystique," Part 2
November 8, 1976
Written by Jimmy Sangster, Barbara Avedon and Barbara Corday; directed by Herb Wallerstein.
The XPJ-1's designer, Peter Knight, is revealed to be a spy as the Nazis try to ply the secrets of Wonder Girl at a hidden warehouse in D.C. Peter, posing as a victim like her, turns on the charm, since this "Wonder Woman" reminds him of the young Drusilla he met the other day. She spills how her bracelets are made of Feminum, a substance found only on Paradise Island. U.S. Intelligence intercepts a signal that the Nazis are preparing a ground force for the location 30' 22" N 64' 47" W — which

Diana immediately recognizes as Paradise Island. She heads there in her invisible plane. Once there, she leads her own force to the Feminum mine at the other end of the island.

The Nazis arrive, and after a few of them get tossed around by the playful Amazons, they finally take control with some knockout gas *(that gas seems to be the only way to take down an Amazon, as evidenced in these early episodes!)*. Wonder Girl manages to escape her captivity, but she has a hard time convincing Steve Trevor what happened when she gets back to the War Department. Steve finally confronts Peter and learns the truth, but he doesn't realize that Lt. Wertz is there on the base, working undercover as Harvey Manning.

On the island, the Amazons are forced to mine Feminum for the Nazis. Wonder Girl arrives on the invisible plane, and she and Diana hatch a plan to take back the island. The Nazis then get their memories erased. But the crisis isn't over. Wonder Woman and Wonder Girl return to the U.S. just as the replacement XPJ-1 is about to take flight — with Wertz in the pilot's seat.

Debra Winger's Wonder Girl is rather adorable in this two-parter, and interestingly enough, the Americans don't get to discover this new superheroine. She's only seen by the Nazis, so she doesn't get the same kind of introduction as her big sis did. Amusing, that the Nazis cannot tell the difference between Wonder Woman and Wonder Girl, not only in the kidnapping, but later on Paradise Island, when Wonder Girl arrives and takes Wonder Woman's place in the captivity at the Feminum mine without anyone noticing. By the way, when she arrives in the invisible plane, viewers might wonder, does that thing have remote control? Well, you could probably say that! In the Wonder Woman comics of the '70s, for instance, our hero refers to it as her "robot plane," and she controls the vehicle through telepathy. Also, the two Amazon superheroines seem to take the long way back to D.C. from their Bermuda Triangle area — they look outside the invisible plane and marvel at the Statue of Liberty! Prolific TV star John Saxon, who would go on to portray Rashid Ahmed on "Dynasty" among many other roles, is the lead Nazi agent, Capt. Radl, in this two-parter. Carolyn Jones as the Queen is much more oblivious to any danger from the outside world than her predecessor Cloris Leachman was.

One of the TV Guide ads promoting the show.

"Wonder Woman vs. Gargantua!"
December 18, 1976
Written by David Ketchum and Tony DiMarco; directed by Charles R. Rondeau.
In Africa, a special ape is undergoing some top-secret training by the Nazis — with Wonder Woman. Or is it? His blond trainer, Erica Belgard, boasts of the animal's abilities as she takes off her Wonder Woman disguise. Flash-forward five months to September 1942, when that ape, named Gargantua, is doing a turn at Turner Circus near D.C. He's touted as an ape "who walks and thinks like a man." Erica aims to rescue an agent who's fallen into American hands. The agent, Conrad Steigler, is being interrogated by Steve Trevor that same day. The Nazis want to know exactly what he's told the Americans.

At a Nazi hideout in an old abandoned D.C. oil refinery, Erica and her cohorts determine Steigler's location, then she sends the superstrong Gargantua into this heavily guarded apartment building. The mission is successful: Gargantua retrieves Steigler and tosses around the military policemen who try to stop him. But before hopping the U-boat back to Berlin, the Nazis decide to wait for Wonder Woman to attempt a retrieval of the agent so that they can nab her, too.

The next day, Steve and Diana consult an animal behavioral expert, Dr. Osmond, suspecting that the circus' "escaped" Gargantua is really the ape one of the MPs, Sgt. Henderson, reported seeing. The scientist reports, from clues found at the scene, that this is a great ape and highly trainable. Osmond inadvertently helps Wonder Woman fall right into the enemy's trap by ascertaining, from crude oil found on ape hair left behind, that the animal is being held at an oil refinery. When the Amazon princess arrives and sees the ape, she develops an affinity for him and tries to soothe the savagely trained animal. Steve and the military police then arrive at the Gillion oil refinery and shoot the gorilla to save Wonder Woman from its grip.

As he recuperates, Gargantua begins to see Wonder Woman as a friend, as well as Diana Prince. But the Nazis figure out that Gargantua is being held at Osmond's lab, and Erica and her cohort Hans seize him and attempt to reprogram him. Wonder Woman — and her kindness — are not far behind.

Wonder Woman mentions Paradise Island as her home — strange, as it was such a tight secret until now, and the Nazis who invaded it even had their memories erased. Robert Loggia portrays Col. Hans Eichler.

"The Pluto File"
December 25, 1976
Written by Herbert Bermann; directed by Herb Wallerstein.
At a research facility in Maryland, Steve and Gen. Blankenship are getting a demonstration from Prof. Warren of the Pluto Project, a device that can prevent — or cause — earthquakes. Meanwhile, a notorious and highly paid mercenary agent, nicknamed the Falcon, slips through customs at New York's LaGuardia Airport. His target in the U.S.: the Pluto File, Warren's research. The people the Falcon has encountered, however, have been coming down with the Bubonic Plague, including his traveling companion, Camilla Moret. He has no idea he's carrying the disease as he's plotting to create a fault line in Maryland.

Disguised as an orderly bringing in a meal, the Falcon attacks Warren and steals his research, landing the scientist in Walter Reed Hospital. Steve and Diana start to put two and two together after the theft, discovering that Prof. Warren's assistant, Charles Benson, was aiding the Falcon when he falls ill with the Plague, as well. They then track the Falcon's movements into Bladensburg, Maryland, to a top-secret atomic lab and its Project 741, a powerful part of the Manhattan Project. The sinister agent plans to use the Pluto Project's earthquake-creating abilities to essentially make the Project 741 lab into a giant bomb that, when it explodes, will destroy all of D.C.

After some of the Falcon's test explosions begin to affect Project 741's reactor, Steve and Gen. Blankenship try to convince Dr. Norris to shut it down. This will require the authorization of Pres. Roosevelt and his rep, James Porter, who realize that they cannot evacuate D.C. in time to avoid this disaster. Wonder Woman stays by the professor's side during this. But the Falcon and his flunky Frank Willis return to the scientist to "tie up some loose ends," just as the Falcon finally begins to feel ill, himself.

"Brady Bunch" dad Robert Reed is quite believable as the sinister Falcon, at turns charming, sophisticated and wonderfully dark. Prolific TV actor Kenneth Tigar is Dr. Barnes, who treats the plague victims; you may recall him as Fritz Heath on "Dynasty" and Dr. Gordon on "Dallas."

"Last of the Two-Dollar Bills"
January 8, 1977
Written by Paul Dubov and Gwen Bagni; directed by Stuart Margolin.
It's September 1942, and the news arrives that notorious agent Wotan is coming to the U.S. No one knows what this top Nazi agent even looks like. Also, an enemy submarine is sunk in Chesapeake Bay. Steve and Diana watch as agents come ashore, then Wonder Woman steps in to duke it out with them. But one man escapes. Diana later recognizes him as he's taking street photos for sale, suckering people for payment. A week later, he's nowhere to be found, to the great dismay of Etta Candy, who really wanted to send that photo of Diana and her to her mom! Diana and Etta check the address he gave, which is the darkroom he was borrowing for the photos, but the clerk there says he doesn't know how to find the guy. Diana is suspicious, so Wonder Woman checks the guy's apartment and realizes he's one of the agents she saw washing ashore.

Steve offers to take Wonder Woman on a tour of the Bureau of Printing and Engraving as he tries to wrap his brain around the clue of a two-dollar bill he recently received. At Nazi headquarters, two agents have been made to look just like the head of the Bureau of Printing and Engraving, Hank Miller, and his fiancée, Maggie Robbins.

Steve realizes the Nazis plan to counterfeit the popular two-dollar bills and thereby undermine the U.S. economy. Hank and Maggie are abducted and replaced with the look-alikes. Steve has sent a secret service agent, Dan Fletcher, to look after the Bureau head, but he's promptly taken out of commission, as well. Then Wonder Woman, who realized that Maggie had been replaced by someone else at her diner, is sidelined, at least temporarily, by the evil agents. Wotan, who was posing as the diner cook, forces her to give up her bracelets and get behind bars with the real Maggie and Hank in the basement of the diner. Steve tries to track down what happened to his man Fletcher, encountering the fake Hank Miller. Wotan frames the real Hank for stealing the plates he wanted from the Bureau.

Wonder Woman breaks her threesome out of their cell and gets her bracelets back. Steve, meanwhile, has discovered his Hank Miller is an imposter — and a Nazi at that — but then gets caught by him and the fake Maggie. He's put into the diner's basement cell, but he escapes and must defuse a bomb at the Bureau where Fletcher is being held. The Nazis head for the shore to catch a submarine that's about to arrive, but not if Wonder Woman has anything to say about it.

This episode includes Wonder Woman's first usage of her tiara as a boomerang, though it flies in its circular form rather than in a boomerang shape. For the tour at the Bureau of Printing and Engraving, we get a rare

We had to wonder, while researching this book, what if any D.C. sites were used for filming. From asking around, we've gathered that the D.C. color was largely stock footage. In "Last of the Two-Dollar Bills," for instance, much of the action takes place at the Bureau of Printing and Engraving. Here's the real building in Washington, which is actually called the Bureau of Engraving and Printing. It's clearly a different building, and it has the freeway nearby, rather than a cute café across the street!

glimpse of our hero in her ceremonial cape and short skirt, the latter of which had only been seen in the pilot's scenes on Paradise Island. For the pilot, however, it was a different skirt, with stars covering the whole of the blue fabric, whereas in this episode, the skirt features only a sprinkling of white stars (much like the bottom half of her uniform would appear in the next season) and a split hem. And speaking of her costume, it's interesting to note that the enemy agents subdue her, and force her behind bars, by merely taking away her bracelets. Her golden belt remains on during her captivity. Even with her super-strength, the threat of a gun is enough.

We also see the writers' aim to maintain Steve's sense of manhood — rather than being saved every time by his lovely Amazon friend, he does get to step in and kick some butt! Fans of the original "Star Trek" series will easily recognize Barbara Anderson, who plays Maggie Robbins here, from the episode "Conscience of the King." She was the very protective daughter of the notorious Karidian.

"Judgment from Outer Space," Part 1
January 15, 1977
Written by Stephen Kandel; directed by Alan Crosland.
It's always risky when you bring space aliens into the plot, but hey, this is already sci-fi / fantasy anyway, isn't it? In an uncharted region of space, a council of advanced peoples is pondering what to do with this Earth place they've been observing. They're considering sterilization of the planet! They send one of their kind, Andros, to Earth to do a final assessment. (We're sensing the show's overall anti-war message is getting amped up a notch or two for this one!)

The War Department investigates sightings of a UFO as Andros lands his ship in a remote wooded area. As he wanders outside the ship, though, Andros comes face to face with Steve, Diana and some soldiers and introduces himself. "I am a visitor, a very peaceful visitor," he reassures them. He wants to speak to the political leaders of this place. When some of the soldiers decide to charge him, Andros uses his pendant to freeze them, then is able to hold an exploding grenade in his hand. Steve and Gen. Blankenship tell him they can perhaps hook him up with a meeting with the President.

Wonder Woman is very enthralled with this Socrates-quoting alien who is an accomplished student of history. A Nazi spy disguised as a Swedish news reporter named Paul Bjornsen is also intrigued. As Gorel, Sakri and the other members of the Council of Planets watch through their intergalactic video linkup(!), Wonder Woman meets Andros at the Lincoln Memorial to learn more, while Bjornsen puts the moves on the vulnerable Etta for his own "research."

At a demonstration of his power the next day, Andros issues a stern warning, saying the Council of Planets is concerned that the savage Earthlings are developing atomic power at Oak Ridge. He gets his meeting with Pres. Roosevelt, then allows Wonder Woman to use her lasso on him to affirm his words. He says if anything happens to him, an orbiting craft will destroy Earth. But the President has ordered that a strike force be formed, if needed. Even as Diana Prince, she pleads his case to the military (sparking her first fight with Steve). As the Nazis apprehend Andros at the Library of Congress and even Wonder Woman cannot stop them, the Council of Planets punishes him for trusting the humans by removing his powers.

Wonder Woman is hospitalized for the first time in this episode, though the American doctors learn her body regenerates. We get to see both her cape and her skirt (the second skirt, with only a sprinkling of white stars) as she speaks with Andros, lending a much more peaceful, diplomatic air to her appearance. Andros realizes right away that this intriguing Wonder Woman and Yeoman Prince are one and the same. This episode also marks the first use of a title screen at the beginning. The writing — despite the space aliens! — is better in this one.

"Judgment from Outer Space," Part 2
January 17, 1977
Written by Stephen Kandel; directed by Alan Crosland.
Wonder Woman finds Andros' ship and gets inside. She makes a plea to the Council with his comm link. Gorel, Sakri and the other Council members hear her plea and call a vote on how to deal with this Andros situation.

The Nazis take Andros to a heavily fortified interrogation center, Schloss Markheim. British intelligence lends a hand in reporting this to the U.S.

War Department, so Steve flies off to investigate. Wonder Woman is right behind him in the invisible plane. In England, Steve gets a hand from Evan Mallory, a secret agent well-trained in relating to the Nazis.

The Nazis tap Prof. Graebner to study Andros' abilities, then try to probe the alien with a charming female, fraulein Lisa Engel. But Andros gets to the heart of the matter with Lisa, telling her details of her life she's shocked he knows. The Council contacts him again, changing their minds about leaving him there but not about destroying Earth. When Wonder Woman arrives to rescue him, Andros doesn't want to leave. He has a thing or two to tell her about these Americans she loves so much, too. Wonder Woman's golden belt is taken away. Steve and Mallory arrive disguised as Nazis, but their cover is quickly blown *(and Steve looked so unfortunately handsome in that Nazi uniform!)*.

The TV Guide ad promoting this two-part episode.

"If you do not outgrow your emotional primitivism, you will destroy yourselves," Andros warns the Nazis. Soon, the Nazis have everybody in custody! They demand to know the secrets of Andros' powerful pendant, as well as Wonder Woman's lasso and belt. Finally, Andros sees just how evil the Nazis are. As Wonder Woman leads the prisoners to freedom, getting a little help from Lisa, the Council gives Andros his powers back. Andros tells Wonder Woman he'll grant the Earth 50 years to disprove the Council's view of their savagery; he'll be back in 1992 *(we must've passed the test!)*. He even tries to woo her into space with him.

This two-parter really evokes Diana's strong feelings about peace and humankind. It's rather humorous that the Nazis keep using a black-and-white 8-by-10 photo of Wonder Woman in the Miss GI Dreamgirl pageant as a point of reference, as it's been seen in other episodes, too. We continue to love that swanky music playing whenever the invisible plane is shown flying. Carter, however, puts it a little more pointedly in her DVD extras interview: "They had the stupidest music playing over that invisible plane!"

"Formula 407"
January 22, 1977
Written by Elroy Schwartz; directed by Herb Wallerstein.
At Fort Frazier Ordnance Testing Facility in August 1942, Steve, Diana, Etta and the General watch a demo of a new formula that makes rubber as strong as steel. The General sends Steve and Diana to Argentina to pick up the formula from its creator, Prof. Moreno. It will be a dangerous mission; though Argentina is neutral in the war, Germany has plenty of supporters there.

The Nazis have gotten wind of the formula and they send their own agent, Maj. Karl Keller, to get it. They're aided by Prof. Moreno's assistant, Maria. The Nazis seize Steve and Diana's car, though Wonder Woman arrives "like the cavalry" to save the day.

At a formal reception that evening, Steve and Diana each get hit on by their Argentinian hosts. Diana's would-be suitor Antonio Cruz is making her skin crawl, but Steve is rather intrigued by the professor's daughter Lydia. Her charm unfortunately leads him right into the Nazi's hands as they're jumped while taking a walk out in the lovely Argentine night. Wonder Woman steps in but gets chloroformed. She and Steve must then bust out of the wine cellar, just as Maria's fiancé Keller is shaking the professor down. Maria feels like a fool for believing her Nazi love. But the professor is feeling worse pain — his daughter's life is in danger if he doesn't give the formula to the Nazis.

Steve and Wonder Woman search the professor's home for any sign of Lydia, to no avail, then meet up with the scientist, who has decided he must give Formula 407 to Keller. Wonder Woman appeals to Maria for help. "I know you made a mistake, and I can understand how that could happen," she tells the distraught woman. Steve convinces Prof. Moreno to pass off a fake formula to the Nazis. But things don't exactly go as planned. Wonder Woman must intervene at the Nazis' beachside rendezvous point.

We wanna know just how long Lynda Carter had to practice swinging that lasso! She's looking pretty savvy with it. It's cute in this episode to see Steve and Wonder Woman continue to flirt with each other, as he insists on not at all seeing a connection between his Amazon infatuation and his able assistant. Just like Rick Mason of "The Secrets of Isis," he's the male

Lois Lane of this show. And for Steve, the attraction is quite mutual; Wonder Woman tips her hand now and then as to her affection for the Major.

"The Bushwhackers"
January 29, 1977
Written by Skip Webster; directed by Stuart Margolin.
The Diamond H Ranch in Texas has been losing heads of cattle to rustlers, and J.P. Hadley *(portrayed by Roy Rogers)* hasn't gotten much help from the local law enforcement, Sheriff Anson Bodie and his deputy, Walter Lampkin. But he has a friend in a high place — Gen. Blankenship. The General sends the lead of his intelligence division, Steve, to investigate, and before he leaves Steve gives Diana a three-day pass from work to get some rest. But we know what Diana's going to do with that time, don't we?

The cattle rustlers are hiding out at a ghost town a few miles from the ranch — and the sheriff's deputies Lampkin and Hanks are part of the scam. Emmett Dawson, working with Lampkin, sets a trap for Steve and imprisons him in an old shaft. With the help of a little mute boy named Charlie, who witnessed the scene, Wonder Woman is able to rescue him. Wonder Woman then heads to the ranch for a new cowgirl outfit and some quality time with J.P.'s "Junior League of Nations" — his multicultural set of war orphans: Linc, Charlie, Freddie, Sen and Babette. J.P. has been suspecting Dawson in the rustling action. J.P.'s son Jeff, meanwhile, has been jealous of the attention his dad has been giving the orphans and thus has been leaking information to the rustlers. Lampkin is effectively playing on Jeff's jealousy.

Our hero's change of costume made it to the cover of this foreign TV book.

After she goes out riding with J.P. and Jeff, the rustlers nab Wonder Woman, stealing her belt and lasso. Charlie secretly witnesses this abduction, and it's enough to make him speak as he runs back to the other kids for help. The orphans work together to bust Wonder Woman out of the ghost town jail, but now Steve has been captured by the rustlers! It takes a collaborative effort to overcome the rustlers, and it requires a remorseful Jeff coming clean with his dad.

We get to see our hero do some real horseback riding in this one. Wonder Woman's Western look of red shirt and white riding pants with her red and white boots, completed by belt, lasso, bracelets and tiara, was reportedly driven by Roy Rogers' aversion to sharing a scene with so much exposed female flesh. In the very (brief) first scene with both of them, our superheroine is draped in her cape, though she promptly removes it. Then, their next scene has her in the Western outfit.

Soaps hunk Kristoff St. John (billed as Christoff St. John here) gets one of his very first roles as Linc. BRBTV votes the exceedingly adorable Charlie Bright Eagle, portrayed by David Yanez, not only the sweetest kid among the orphans, but also the MVP of the first season. And while we're at it (!), for the multicultural makeup of the war orphans, their heroics during the episode, Wonder Woman's snazzy Western attire, and even the fact that our boy Yanez can ride a horse like nobody's business, BRBTV votes this episode second best of the series. And if we didn't have such a sentimental childhood attachment to the "Von Gunther" episode, we'd vote this one first!

"Wonder Woman in Hollywood"
February 16, 1977
Written by Jimmy Sangster; directed by Bruce Bilson.
Morale-sparking war films are being produced by Mark Bremer in Hollywood, with proceeds going to war bonds, and war hero Steve Trevor is called into "action!" On Paradise Island, meanwhile, the Queen wants Diana to come home for their bimillennial celebration, the 2,000th anniversary of their arrival on the island. She reluctantly agrees to let Drusilla go fetch her older sis. Dru meets up with Diana on the Hollywood movie set, just in time to witness the attempted abduction of one of the film's other war-hero stars, Cpl. Jim Ames. Wonder Woman stops it.

Diana is concerned that someone is trying to sabotage this film project. She takes Dru to a Hollywood party that night. Two other war-hero stars of the film, Lt. Bill Rand and Sgt. Harry Willard, also attend. Lt. Rand promptly disappears after chatting with a "slinky" blond starlet, Gloria Beverly. The party's host, the film's producer, Bremer, is really a Nazi collecting U.S. war heroes to ship to Germany to stand trial for war crimes. And after the Nazis have won the war, Bremer plans to control the entire U.S. film industry.

Dru hangs out with the young Cpl. Ames at the soda shop, then must change to Wonder Girl when a couple hooligans hassle her new friend. Ames leaves out the little detail that someone else saved him as he relates the story to Dru, making Dru suspect this "war hero" is not that heroic. Back at the movie set, Sgt. Willard disappears. Steve calls for reinforcements, forcing the Nazis to step up their plan.

Both Steve and Ames are kidnapped — with the help of Ames, who's been blackmailed by the abduction of his parents. Wonder Woman tracks down Gloria and compels her with the golden lasso to reveal where the prisoners are being kept. Wonder Woman and Wonder Girl then head to Bremer's estate and attempt to free the prisoners. Wonder Woman actually appears to have been caught by surprise and taken a bullet, but she's really giving a chance for Ames to redeem himself.

What a way to end the first season! Too bad we didn't see Dru again. She certainly has a pixie-like, arms-down spin. This is Wonder Girl's first real appearance to the Americans, but there's no explanation as to who she is. Carolyn Jones stays in the role of the Queen for another episode. One of BRBTV's fave actors, Barry Van Dyke, is barely recognizable as Freddy, one of the punks who hassles Ames at the soda shop. Christopher Norris of "Trapper John, M.D." and "Santa Barbara" is starlet Gloria.

Season 2

"The Return of Wonder Woman"
(90-minute season premiere)
September 16, 1977
Written by Stephen Kandel; directed by Alan Crosland.
The show gets retooled for the second season to set it forward 35 years to modern times. The opening still carries the theme song, slightly reworded, with the comic book images borrowed from the Season 1 opener and the animating to "life" for the two core stars (but sorry, Steve — that three-piece suit and puffy hair just ain't cutting it! you're much manlier than that!). The show's title screen now reads "The New Adventures of Wonder Woman," and the writing and directing credits are moved from the musical sequence to the opening shots of the episode. Our hero's outfit also reflects some revamp: gone are the "bullet breasts" Lynda Carter lamented about in the Season 1 DVD features; this new eagle-clad corset has a little more breathing room! And the white stars on her now-high-cut blue bottoms are pared down to just a sprinkling. Her golden lasso now has powers of forgetfulness as well as truth-telling, and the star in her tiara is said to contain a ruby she can use to contact Paradise Island if needed. Her bracelets are now gold rather than silver, and the Wonder Woman spin has again sped up! The invisible plane has a new shape, too.

In the story, Steve Trevor is meeting with some associates aboard a plane, discussing recent terrorist activity, as the plane enters the Bermuda Triangle en route to Samarra, Latin America. They're being secretly watched by a Dr. Solano and his partner back in D.C. The plane encounters interference and appears to be in danger. Everyone on board passes out, thanks to some noxious gas.

Below, on Paradise Island, Diana and fellow Amazon Evadne (her cousin, it turns out) watch the plane in the sky, aware that it's in danger. Somehow the Amazons are able to take control of the plane remotely and land it (they've advanced in technology, evidently!). Diana boards the plane and recognizes a familiar face among the unconscious passengers — but it can't be Steve, because he'd be more than 60 years old! She and the Queen learn that this is Steve Trevor's son. Again, Diana wants to venture to the outside world to put things aright. Her mother opposes this but is outvoted. After a brief bullets-and-bracelets challenge from Evadne, Diana is once again on her way to America.

Steve's plane lands safely in Samarra, and he and his new "associate" *(not assistant! woo-hoo!)* Diana attend a meeting representing the U.S. in a plan to airlift a nuclear plant. But the man at the heart of it all, Dr. Solano, has evil aspirations of his own, and his partner Gloria Marquez realizes that he'll start wars if he needs to.

Diana meets IRAC — the Information Retrieval Associative Computer — and promptly programs her own faked credentials into it. She acclimates herself to a new life in Washington, D.C., fully equipped with a comfy new apartment (she did get $25,000 each for those rare old Syrian coins her mother sent with her, after all), and this time her social commentary is about inflation, not bureaucratic paperwork. But she's followed by Gloria, then her apartment gets broken into — and bugged — just before she reports to work at the IADC (InterAgency Defense Command).

The Season 2 DVD set features a bonus documentary, "Revolutionizing a Classic: From Comic Book to Television."

Wonder Woman saves Steve after an ambush by terrorists — led by the evil Dr. Solano. Gloria takes special note of this amazing Amazon, recording her on a video camera. The bad guys do a little digging on our hero, uncovering her past fighting the Nazis in 1942-1945. Having developed lifelike robots trained to fight, they craft a duplicate of Steve Trevor and swap him for the real thing at an embassy shindig. But when he puts the moves on Diana back at her apartment, she knows something's up. She subdues him and finds the real Steve, and together they must thwart Dr. Solano's plan to divert the airlift of the nuclear plant.

For her new IADC job, Diana even gets an office, reflecting her advancement in this new era of greater opportunities for females. This is the fifth and final episode featuring Paradise Island, and the look (and music) of it remain the same from the first season. Beatrice Straight is the third actress to take on the role of Queen Hippolyta, and she plays it shrewder and sharper in tone. Jessica Walter guests as Gloria. As Wonder Woman and the new Steve chat for the first time, he mentions that his dad raised him on stories of Wonder Woman and their adventures. She reveals that she'll be 2,527 years old on her next birthday. Wonder Girl seems to be out of the picture, though, because when Steve asks her if there's an "organization" of Wonder Women, she says it's only her. Plus, there's no reference to Wonder Girl or Drusilla on Paradise Island. BRBTV's fave line, after Diana discovers an intruder in her apartment and tells her, "You're a woman; we shouldn't be enemies." The woman replies, "I don't know where your head is at, baby; women are naturally enemies!" And so fun, by the way, that the second season kicks off with a catfight just as the first one did.

"Anschluss '77"
September 23, 1977
Written by Dallas L. Barnes; directed by Alan Crosland.
Wonder Woman's return after so many years is causing a media splash. But Steve and Diana must turn their attention elsewhere: modern-day Nazi activity has been detected in Cordova, South America, led by surviving Nazi officer Fritz Gerlich. They fly there to investigate. Steve gets hit by a street thief, and when he chases him down, Wonder Woman steps in to help *(gotta love his surprise: "Wonder Woman, what are you doing in South America?").*

They meet with the local police captain, Gaitan, then trace a lead to the home of a Dr. Stern, who they learn was doing research on cloning. Diana is kidnapped from the house and taken to an abandoned mine shaft. One of her captors is Gerlich, who shows her the brand-new leg that replaced his missing leg of four decades earlier. She's then left there to die in an explosion, though Wonder Woman escapes and hitches a ride on the Nazis' helicopter to their secret camp. She then hurries back just in time to make an appearance as Diana to Steve, who has tracked her to the mine.

Back at the Nazi base at Campo Grande, Dr. Stern reveals to Gerlich, as well as to the sons of the Nazi men he worked with decades earlier,

Behind the Scenes: Bronson Canyon

The helicopter stunt you see in "Anschluss '77," as well as the explosion scene preceding it, were shot at Bronson Canyon. The canyon, also called Bronson Caves, is a section of Griffith Park in Los Angeles that has served as a filming location for a large number of movies and TV shows, from the early days of motion pictures to the present, according to Wikipedia. Its craggy and remote-looking setting, but easily accessible location, has made it a prime shooting choice. Its tunnel was famously used as the exterior for the Batcave in the 1960s "Batman" series starring Adam West.

The Bronson Caves are man-made, and were probably created back around 1900, when the area was a rock quarry, according to Seeing-Stars.com. (Some say the caves themselves were created especially for the 1922 version of "Robin Hood" with Douglas Fairbanks.)

Griffith Park is also the setting for the tense meeting with the perp before Farrah Fawcett's famous skateboarding scene in the 1976 "Charlie's Angels" episode "Consenting Adults." The skateboard chase was shot throughout the sidewalks and hilly zones of Griffith Park's far east side, according to CharliesAngels.org.

The 1948 Kirk Alyn Superman also saw shooting there — making that no less than three Justice Leaguers who've starred at this location, as pointed out by Scott Sebring in his YouTube tour of the Batcave!

The exterior used for the Batcave, Griffith Park. Photo by Mike Serrico.

Strasser and Rogel, that he actually preserved some cells of the Fuhrer for just this moment ... to be cloned. *Egads!* Steve and Diana surveil the secret camp, and Diana takes the Jeep to report it to the local officials. Steve then infiltrates the ranks, garbed in the brown-shirted Nazi uniform, addressed by the clone of the Fuhrer himself, as Wonder Woman secretly watches in horror. Steve and Wonder Woman then get to Dr. Stern — learning his true name is Heimlich Von Klemper — and compel him to give the directions for reversing the cloning. Afterward, Wonder Woman is able to destroy his cloning lab.

This is a bit of a dark episode, and it's surprising that they actually went there, depicting a clone of Hitler. Still, it's nice to see the Nazi intrigue return, if for nothing more than to solidify the continuity between these first two seasons. Wonder Woman seems to have her own memories of the Nazi regime, and it was referenced in the previous episode that she had remained in the United States from 1942 to 1945. It's rather amusing that the first thing Diana does when the Nazis leave her in the abandoned mine shaft is try to spin, but it's kinda tricky while her torso is bound. You might recognize the actor who portrays Gerlich's hired hand Koenig in this one; Kurt Kreuger also portrayed a Nazi officer named Henchler in "The Feminum Mystique" in the first season.

There's a scene in this episode where Wonder Woman grabs the underside of the helicopter that the Nazis are flying to escape the abandoned mine shaft. She hangs from the copter as it lifts and takes off. This was a great shot though quite controversial for the actress, who was determined to get the stunt done. "We were losing our light," she says in the Season 1 DVD extras. "We were in a canyon. The camera couldn't get far enough back. They were seeing that it was Jeannie Epper or whoever hanging on that helicopter. ... And I just ran in and grabbed the underneath strut or cross thing of the helicopter and told them to go up, and they did, and then they just went up about 30 feet or so, and maybe more, and then they put me right back down. They got the shot. And the next day I got into big trouble."

"The Man Who Could Move the World"
September 30, 1977
Written by Judy Burns; directed by Bob Kelljan.
Steve and Diana attend a late-night briefing on Dr. Kenneth Wilson, who retired from the space program and delved into research on psychokinesis, but has now vanished. They go to his office at the Washington Institute of Behavioral Research and find it ransacked — then an alarm goes off downstairs. One of Dr. Wilson's fellow staff members, Taft, has been trapped in the vault and is losing air. Wonder Woman steps in to break him out, then he tells how he was grabbed at the same time Dr. Wilson disappeared. Diana finds a tape showing Dr. Wilson experimenting with a Japanese man named Ishida, who demonstrates his power to move objects with his mind but who then turns on Dr. Wilson to take his brain wave machine.

Diana — then Wonder Woman — investigates at Takeo Ishida's home, where she finds an assortment of Wonder Woman paraphernalia *(it's a smashing sort of tribute to the show and the icon — even including a Mego 12" doll like the one this author got as a girl, of which Wonder Woman comments that "only a few sold during the Second World War, for charity")*. Diana does some digging into Ishida's past. Ishida then lures Steve to Los Alamos under the guise of a letter "from Wonder Woman." On the way, though, Steve gets a scare when Ishida takes control of his Jeep, leading him to a former World War II relocation camp for the Japanese. Ishida was once a resident there, himself, it seems, and his memories are haunting him.

As Steve wanders around the camp, objects fly all around him, then Ishida appears and confronts him. But it's Wonder Woman he really wants to confront. He faults her for the death of his older brother Masaaki all those decades earlier, when the two tried to escape the camp as young boys. Wonder Woman tried to save them from the artillery fire, but Masaaki was hit.

Wonder Woman hops her invisible plane toward Los Alamos (getting a bit of grief from the air control officer for not having a flight code). Later, as the captive Steve and Dr. Wilson watch, Ishida forces Wonder Woman to walk toward a landmine. Her power shorts out the brain wave machine, at last, and Ishida learns a little more about why you should use your powers for good!

Dr. Wilson's first name is given as Kenneth in the episode's beginning, though the credits list it as Theodore. You can see Lynda Carter, who commented in the first-season DVD extras on how "green" she was in this role, coming into her own in the second season. Almost as if a parallel to Diana Prince's new IADC job, which more appropriately matches her capabilities, the actress herself is markedly more confident in the role. This episode serves nicely to further bridge the gap between the first two seasons, showing Wonder Woman in a "flashback" scene with the two young boys. It would've been even better if she were wearing her first-season costume rather than the redesign. That Mego 12" doll shown at Ishida's home, by the way, is a variation of what was actually released in 1977. Her red boots, for one thing, have the white detailing, whereas the dolls didn't as sold. Steve remarks that the doll is a collector's item. Yea, if he only knew!

"The Bermuda Triangle Crisis"
October 7, 1977
Written by Calvin Clements Jr.; directed by Seymour Robbie.
The show ventures into the "Devil's Triangle" once again, as Diana, Steve and Joe Atkinson are summoned into the briefing room to learn about a sabotage operation at sea. Diana is more concerned, actually, about an experimental nuclear facility planned for the vicinity of Paradise Island. She contacts the Queen via the ruby in her tiara *(we were wondering when that was going to show up!)*. Her mother advises her to watch for "the heart of darkness."

Diana and Steve fly to the Triangle in search of terrorist Raymond Manta, whose team of operatives has been throwing aircraft off-course for years. Manta's antics force a malfunction of their plane, and they parachute onto an island that turns out to be the base of Manta's operations, ICOPE (International Confederation of the Power Elite). They sneak up to the base to send out a radio signal for help. But when they spot Lt. Cmdr. Robert Mansfield, a kidnapped U.S. pilot whose plane had gone down, they then infiltrate the base in disguise to rescue him (the shapely Diana struggling to look manly in her uniform!). As they try to take Mansfield away in a Jeep, they're stopped.

Back at IADC headquarters, the radio signal tips off Atkinson that Diana and Steve are still alive. He deploys a Naval search mission, but Manta

BRBTV's own Wonder Woman Mego doll from the '70s, with Diana Prince outfit. It's been played with a little, of course. By BRB. As a child!

activates his undersea weapon, Sting Ray. He has Steve and Diana locked up behind bars, but Diana devises a ruse to escape. Wonder Woman then takes to the sea *(in a snazzy, spandex, red, white and blue diving outfit — marking the first use of that)*, where she sabotages Manta's sabotage, saving the destroyer Jefferson that Atkinson deployed. But Manta moves on to larger terrorism, rigging the whole island to explode.

Beatrice Straight hangs onto her role of Queen Hippolyta from a few episodes ago. You've gotta love Diana's '70s fashions. She departs from her theme of dresses in this one for yellow bellbottoms (later cut into shorts!), a thin rainbow-patterned tank top and a flurry of necklaces on her tanned décolletage. Rockin', man.

"Knockout"
October 14, 1977
Written by Mark Rodgers; directed by Seymour Robbie.
Diana comes home one night to discover two thugs trying to break into her apartment. She learns from Joe Atkinson that Steve was abducted on his way to a vacation in Los Angeles. She flies to L.A. to investigate. Her cab driver, Pete Johnson, lends a hand (a fist, actually, punching the bad guys who are following them) just before Wonder Woman arrives to find out why these guys were menacing Diana Prince. After she finally gets to the Camden Hotel, a creepy guy in an elevator follows her.

She phones up her IADC contact in L.A. and tells him that she wants some time to figure out just what's going on with Steve. She tracks the investigation to the run-down apartment building of terrorist Angel Velasquez, where she uses her lasso to learn from Angel of "The Movement," a secret organization that has captured Steve. One of its members is an ex-cop named Carolyn. Diana finds a place to hang with Pete and his young son Ted, but the creepy guy, a member of The Movement, is still following her.

Back in D.C., Joe learns that the mysterious Carolyn Hamilton once worked with Steve. At The Movement's hideout, Steve asks Carolyn just what happened to her since they last met, when Steve saved her life. She does appreciate that whole life-saving thing and has reservations about Steve's abduction. Diana, meanwhile, tells the L.A. IADC that she wants the chance to save Steve. But The Movement then kidnaps young Ted as added leverage, forcing an exchange with Diana.

In his captivity, Steve keeps working on Carolyn's allegiances, and it's revealed that L.A. IADC agent Tom Baker is really working for The Movement. The group has plans for the international Trade Conference being held in L.A., a prime opportunity to make some demands. Wonder Woman thwarts their effort.

The series ventures to the West Coast, and that sunny setting would certainly recur in the coming episodes. Ted Shackelford, who would go on to the role of Gary Ewing on "Dallas" only a year or so later, plays the street-smart, and California-blond-handsome, Pete. Jayne Kennedy adds some much-needed color to the series as Carolyn. Wonder Woman does her third tiara throw in this one, and like the first throw, the tiara remains in its circular shape. In the second throw, a couple episodes back, the tiara straightens as a boomerang. And in this one we get to see her use the golden lasso for the first time to make someone forget.

"The Pied Piper"
October 21, 1977
Written by David Ketchum, Tony DiMarco and Brian McKay; directed by Alan Crosland.
Rock 'n' roll star Hamlin Rule *(a surprising Martin Mull in Elvis-like attire)* is the newest sensation, with a stage act that includes a mesmerizing flute routine. His concert receipts, incidentally, are getting stolen. Joe Atkinson is feeling a generation gap with his UCLA-coed daughter Elena, who barely talks to him and has been taken in by Hamlin Rule. Thing is, Rule has been hypnotizing his young fans to commit the thefts.

Rule's heavy Carl Schwartz tries to shake down venue manager Amos Hoffman for the cash from the latest concert, which he, of course, doesn't have. Then he joins Rule at his poolside pad on the West Coast. Diana *(sans Steve, for the most part, this episode)* flies to L.A. with Joe Atkinson to investigate Rule. She enters a costume contest (as Wonder Woman!) to become his on-stage "girl in the golden basket," but it's Elena who wins. When Diana tries to talk to her, Rule doesn't appreciate her sniffing around. After talking to her college friend Louise, Diana tracks Elena to the Elura recording studio, where Rule tries to turn his Pied Piper routine on her. She's able to secretly change into Wonder

Woman (in a spinning chair!) and duke it out with the entirely thuggy Carl. Afterward, she finds a clue that Rule and his crew are behind the robberies.

Rule, meanwhile, indoctrinates Elena to his behind-the-scenes operation, showing her the gizmo his crew has been using that causes objects like door locks to disintegrate before your eyes. Then, at Rule's gig at Cleft Concert Hall in L.A., the band of bandits strikes, dousing Wonder Woman with knockout gas to escape. Elena's not too keen on her new "job." Joe and Diana learn a bracelet belonging to her was found at the crime scene and realize she's involved. It takes Wonder Woman breaking into Hamlin's plush pad to rescue Elena and learn through the golden lasso just what has been motivating Rule's actions.

Eve Plumb of "The Brady Bunch" is Joe Atkinson's daughter Elena, who, incidentally, was mentioned briefly in a previous episode. A familiar-voiced Bob Hastings is the gatekeeper at Hamlin Rule's estate.

"The Queen and the Thief"
October 28, 1977
Written by Bruce Shelly; directed by Jack Arnold.
Who needs a car when you can race to work as Wonder Woman? Diana gets summoned to the secure IADC briefing room early in the morning, and we see her navigating the long stretch to get there. It seems hall-of-fame thief Evan Robley is the new prime target for her, Steve and Joe. And his prime target? Queen Kathryn of Malakar, a Princess-Grace-like monarch who's now lingering around the "millionaire's sandbox" of Palm Beach. So it's off to Florida, where Steve and Diana go undercover.

Diana, as a maid, encounters Robley right off the bat, posing as a count and cousin of Kathryn, then as an agent sent to protect the queen. It's Kathryn's royal jewels he's after. Wonder Woman watches secretly as he works the queen for information, then she transitions to Diana to serve them tea. This devious fake agent, meanwhile, has gleaned from the queen that the jewels are being kept not in the vault as assumed, but in a hidden safe.

With the knowledge Diana also has gained, Steve confronts Robley directly, expressing interest in buying the crown jewels from him. Robley dispatches him with knockout gas and learns who he really is. With the queen, he then passes Steve off as the infamous jewel thief Evan Robley, detaining Steve in the basement. Diana must do considerable damage control with the queen, both in her maid's uniform and as Wonder Woman. But it's too late — the hidden safe is empty and the jewels are gone.

Wonder Woman goes to Robley and uses her golden lasso on him, and he says he didn't steal the crown jewels. Turns out, he was right — what he stole were fakes! He offers to work with her to expose the real crooks — for a little amnesty, that is. Together with Steve they get the actual jewels from the safe at the consulate (and Wonder Woman does a stunning retrieval hanging by her lasso!).

Actress Juliet Mills at a fan festival in 2004. Photo by Jennifer, from Wikimedia Commons.

Disney mainstay Juliet Mills guests as Queen Kathryn. Fans of the "Dynasty" spinoff "The Colbys" will recognize Evan Robley as David Hedison, who portrayed Roger Langdon. (Mills, incidentally, is married to one of Hedison's "Colbys" costars, Maxwell Caulfield, and she also appeared on "Dynasty.") And John Colicos is highly recognizable as Ambassador Gregory Orrick — he has a long television resume, notably the evil Mikkos Cassadine on "General Hospital."

"I Do, I Do"
November 11, 1977
Written by Richard Carr; directed by Herb Wallerstein.
Steve Trevor is serving as best man for a nervous groom, White House adviser Christian Harrison. And who is it that Joe Atkinson escorts down the aisle, clad in flowing white so elegantly ruffled at the neck? None other than Diana Prince! What gives?

As the ceremony takes place, a sinister-looking guy places a homing device under the fender of the cool-blue Mercedes convertible that the newlyweds will be driving. Chris and Diana then head off to their honeymoon. En route, Diana discovers a man rifling through their luggage, and she changes into Wonder Woman to stop him.

Later, after their convertible pulls up to the Hacienda Health Spa, their plan is revealed: They staged the fake and rather public marriage to smoke out a secret informant working from the Hacienda. This information broker, David Allen, uses the gentle art of massage to ply his female victims — the wives of Washington's powerful figures. Christian and Diana consult with Sam Tucker, who first told Joe Atkinson about this scheme and whose wife Dolly has evidently and inadvertently leaked out important information to this David Allen.

Soon Allen's sights are set on the new bride of presidential adviser Christian Harrison, as Diana circulates herself at the Hacienda, playing on the tennis courts and hanging in the steam room. The latter activity knocks her out, quite literally, and she's taken away by Allen's cohorts. Fellow prey Dolly, meanwhile, is on to Allen, thanks to a chiropractic adjustment that left her nerves impervious to his hypnotic touch. She wants to blackmail David into getting her hubby Sam out of the Washington rat race, even if it means discrediting Sam. David prefers to go about things another way; he sets up Dolly for a ride on a dangerously trained horse *(named Satan — yikes!)*. He then sets to work on Diana, but she's too wise for him. After rescuing her "husband" and Dolly's husband from a rigged runaway golf cart, she saves Dolly from the horse.

It's the first time we see the pale-blue Mercedes convertible that Diana will be driving often in the series. Diana seems to be wearing her eyeglasses less and less. She doesn't have them on for the fake trip down the aisle, and she has no problem leaving them off around Christian, even though he's also met Wonder Woman. Henry Darrow, who was Walter Lampkin in "The Bushwhackers," returns to play another bad guy, this time David Allen. Celeste Holm portrays Dolly Tucker.

"The Man Who Made Volcanoes"
November 18, 1977
Written by Wilton Denmark, Brian McKay and Dan Ullman; directed by Alan Crosland.
The show's opening music sequence is streamlined and recast, and it now occurs after a slice of the action: Gone are the animated, comic-book-like images, replaced by live-action shots from the episodes. The place-setting boxes in the corner of the screen have disappeared, too. At the show's closing is simply a shot of a smiling Wonder Woman under the credits.

Diana does a rendezvous with Steve at the airport for a new assignment: investigating a suspicious Chinese volcano, the origin for which seems to be a spot in Mexico. She hops a dune buggy to the Vista Bonita hotel in Baja California *(Steve certainly has a reduced role in these episodes, explained as a job promotion)* and ticks off the radar of some bad dudes. They know she's an IADC agent and decide to get rid of her. Diana, meanwhile, checks into the same room, No. 7, as the previous IADC agent sent to investigate this activity, Dave Pruett. When she searches the room, she finds a map hidden in the bedpost. But then the floor falls out from under her, and she gets thrown into a dungeon with walls closing in to crush her. Wonder Woman, however, escapes.

Baja California is getting to be a busy place. China has sent two agents to investigate the volcano business, which they think the U.S. is behind, and another volcano, in Russia, has prompted the arrival of two Russky agents known as the Twins. The next target for the volcano terrorists is Maryland, just as all five agents are making their way up the mountain near the Vista Bonita where the volcanic weapon is located. The agents inevitably bump into each other along the way, and the two Chinese agents — a competitive and continually barbing male and female — capture Diana for a time, then let her go. They then meet up with the Twins, who encounter Wonder Woman, who tries to convince them the United States is not behind the volcanic activity.

It's to Diana's disadvantage that one of the perps, the hotel manager Jack Corbin, has a little crush on our gal. He takes Diana to his boss, physicist and inventor Arthur Chapman, who says he is actually wielding his weapon in the name of world peace. Peace is her gig, after all. But she certainly doesn't approve of his methods. He issues a three-hour ultimatum to the world's superpowers to disarm, threatening to turn the entire planet into a volcano.

There is a sense of some time passing here: Diana and Chapman talk about how it's been two years since they saw each other, though we're only nine episodes into Diana's return to the U.S. So funny to see the Asian agent at the airport giftshop pretending to look at a Slinky toy as he spies Diana. A largely bespeckled Roddy McDowall does his first guest spin as the bad guy, Prof. Arthur Chapman.

"Mind Stealers from Outer Space," Part 1

December 2, 1977
Written by Stephen Kandel; directed by Michael Caffey.
Some notorious aliens called the Scrill are heading for a planet called Terra (that's Earth, ya know). The Council of Planets decides to dispatch Andros — son of the Andros that Wonder Woman knew in the '40s — to prevent the Scrill from wreaking havoc. They're setting a deadline on his mission, though: six days.

At the IADC, the entry of the aliens has been picked up on monitors, so two investigators, George Hess and Ruth Blaine, are sent out. They meet with the Scrill in a wooded area, where the aliens freeze them then place egg-shaped gizmos on their foreheads to drain their brains. Diana Prince tracks the action to the same location, detecting the unusual, high-pitched squeaks of the aliens before finding the two unconscious agents as Wonder Woman. Diana then takes George and Ruth to the hospital, where Dr. Rand determines they essentially have no brain activity.

In the same forest region, some college students are examining the native flora. Bad move. The Scrill feast on a couple of their brains, as well, then take over their bodies! Andros arrives *(in the body of hunky Dack Rambo of "Dallas," by the way)* and meets up with Wonder Woman, intercepting a Scrill attack on her. The aliens in the bodies of coeds Debbie and Johnny Chambers, meanwhile, steal a truck and lure Capt. Parelli and his fellow law enforcement to witness the truck jumping off a cliff.

Back at her apartment, Diana learns from Andros that the Scrill are stealing human knowledge to sell for a high price elsewhere in the universe. Steve calls and tells Diana that the military is only giving Andros until the next morning to prove he can more effectively deal with the alien threat.

At the meeting, Andros recognizes the military commander Gen. Miller as a Scrill, and all you-know-what breaks loose. Wonder Woman manages to capture the alien-possessed Debbie. She uses her lasso to learn more about the Scrill, like where they're hiding during their brain-drain mission. Back at the Scrill hideout, they've figured out what no one else apparently can (!) — that Diana Prince and Wonder Woman are one and the same. Two Scrill in human hosts, Kim and Karen, con the cleaning lady into letting them into Diana's apartment. Diana is able to toss them around a while, until their secret weapon arrives: A really big Darth Vader-looking robot-type guy.

Seriously — the aliens have red Christmas garland on their silver outfits?! But we'll forgive that, since Diana wears an incredibly fab brown leather blazer that we REALLY want to find at a vintage clothing shop someday. Earl Boen portrays one of the planetary council members, Chaka.

"Mind Stealers from Outer Space," Part 2
December 9, 1977
Written by Stephen Kandel; directed by Alan Crosland.
Diana's alien intruders, with their giant Darth Vader-like predator called the Sardor, waste no time tearing into her. Andros arrives just in time. Back at the Scrill lair, the aliens are next targeting a think-tank for intelligent minds to harvest. Steve tells Diana the Scrill have been detected in an abandoned building downtown. Andros goes to check it out, and after Diana sits on pins and needles waiting, a worried Wonder Woman follows.

The Scrill destroy the building with Andros and Wonder Woman inside, but they survive. The Scrill go about grabbing unsuspecting think-tank members right and left, such as Sen. Wainright, famed sculptor Carla Burgess and Prof. Paul Eidleman. At the IADC, Steve and Diana realize Andros is working against a deadline set by the Council of Planets, and that after this deadline the Council will take matters into its own hands with a "decontamination" measure that will leave a portion of Earth's inhabitants insane. They convince Andros to appeal to the Council to let the humans deal with the Scrill on their own. The Council refuses.

Steve and Diana turn to the United Nations, where Wonder Woman and Andros explain the danger to the General Assembly. The Scrill terrorize the scene and are able to attack Andros. With his pendant, Wonder Woman contacts the Council of Planets and tries to convince them not to decontaminate the Earth to deal with the Scrill. Nope, again. They're quite the tough bunch.

Wonder Woman realizes it's up to her to capture the Scrill. She tries to get more information out of the Scrill in custody, and finally learns where they are hiding. She charges in, fights off the Scrill (including another face-off with the Sardor) and is able to retrieve the storage device containing Andros' stolen mind. With his powerful pendant, Andros banishes the Scrill light-years away.

Diana mentions that the last time she said goodbye to Andros was 1943. She said goodbye to his father in 1942, when that Andros made the point that he'd return to Earth in 50 years — 1992. She has some history with both father and son. So sweet that the son calls her Princess. Steve instructs his assistant Eve by name via phone in this episode; she'll be on-screen in future episodes. At the end, we see Diana enjoying some of IRAC's attempts at humor, and we also get a hint that the precocious computer knows her secret, telling her as she leaves the room, "Goodnight, Ms. Prince ... ess."

"The Deadly Toys"
December 30, 1977
Written by Anne Collins and Carey Wilber; directed by Dick Moder.
Dr. Royce Tobias, a scientist working on the dangerous weapon Project XYZ, is replaced by an android that melts down in the middle of a team meeting. Diana investigates at the lab, finding an intruder that turns out to be another android. Steve arranges for the project's other key scientists, Dr. Prescott and Dr. Lazaar, to be secreted away. Prescott gets a special delivery of toy soldiers (turns out, all three researchers have a penchant for war games) and is poisoned and hypnotized to leave the hideaway. The MP at his door takes a snooze after a visit from a yipping little toy puppy. Prescott is replaced by an android double.

Meanwhile, it's Christmastime. A toymaker gets his own special delivery — the real Dr. Prescott. IRAC the IADC computer (who's being programmed with more and more attitude these days) is advising Steve on the case. (In a humorous moment, Steve asks IRAC what to get Diana for Christmas, and he suggests asking Wonder Woman. "You're a big help," Steve disappointedly replies.)

Diana drops in on Dr. Prescott, who's really the android double. She realizes this and reports it to Steve. She then visits the project's third scientist, the exceedingly cranky Dr. Lazaar, and is clued in to the toy soldiers the scientists all share. She visits the toymaker's shop in Georgetown. After she asks questions and leaves, the toymaker, Orlich Hoffman, sends a deadly toy plane after her. Then he constructs an android of Wonder Woman.

The XYZ project's originator, Maj. Dexter, is getting antsy, especially since he's secretly working with Hoffman. Diana finds a connection between Dexter and the toymaker. Dexter asks for a meeting with Diana, and she comes face-to-face with Wonder Woman! The two go to the toyshop, where Diana is drugged. Dexter and Hoffman learn from her the location of Dr. Lazaar — her apartment. But Diana is able to change into Wonder Woman and bust out of her cell. She then steps into the android's role to bring down the bad guys. She pulls another android switcheroo to thwart the whole Project XYZ sabotage plan.

We learn that Diana lives in Apartment 410 of the Spruce Building. The Riddler of the '60s "Batman" series, Frank Gorshin, plays it a bit older as the toymaker, Hoffman.

"Light-Fingered Lady"
January 6, 1978
Written by Bruce Shelly; directed by Alan Crosland.
Diana, posing as a thief named Lil Faxton, is infiltrating a gang planning a big heist via its hunky thug Tony Ryan. While the boss, Anton Caribe, is checking her out, Steve makes sure she has a "record" with the police department. But the boss *(Greg Morris of "Mission Impossible")* is still skeptical and has Lil tailed and ordered killed if she does anything suspicious. She secretly changes into Wonder Woman to break into a secure facility and photograph some plans, No. 10355 for a state-of-the-art alarm system, then, as Diana, delivers one set of film to Caribe, claiming to have shaken Wonder Woman off her trail. The second set of film she delivers to Steve, who has it analyzed by IRAC, but it's still unclear just what these heisters are heisting. Caribe then tells all to Lil:

They're going to lift some infamous loot from a 1976 Beirut job, out of the possession of the infamous Michael Sutton.

Caribe's flunky Leech keeps digging for dirt on Lil, finding a former cellmate, Marge Douglas, and arranging for a "reunion" between the women. But Steve has that one covered. On to the operation. Caribe makes Sutton think he's stolen a valuable Egyptian sarcophagus from him. Lil is hiding inside as it arrives at Sutton's home. Sutton thinks so highly of the treasure that he has it placed in his vault. When she hops out to disable Sutton's alarm system, she encounters guard dogs. She changes to Wonder Woman, who has a certain rapport with animals.

She's able to get to the alarm, then gives the signal to the rest of the gang. Her cohorts move in to hit the safe. But they don't get out of there fast enough — the guards reactivate the alarm, and Lil inadvertently trips it. The other thugs leave her behind, and she transforms to Wonder Woman again to get out of this mess, even getting a little hand (paw) from the dogs to fool Sutton and his men.

Caribe is surprised to see Lil join them at the hideout a little later — and even more surprised when she tells them who she really is. She and Steve take down the crooks.

Lynda Carter plays it tough and seasoned as Lil. We get our first glimpse of Steve's assistant Eve, at the IADC offices then in the back seat of the car, though she's not called by name. Wonder Woman wears her diving suit at the beginning of the episode, when she secretly swims ashore from a boat to catch a meeting with Steve. Bubba Smith's character Paul Rojak is a former football player.

"Screaming Javelins" *(sometimes listed as "Screaming Javelin")*
January 20, 1978
Written by Brian McKay; directed by Michael Caffey.
A package is delivered to Diana's door, and as soon as she examines it, she changes into Wonder Woman and hurls it into the sky — it's a bomb. Athlete Bill Bethude is then kidnapped, phone booth and all! A defected gymnast, Nadia Samarra, meanwhile, can't seem to convince her American boyfriend Tom Hamilton *(hottie Rick Springfield, so youthful!)* she's being followed.

It's the evil madman Marion Mariposa, and Diana and Steve discuss him along with the case of the missing Olympic athletes. Mariposa fancies himself the emperor of Mariposalia, and he intends to get some global recognition through the top-notch Olympic team he's assembling via the kidnappings. IRAC has pegged Nadia as the next one to get nabbed, so Diana keeps an eye on her. Nadia is a worried mess, and for good reason — one of Mariposa's hired men, Bo Taggart, tries to break in to her apartment to grab her. It's an unsuccessful attempt, thanks to Wonder Woman. But the scared Nadia runs away from her apartment, which puts her in further danger. She falls right into Mariposa's grasp.

As the kidnapped athletes are forced to train at Mariposa's compound, Diana, then Wonder Woman, tracks down Nadia's boyfriend Tom. She and Steve realize none of the loved ones of these athletes are talking to the authorities.

Over at Mariposa's camp, a plan is hatched to capture Diana Prince in order to bait Wonder Woman, since the latter always seems to appear when the former is around, and the latter would be great for the team! They choose the ruse of flowers — of the slightly gaseous variety. Diana changes into Wonder Woman to break out of her Mariposalian prison cell, then rushes to Tom's place to save him from the hit that Mariposa ordered. She then returns to the madman's lair. Though she frees the athletes, Mariposa slips her grasp, again (he and Diana have a history, evidently).

Wonder Woman mentions in this episode that she hasn't lost her temper in 500 or 600 years. She also gets to try out a few gymnastics as she chases Tom around the university gym. In an amusing chick moment, after Mariposa orders his twin blond henchwomen to "get" Wonder Woman, our heroine tersely tells the ladies to "have a seat." They promptly comply as she marches past them to pursue their boss.

Would you believe ... a dollar store? Seriously. Maybe we should've gotten a few more.

"Diana's Disappearing Act"
February 3, 1978
Written by S.S. Schweitzer; directed by Michael Caffey.
A magician has a machine that changes bars of lead into gold. Right now, though, he's very interested in a pendant that was recently sent to Diana Prince. Another magician, Jezreel, appears at a reception honoring a powerful emir, Mustapha ben-Hassan, and Diana is also in attendance. She's busy getting hit on by a man who lives near her, Harold Farnum *(Ed Begley Jr.)*. Then she gets called on stage for Jezreel's disappearing act — a ruse to abduct her for the pendant. Harold worries when Diana doesn't return in the act. But Wonder Woman is able to break out of the crate she's being driven away in, and Diana walks back into the reception.

Steve and Eve have Diana's pendant analyzed by the Nobel Prize-winning Dr. Hutchens. Before he can report his findings to Diana and Steve, he's drugged by an evil mime at the university (!) and taken away. Diana reluctantly lets Harold, who has an interest in magic, help her look for the evil mime. They wind up at a magician's symposium. The event includes a performance by Count Cagliostro, who trips Diana's radar. Jezreel is there, as well, colluding with Cagliostro, and Diana changes to Wonder Woman to chase him to the roof, where he throws her his briefcase, containing a bomb. She hurls it into the sky *(just like last episode!)* then uses her golden lasso on him.

She finds the pendant in the safe at Hutchens' lab — but the necklace is now lead! It seems Cagliostro's magical machine's golden transformations are only temporary. Diana learns that the emir and leaders of other oil-producing nations are setting aside stacks of cash in their Swiss bank accounts to buy Cagliostro's "gold" at a cheap price. This, meanwhile, is raising the price of oil. Cagliostro is the descendant of a swindling alchemist Diana recalls from a couple centuries earlier. He kidnaps Harold to get his help capturing Diana. Wonder Woman rescues Harold and Dr. Hutchens, with the help of Cagliostro's assistant Morgana.

This episode marks the second appearance of IADC agent Eve. BRBTV is disappointed that the adorably geeky Harold, who does make another appearance in the third season, was not made a recurring character. Cagliostro pulls a first-season trick on Diana — a voice impersonation over the phone. Her own voice impersonations were abandoned after the first season.

"Death in Disguise"
February 10, 1978
Written by Tom Sawyer; directed by Alan Crosland.
A man disguised as a woman is out to kill Diana Prince. Our heroine, on a horseback ride to get some info for the IADC, is then led into an ambush. She changes to Wonder Woman to save herself and is able to question one of the perps, though the others get away. She and Steve discuss the situation back at the IADC, realizing that the prime target of the assassin(s) has the initials CARI. Soon Diana has her own target: the notorious assassin Woodward Nightingale.

Diana is assigned to protect Carlo Indrezzano, whose life might be in danger; Steve and Diana suspect he is "CARI." Indrezzano is miffed at being assigned a bodyguard — until he meets the lovely Diana. But Indrezzano is abducted from the restaurant where he and Diana were dining (the perps thought they were nabbing Diana). Wonder Woman gives chase and retrieves her charge. Steve and Eve check with IRAC on who might want Indrezzano dead.

Maj. Anita Finley, an engineering expert, is intercepted as she's reporting in to the IADC. The man with a talent for disguising himself as women, Starker, stands in for her to collect some important building plans. Nightingale's thugs get into Diana's hotel room to finish their job, but Wonder Woman has outsmarted them — they're just shooting into pillows on her bed. She nabs 'em with her lasso and then stashes them aboard a bulldozer's scoop. She next breaks into Nightingale's office. He aims a small cannon at her, and she catches the ball in midair! She wants to know who Nightingale's real target is. Through the typing ineptitude of his dyslexic secretary Violet, the real victim is revealed to be ... IRAC!

Wonder Woman rushes back to the IADC and stops the hit. But the hit "man" Starker is about to get away. Not so fast — Wonder Woman busts "her" cover. When all is said and done, Indrezzano wants to reward Wonder Woman with a big ole diamond! She, of course, can't accept, and neither can Diana.

Joel Fabiani of "Dynasty," "Dallas" and quite a few other soaps over the years is Nightingale. His "Dynasty" castmate Lee Bergere (Joseph Anders) is Marius. George Chakiris of 1961's "West Side Story" is Indrezzano. In this one we hear IRAC's voice switch to Tom Kratochvil, the voice by which we know him best, though it's not credited until later.

"IRAC Is Missing"
February 17, 1978
Written by Anne Collins; directed by Alex Singer.
A leading computer maker, Everright, is introducing a "brave new world" to prospective buyers when the host computer is sabotaged and its central memory bank wiped out. Steve and Diana realize their own IRAC is also in the line of fire. Diana, meanwhile, meets "Rover," the new roving computer the guys at the lab have been working on. It's IRAC's little programmed pet, it seems.

IRAC surmises which computer system will get hit next, and Diana goes to the business that owns it to prevent the crime. She changes to Wonder Woman and lassos the perp, but after a diversion he gets away. His boss, William Havitol *(a growling Ross Martin of "The Wild, Wild West")* is none-too-pleased at Wonder Woman's interception. He sets his sights on an impersonation *(a la Artemis Gordon!)* of an associate of Steve's named Dr. Hinkley Bernard.

As Bernard, he gets access to the IADC offices and the room where IRAC is located. A fire alarm then goes off. Diana changes to Wonder Woman and addresses the problem, soon realizing it was just another diversion. IRAC has been computernapped. Havitol wants IRAC's satellite information. But there's a deeper danger here — IRAC just happens to know one crucial secret about Diana Prince that no one else knows!

Rover is also nabbed in the scheme, then suddenly Diana sees two Rovers! One is carrying a bomb, which Wonder Woman uses her lasso to subdue (by wrapping it around the bomb — a new usage for the lasso, for sure).

Back at Havitol's lair, IRAC has a friendly chat with the cute secretary robot, Cori (who has two big modules on "her" chest — so precious!). Diana finds the "good" Rover waiting for her in the front seat of her car; it turns out, IRAC programmed its pet to find IRAC through a homing device. As Rover directs, Di drives her cool blue Mercedes to the location. Havitol is busy accessing IRAC's data as his thugs find Diana outside and lead her in by gunpoint. Havitol explains his evil plot for — you guessed it — world domination. But look out, Havitol — Rover bites! Then it's Wonder Woman who must defuse a bomb that Havitol has set.

William Havitol's first name is listed as Bernard in the credits. The intention was no doubt to indicate that Ross Martin portrayed Hinkley Bernard and William Havitol. Though Eve does not appear in this episode, Steve references her. In an ironic moment in this 35-year-old episode, Steve laments to Diana that he never realized how much computers affect their lives.

"Flight to Oblivion"
March 3, 1978
Written by Patrick Mathews; directed by Alan Crosland.
While he's with his fiancée and fellow officer, Capt. Anne Colby, Maj. Alan Cornell gets a mysterious phone call. On the other end of the line is a voice that soon has him hypnotized. He drives off.

Diana poses as a military photojournalist at the San Remo base *(and gets to wear a navy blue uniform once again)*. She reports in to Steve (who's piloting a plane again — this episode is like a flashback to the first season). She then checks in with Capt. Colby. But her communication to Steve is caught by the hypnotized Maj. Cornell, who reports it to his mysterious contact, who happens to be in the bus of a band about to perform at the base.

Diana is pursued by an obnoxious officer and must change to Wonder Woman to elude him. She then encounters another officer, who's in his own daze, and tells her, "When the snow falls, I must obey."
Steve lands his plane at the base, and Diana relays to him her latest adventure. They surmise that the planned test flight of the Z400 aircraft is in peril.

That night, Sgt. Prince photographs the live concert at the base. Maj. Cornell wanders off mysteriously during the concert. Diana meets the band's creepy manager, Edmund Dante, and realizes the band, called the Hull City Howlers, has played all the other bases she and Steve have been looking at in the Project Z400 threat.

The perps are on to Diana and try to throw her off: Maj. Cornell is spotted on the base with some explosives. Just as he's about to be apprehended, Wonder Woman steps in and lassos him, realizing he's been hypnotized. She clanks her bracelets together to bring him out of his daze.

Dante hypnotizes the obnoxious Lt. Stonehouse, who then lures Steve into an ambush. Steve realizes Dante is the notorious Otto Franz, a formerly respected officer who was responsible for the death of a pilot. He tells Steve he will be blowing the Z400 "to oblivion" as it approaches San Remo on its test flight. He hypnotizes Steve, and Steve gives it his best effort to fight the daze. Wonder Woman, meanwhile, chases down the band's tour bus to stop Dante / Franz. But she must stop the missile aimed at the Z400, as well.

The band in the episode is actually called Nightwind.

"Séance of Terror"
March 10, 1978
Written by Bruce Shelly; directed by Dick Moder.
A little boy takes Polaroid pictures "from another world," snapping a shot of a foreign political leader — with the man's dead wife. When the boy helps whisk Secretary Bakru away in a car, a curious Diana follows, but then gets "detained" by two thugs on the roadside, having to change to her alter ego to escape.

Steve is worried about the other foreign ambassadors, who are in town for the peace conference, and he sends Diana over to keep an eye on them. The little boy next photographs Deputy Minister Kell with her dead son Eric. As Diana tries to investigate, she gets waylaid by some chloroform gas. It only worsens the tension between her and the security official for the event, Col. Dekker, who has no problem complaining to Steve and the higher-ups about Diana's work at the peace conference. Steve yanks her from the case and cuts off her access to IRAC, though a little sweet talk coaxes out of the computer some info about the boy from a photo Diana found at the scene. His name is Matthew Koslo. It seems Matthew's Uncle Lawson and Aunt Theodora are using the boy's psychic abilities to run a con that involves assembling several key ambassadors from the conference for a special séance.

Diana is not scaring off the case so easily. She dodges a car bomb, then as Wonder Woman lassos a couple thugs, only to be thrown later into a spooky ruse. She dons the disguise of "Carol Littleton" to infiltrate the home where the ambassadors have been secreted away, presumably to contact her "dearly departed (wealthy!) husband." "Carol" lays out the bait of a supposed hidden treasure, of which her husband knew the location, and is promptly shown a room at the home.

Diana is able to privately warn Matthew about the séance, and that his aunt and uncle want to make the foreign leaders do something that's wrong. When Matthew takes her picture, it reveals that she's there in disguise. Later, she hears the "spirits" calling out her name then falls through a trap door, getting doused with sleeping gas.

The séance begins. The deceased loved ones of the ambassadors appear, urging them to end the peace negotiations. At last, Diana manages to change to Wonder Woman and thwart the technological tools of the séance's trickery.

Near the episode's beginning, Diana changes to Wonder Woman while rolling down a hill — that's a new one! Todd Lookinland — bro of Mike Lookinland of "The Brady Bunch" and quite similar to him in facial features — portrays Matthew.

"The Man Who Wouldn't Tell"
March 31, 1978
Written by Anne Collins; directed by Alan Crosland.
Alan Ackaroy, a student working his way through college as a janitor, is cleaning up at a lab at the Whitaker Building one evening when he mixes up some chemical solutions and accidentally discovers the formula for a powerful explosive. The building burns to the ground as a result. Hopewell International, the company that was researching the formula at the lab, realizes that someone was observing their progress and trying to steal the work. That someone is Rudolph Furst of Hopewell's competitor, Furst Enterprises. They figure they need to get with this Ackaroy guy.

Alan realizes he's a target and scrams. Diana flies to Los Angeles and pursues him as she works on the case. She follows the trail to a Laundromat, where she encounters Furst's thugs and must change into Wonder Woman to learn what's going on.

Alan goes to his ex-girlfriend Meg for help. Diana pays a visit to Furst to try to shake him down for information. Hopewell then tries unsuccessfully to abduct Alan. Steve has IRAC profile Alan and tells Diana he may run to Bakersfield and may be using disguises from his background in theater. Diana finds him at the airport, in disguise, and chases him down as Wonder Woman. Furst's associates are able to nab him, though.

Diana goes to Meg to try to relocate Alan, then encounters one of Hopewell's flunkies, B.W., trying to sabotage Meg's car. Furst and his men, meanwhile, want Alan to tell them exactly what he was mixing that night of the explosion. They've even replicated the lab of the Whitaker Building — complete with his janitor's cart and supplies — to help jog his memory. When Alan won't spill what he knows, Furst's men kidnap Meg, along with Diana, who was with her at the time.

Diana is left bound and under guard upstairs while Alan and Meg are taken to the replicated lab. Diana tries to bluff her guard, telling him it isn't the real Alan they've captured. She is able to shake the guard loose and change to Wonder Woman, then rescue Alan and Meg at the lab. And the quirky lovers even get to make a quirky new start!

Gary Burghoff of "M*A*S*H" is Alan, while a pre-"Miami Vice" and altogether-sinister Philip Michael Thomas, sans middle name in the credits, is Furst.

"The Girl from Ilandia" *(sometimes listed as "The Girl from Islandia")*
April 7, 1978
Written by Anne Collins; directed by Dick Moder.
A newspaper publisher, Simon Penrose, is out on his yacht when he encounters a little girl drifting on a raft. He rescues her, then calls his acquaintance Diana Prince, who flies to Long Beach to help. The young girl is a mystery, especially considering the men who try to abduct her from the hospital, and the unusual necklace and bracelets she wears. Simon takes a protective interest in the girl, calling her Tina.

As Simon is arguing with Diana about her treatment, Tina runs away from the hospital. She goes to the ocean shore, where she wishes she could go home, and she finds a dog.

Diana, who as Wonder Woman has used her abilities *(telepathy, evidently — a rare usage of that for the show)* to learn where the girl is from, suspects the notorious Bleaker as the one who is pursuing her. But the girl does a good job fending for herself, with the power of her jewelry. The police then find Tina, who's placed in Simon's custody.

IRAC's profile on Bleaker implicates him in recent oil tanker sabotage by submarine. Wonder Woman visits Tina at the Penrose estate, and the girl begs her to take her back to her home. It's revealed that the girl is from another dimension, Ilandia, though she's reluctant to reveal her real name, Emma-Donna. She and Wonder Woman have a casual, impromptu match of their physical abilities, and the girl keeps up just fine. Wonder Woman teaches her how to make an invisible shield around her body. For added protection, Diana communicates with Tina's dog, Tiger, with instructions to come find her if Tina is ever in trouble.

Right afterward, Tina is kidnapped. The evil and highly intelligent scientist Bleaker, the one who brought her through a portal from the other dimension, tries again to harness the girl's power.

With the help of Tiger, Wonder Woman tracks down Bleaker's seaside lair. She demands that Bleaker send the girl back home. But after an explosion in his lab, Bleaker flees by sub. Wonder Woman encourages poor Tina to try to adjust to life away from home. She also uses her lasso to erase the memories of Bleaker's men.

Simon Penrose drives a light yellow Mercedes convertible just like Diana's light blue one. Tina / Emma-Donna is played by Julie Anne Haddock of "The Facts of Life." This episode feels strangely like a pilot for a spinoff — and indeed it was meant to be. The show focusing on Haddock's young character from another dimension just never got off the ground.

"The Murderous Missile"
April 21, 1978
Written by Dick Nelson; directed by Dick Moder.
While out for a drive in her powder-blue Mercedes convertible, Diana gets 'jacked. But this guy is no match for Wonder Woman. She changes back to Diana before the local constable arrives to find her carjacker knocked out at the wheel. The sheriff insists on Diana following him into town to give her statement on the crime, and we get the idea that this is some kind of sinister small-town trap. The sheriff is actually connected to the 'jacker, Mac MacDonald, who's promptly thrown into the local jail to get him out of the way.

Diana hangs out in this town of Burrogone, growing restless at missing her scheduled time at the nearby Red Mountain Army missile testing range. The sheriff leisurely takes her statement over coffee and doughnuts at the town diner, then the local mechanic Ernie fiddles under the hood of her car, saying the fuel pump is leaking. She then meets the peculiar "just George," whom she quizzes on alternate forms of transportation.

Back at the jail, Mac manages to bust out of his cell. Diana sees satellite dishes on the nearby hill, then is pursued by strange men in Jeeps. She tracks down the town's switchboard operator, Flo, and learns there is strange static in the air, as if someone is jamming communications.

Sheriff Beal and his deputy Luther try to track their missing inmate, who runs to Flo's house and warns Diana through the window that Flo has laced that tea she's serving with an extra-special ingredient. Diana hurries out, then meets up with her new benefactor, Mac, who tells his story: A former resident of Burrogone, he returned recently to discover its residents whisked away and a generator placed in a barn at the end of town. Diana realizes they must be trying to sabotage the missile test at Red Mountain, where one of the missile's control helmets is missing. Diana finds the generator then changes to Wonder Woman, but she is tricked and knocked out with gas.

The missile launches, but it soon veers out of control. The conspirators at Burrogone land it with their stolen control helmet. The mastermind behind it all turns out to be the innocent-seeming George, who plans to cash in on this helmet. Wonder Woman breaks out of captivity to pursue George as he speeds away on his dirt bike *(changing into her spandex biking suit — a variation of her spandex diving suit!).*

Mark Withers, who plays Luther here, would go on to play Ted Dinard on "Dynasty" three years later. Minus the country-bumpkin voice, of course.

Behind the Scenes:
The IADC Building Paradise Island

For the exterior shots of the IADC building in the second and third seasons of "Wonder Woman," the Inglewood City Hall was the star. The building, located in Inglewood, California, was also used for the show "Quincy."

Photo by Robert Washburn.

For Paradise Island, the Los Angeles County Arboretum & Botanic Garden in Arcadia, California, was used. The IMDb notes that this location was also used in "Charmed," "Buffy the Vampire Slayer," "The Lost World: Jurassic Park," "Roots," the 1960s "Mission: Impossible" and many others. It's a 127-acre botanical garden and historical site jointly operated by the Los Angeles Arboretum Foundation and the Los Angeles County Department of Parks and Recreation, according to its official site, Arboretum.org.

Photos from the collection of the Los Angeles County Arboretum & Botanic Garden; courtesy of the Arboretum.

Season 3

"My Teenage Idol Is Missing" *(sometimes listed as "One of Our Teen Idols is Missing")*
September 22, 1978
Written by Anne Collins; directed by Seymour Robbie.
Just as an autograph-seeking girl sneaks into a hotel suite to see the current hottest teen heartthrob, Lane Kincaid *(Leif Garrett in a true-to-life role)*, she sees him taken away by thugs. She has a hard time convincing her dad, Benjamin Springfield, however, that the teen idol has been kidnapped. Her dad's associate, Diana Prince, is about to return to D.C. from L.A. and hears their conversation. Later the girl, Whitney, tracks down Diana in her cab and diverts her from the airport, begging her to investigate the supposed abduction.

The kidnappers demand $2 million from Kincaid's manager, Ashton Ripley, meanwhile. Wonder Woman sneaks up to Lane's hotel room (scaling the side of the tall building with her golden lasso, in her ceremonial cape, even) and spies through the window ... Lane? It seems Whitney is sorely mistaken, but Diana is willing to do some more digging. What's really going on, we know, is that Lane has been replaced with a double, whom we learn is a twin brother he hasn't seen in 10 years. The two were separated at age 5.

Diana dials up Steve Trevor at IADC headquarters, and IRAC joins the investigation. The name Raleigh Crichton surfaces. He's notorious for kidnappings that involve doubles. Diana tracks down Ripley to stop the ransom exchange. She must change to Wonder Woman, but she's still unsuccessful, largely thanks to Ripley's own machinations. Ripley later tries to convince Crichton that there was no double-cross and he didn't contact Wonder Woman.

That night, Diana and Whitney go to Lane's concert, where twin Michael takes the stage to lip-synch his way through Lane's songs. His awkward faking is quickly booed, but he recovers by queuing up some music of his own, which goes over much better! Crichton is none-too-pleased but is able to switch gears in light of this new twin talent.

Lane, who has been held at Marina del Ray on a boat called Your Just Reward, is moved via car. Diana decides on a hunch to return to the

The third and final DVD set includes Lynda Carter's commentary on the season premiere, as well as a documentary called "Wonder Woman: The Ultimate Feminist Icon."

previous rendezvous point, a junkyard, but has car trouble on the way. Stowing away in her car, incidentally, is the precocious Whitney, whom Diana quickly shoos off. Wonder Woman then dons her motorcycle outfit (in a rapid-fire double-spin) and grabs a nearby motorbike to make it to the junkyard and bust up the scene with some pretty fancy moves.

Soon afterward, both twins are on stage, performing together to adoring fans.

This third-season premiere features an episode title screen at the beginning, something that was only used once in the previous two seasons. The opening credits also intersperse some new images, including a well-timed bark from Rover (or is that a wag?). Our hero's spins are no longer accompanied by her theme music for this final season. Leif Garrett, who was just shy of 17 when he did this episode, was already a hot sensation; Lynda Carter comments in the third-season DVD set that fans went crazy during any of the outside shooting they did. The kid is not bad at contrasting a confident Lane with a submissive Mike. His sister Dawn Lyn, meanwhile, displays her own acting chops at only 15 in the role of Whitney, who's savvy beyond her years.

"Hot Wheels"
September 29, 1978
Written by Dennis Landa; directed by Dick Moder.
A 1935 Rolls Royce with platinum hood ornament, which Diana is picking up for the IADC, just happens to drive off without her. She changes to Wonder Woman to try to track it, but to no avail. Inspector Tim Bolt, who was also at the scene investigating a car theft ring, is not too happy that his own operation was botched, and he lets Steve and Diana know it later at the IADC offices. Still, Diana and Bolt decide to work together on the case. Steve has some cool surveillance toys for them, such as a microphone brooch and a "ball-point tape recorder."

The car thieves are filling an order for an ophthalmologist, Dr. Samson. Diana tracks him down and pays him a visit, knowing that he's been seeking a certain classic car. She works out a trade for that fancy classic Rolls the dentist just acquired, though the deal is intercepted. Diana, behind the wheel of the 1934 Duesenberg that was set for the trade, must make a break for it, leaving Bolt there with the crooks.

Bolt really works-it with the thieves, posing as "Arnie Lippincott." After a smooth shuffle at the car wash, he is able to rendezvous on a rooftop with Diana to deliver camera film, a tape recording and some fingerprints. But he realizes he was shadowed, and after Diana leaves, he has a fight on the roof with the guy. Bolt gets knocked over the side of the building — only to be caught by the more-than-capable Wonder Woman.

At the IADC, IRAC analyzes the evidence, which points to a swindler named Otis Fiskle. Diana goes to meet Bolt but is abducted by the crooks. She's still wearing her microphone brooch, however, so she's able to feed some crucial audio to Steve back at the office. Bolt, with Steve's help, finds the car that's carrying Diana, but then discovers that a bomb has been planted in his own car! He narrowly escapes, then Wonder Woman enters the scene. Steve follows (a rare trip out of the office for him these days, it seems).

Diana and Steve finally obtain their real target: some valuable missile plans hidden inside the Rolls' hood ornament.

"The Deadly Sting"
October 6, 1978
Written by Dick Nelson; directed by Alan Crosland.
While attending a football game, Steve witnesses some peculiar behavior by the players. We see that they're being shot with darts by a mysterious man in the stands. Steve and Diana later wonder, along with Bill Michaels of the Physical Fitness Council, if organized gambling has found a way to control the outcomes of these games.

One mobster suspects another, meanwhile: A heavy named Beamer pays a visit to Angelo ("Angie") Capucci. IRAC scans files in search of a bookie who's seen consistent betting against the odds and comes up with the name Lou the Lithuanian. But a couple of thugs get to ole Louie before Diana and Bill can. And when Wonder Woman helps out in a scuffle, Bill takes quite a shine to her.

Capucci's bad guys have Louie call around to find out who this mysterious game-rigger is. Come to find out, he's a scientist named Brubaker, and he's soon located. He says he's only fixing the games to fund his research.

The thugs use Prof. Brubaker to peek in on a dinner event for the football players, drilling holes in the wall from the next room. Diana is also attending the dinner, getting hit on by some of the players just before the players are getting hit on by Brubaker's darts! From the other side of the wall Brubaker is able to control their behavior with the darts, and some hearty fights break out at this dinner.

Next, Bill unknowingly gets shot with a dart at his hotel room, and he flies into a rage with Diana later. She's able to fish the dart out of his neck after he's knocked out. She gets a look at the tiny arrow just before it disintegrates. She and Bill then go to Brubaker's lab, and Wonder Woman uses her lasso on the mad scientist. He tells her that mobster Capucci is going to use his invention to win big on a game.

As one of the teams playing in the game rides along on its team bus, some specially trained hostesses, Phyllis and Glinda, distribute specially prepared drinks. Wonder Woman must find Capucci at the game to stop this evil mess.

Behind the Scenes: Ron Ely

Ron Ely, who has taken on the roles of Tarzan and Doc Savage, plays Bill Michaels in "The Deadly Sting." This author had the opportunity to meet him in October 2012 at an appearance in Gaithersburg, Maryland. We asked him what he recalled about the episode. "I do remember a couple of things," he said. "It was shot at the coliseum where USC plays. There were a lot of USC players. I remember having a scene where I kinda went berserk." (You were shot with a poison dart, BRBTV reminded him!) "I remember tearing up a room," he said. "We had a very good cast for that one. Craig (T. Nelson) hadn't quite hit it yet."

Ely joked as we reminded him about the episode's plot, "You know a lot more about it than I do." Ely loved working with Lynda Carter and noted that he worked with her again in her "Hawkeye" series. He's also friends with Lyle Waggoner. He said the brother of Carter's stuntwoman Jeannie Epper, Tony Epper, was the one who doubled him for his "Doc Savage" movie. "Tony was my dimensions exactly," Ely said. "Very dear friend of mine. Just passed away."

Photo of the author with Ron Ely by James R. Green Jr.

Craig T. Nelson of "Coach" plays one of the bad guys, Sam, while real-life football players Roman Gabriel, Deacon Jones, Eddie Allen Bell and Lawrence McCutcheon play themselves. In this one, Diana references Eve, though she hasn't been seen for a while.

"The Fine Art of Crime"
October 13, 1978
Written by Anne Collins; directed by Dick Moder.
Roddy McDowall guest-stars again, this time as sculptor Henry Roberts, who's opening an exhibit of highly lifelike statues called "Here We Stand" at the Putney Museum. Diana's neighbor Harold Farnum *(Ed Begley Jr. reprising his role)* drags her to the opening. Afterward, when Harold goes out to the parking lot to bring Diana's car around, he meets a man fiddling around inside the car. The man leaves a cryptic note for Diana before he scrams. Come to find out, he's under Roberts' employ.

Diana poses as an agent for well-known buyer Bob Bertalucci as she inquires about some valuable Hollenbeck crystal. The dealer Shubert, though, tells her the crystal has been stolen, then a couple thugs try to accost Diana at her car. Wonder Woman intervenes.

A wealthy man named Tad Ellsworth gifts his wife *(it's Gavin MacLeod of "The Love Boat" with wife Patti MacLeod)* with an original Roberts statue, as Steve and IRAC investigate the recent art thefts. Then a $100,000 ram medallion is stolen from the Ellsworth household. Roberts, meanwhile, is trying to fend off the aggressive Harold, who wants to know just how Roberts makes these interesting statues, since he's writing a term paper and all.

Wonder Woman intercepts the exchange of the ram medallion with fence Carmichael Goodman. Harold asks Steve if he can use IRAC to analyze Roberts' statues, but IADC policy forbids it. Harold still tries to get access, falling prey to little Rover's joke. Then he decides to break into Roberts' storage area for his research, and amazingly these lifelike statues come to life!

Another valuable piece of art is stolen (a golden bull), this time from the Putney Museum, where Roberts' statues are still on display. Back at Roberts' lair, Harold has really stepped into it — the artist uses a gizmo to "suspend his animation" and make him into a statue, too.

Diana consults with IRAC and figures out that Roberts plans to use the twin statues Romulus and Remus — commissioned by the Italian government — to make a big heist. Wonder Woman breaks into Roberts' base but finds that the sculptor has lured her there purposely. The next statue planned for unveiling? Wonder Woman! And the fact that Harold is a statue himself provides a little extra leverage against the Amazon princess. But Wonder Woman is still smarter than that, outwitting the real mastermind behind the scheme, Lloyd Moreaux.

This is the first episode that does not feature the Wonder Woman spin, if you don't count the second half of "The Feminum Mystique," which did show a spin in its recap of the first half.

"Disco Devil"
October 20, 1978
Written by Alan Brennert; directed by Leslie H. Martinson.
Disco patron Tony Borden is led to a secret room full of mirrors, where he's accosted by a mysterious man who seems to have telepathic abilities. Diana, meanwhile, is checking out a nuclear facility, hosted by a military colonel *(Russell Johnson of "Gilligan's Island")*. A dangerous detonation is about to occur, but it's stopped by Wonder Woman. The nuclear engineer responsible for stopping the detonation, Borden, has completely forgotten the sequence!

At the disco, the telepath recalls the critical information he got from Borden, then later he and his fellow con Angelique realize that Diana is investigating Borden's sudden amnesia. They decide to keep an eye on her. Diana tracks down an expert in telepathy / psychic abilities, Del Franklin, just as he gets fired from his trucking job after almost causing a fatal accident. Franklin demonstrates to her his ability to "steal" a memory from a person's mind, an ability he's not so happy to have. Diana hires him to help on this case.

Back at the disco, which is called "The Sticks," the cons again compare notes. They set a trap for Del with their pretty blond weapon, Kathy Munro, luring him to the disco. But Del leaves before they can get him to the mirrored room. He goes to Diana's place, where he finds that she's being menaced by a thug with a gun. Del was followed, so soon there are two thugs with guns pointed at them! Diana manages to escape and change into Wonder Woman. But she and Steve realize they better get some protection around Del.

Steve has Del attempt to retrieve memories from Borden's head. During the attempt, Del sees images of the cons at the disco, including a ringleader named Angelique McKenna and Del's fellow telepath Nick Carbone, with whom he spent time at a research institute. Steve realizes The Sticks is the base for the criminal operation.

Carbone scams his way into Steve's office with his psychic abilities, then learns where Del is being kept. Later, the two telepaths confront each other at The Sticks, and Angelique doesn't like Nick's new attitude. She decides Del can be of some use but Nick is highly expendable. She sends another of the cons, Lance, to dispose of Nick, but Nick gets the better of him.

Diana heads to The Sticks, gets hit on while on the dance floor, then sneaks upstairs to find Del. She soon finds herself trapped in the mirrored room, but she changes to Wonder Woman and busts her way out. Back down on the disco floor, she's got some fancier moves this time as she brings an end to the scam.

Wolfman Jack guest-stars as the disco's DJ, Infra Red. Kerry Sherman of the '80s daytime soap "Santa Barbara" is Kathy Munro. Though Tony Borden is referred to as "Tony" and "Anthony" in the episode, he's listed in the credits as Andrew Borden.

Writer Alan Brennert tells BRBTV: "I spent very little time on the set of 'WW' — met Lynda Carter briefly at a disco on La Cienega Boulevard where they were shooting 'Disco Devil,' and had an empty Coke can lobbed at me by Lyle Waggoner during a night shoot for 'Girl with a Gift for Disaster.' (Lyle, with a grin: 'You! This is all your fault we're all here tonight!' Me: 'I'm sorry, Lyle, I tried writing a blackout set during the day and it just wasn't the same.')"

"Formicida"
November 3, 1978
Written by Katharyn Michaelian Powers; directed by Alan Crosland.
A mysterious woman in a parked car seems to have telepathic control over an ant colony, causing the ants to take down a nearby building. The target behind this and other recent building collapses appears to be pesticide manufacturer GDH Enterprises. The woman, Formicida, wants GDH to shut down one of its chemical plants.

Dr. Douglas Radcliffe, a chemist, dials up Diana, nervous that he's being followed. Formicida overhears their exchange — or rather, one of her ants does — and she sends men to intercept Doug's meeting with Diana. Wonder Woman appears and tangles a bit with this slinky-leotard-clad ant-whisperer.

But Doug is still taken prisoner. His old partner, Irene Janus, is behind the corporate sabotage and the kidnapping. She's upset that Doug sold the pesticide formula they developed to GDH. The company is about to market the pesticide, called EF-11.

Steve and Diana have IRAC analyze the carpenter ants Diana found at the scene. IRAC then programs Rover for a special role in this case.

Formicida / Dr. Janus is poised to strike again, terrorizing GDH bigwig Gideon D. Harcourt by phone. Diana goes to Harcourt's offices and is mistaken for the terrorist. Formicida has had an army of ants delivered to the building, meanwhile, and they wreak huge havoc on the executive's office. Diana reports to Steve what's happened. IRAC turns up Irene Janus' name in the investigation.

The TV series tended not to focus on mad, costumed supervillains like the comics did, as shown with Cheetah here in issue 230 of Wonder Woman, *April 1977. So the episode "Formicida" may seem more like the comics than the others.*

One of Harcourt's researchers learns that EF-11 is extremely harmful to humans and warns the exec, who's unfazed. Diana takes Rover, who with IRAC's programming can now communicate with the ants, to Dr. Janus' home. She confronts Irene, who quickly summons her gun-toting flunky Aldo. Irene then demonstrates how drinking a hormonal formula she developed transforms her into Formicida. It's the powerful alter-ego that this mousy scientist would rather be, it appears. She tells Diana how EF-11 will seep into the food chain in a few years and do irreparable harm. She unleashes the ants on the bound Diana and Doug, but Rover saves them. Wonder Woman then rushes with Rover to Harcourt's chemical plant to stop Formicida from destroying the building.

For a show that has relied on mad scientists and other more typical human vermin for its villainy rather than costumed comic-book villains, this story feels like it came straight out of a comic book. Rover gets the MVP Award from BRBTV for this one. We can't help but like the little guy.

"Time Bomb"
November 10, 1978
Written by David Wise and Kathleen Barnes; directed by Seymour Robbie. On November 10, 2155, a scientist and a historian *(Ted Shackelford and Joan Van Ark of "Dallas" and "Knots Landing")* are monitoring the controls of a time portal. The historian, Cassandra Loren, decides she wants to do a little more hands-on research into this 1970s era she's been studying, where people were allowed to accumulate so much personal wealth. She travels back through the portal, and Adam Clement, the scientist, must follow her, concerned that something she might do will affect the future.

Cassandra puts the moves on her target right away: MacConnell Mining Corp. and one of its execs, Dan Reynolds, as well as its owner, J.J. MacConnell. She tells them that they're sitting on a valuable new energy source. When MacConnell doesn't buy her story, she lists off several events that will occur the next day.

Adam calls up the IADC, where his grandfather once worked (or will work!) and speaks with Diana. They arrange to meet, but at their rendezvous point, the planetarium, shots ring out. Wonder Woman stops the sniper, but Adam is long gone.

Cassandra has MacConnell's attention the next day when he reads in the newspaper that her predictions came true. She cuts a deal with him for the radioactive cabrium-90 that's buried at one of his properties. At the same time, she's dismayed that the hit she put out on Adam failed.

Adam disrupts a tour at the White House to try to get a meeting with the president. Diana finds him and takes him back to her place, where she hears his whole story at last. They decide he needs to try to build a makeshift time portal right there, in 1978. But Cassandra has already anticipated Adam's moves and hires a thug named Reves to take care of him. Then she tests out the cabrium-90 (which looks quite a lot like quartz!) at the mine.

Adam meets the "quaint, antique" (and quite temperamental) IRAC at the IADC offices to get some data together, while Diana orders the parts for the time portal, and then she and Adam narrowly miss a bomb detonation at a manufacturer's site. To take the heat off, they let the newspapers report their deaths. Adam realizes Cassandra is after the cabrium-90 at a mine in Arizona, not far from Phoenix.

He and Diana arrive at the mine on horseback but are soon apprehended by Cassandra's men. Adam tries to remind Cassandra of the historical explosion that happened near Phoenix when cabrium-90 was first mined. But Cassandra desires her 1970s wealth too badly to listen.

When the blast goes off, Diana and Adam have escaped from their bonds, and Wonder Woman is able to diffuse the explosive gas. She next captures Cassandra as the futuristic scammer is trying to escape on one of the horses.

There seems to be much more local D.C. color in this episode, though the second and third seasons of the show relied heavily on California storylines. This one also makes reference to Wonder Woman's immortality: Cassandra complains that the Amazon princess is just as "meddlesome" in the 20th century as she is in the 22nd. Adam mentions a 2007 nuclear holocaust, interestingly enough.

This episode first aired on November 10, 1978, just a couple months after Joan Van Ark made her debut as Valene Ewing on "Dallas," though the Gary Ewing she played to at that point was David Ackroyd, not Ted

Shackelford. She and Shackelford "reunited" on screen a year later in the series, in 1979, when he took over the role of Gary.

"Skateboard Wiz" (sometimes listed as "Skateboard Whiz")
November 24, 1978
Written by Alan Brennert; directed by Leslie H. Martinson.
Diana heads to Santa Corona, California, for a vacation to see former coworker Leslie O'Neill and her teen daughter Jamie. At the Santa Corona Beach Club, meanwhile, mobster Evan Donalsen is trying to shake down the owner. A couple skateboarders, including Jamie, head into the club's arcade, oblivious to the fact that there's a secret backroom there full of illicit gambling.

Diana arrives at Leslie's house and sees Jamie's excitement at entering a skateboard contest. Afterward, Diana runs into Skyler Markham, a former cop she once worked with on a case. She then witnesses an explosion at a nearby building — more of Donalsen's pressure tactics — and changes to Wonder Woman to put out the fire. Donalsen doesn't appreciate that, and neither does his swindling partner — Skyler Markham! Skye is suspicious of Diana's "vacation."

One of the regulars at the gambling hall, Duane Morrisey, spots a progeny in Jamie when he sees her arcade-game prowess and calculator brain. He talks her into "helping" him at the gambling table.

At the beach, two hoods try to drown Diana. She changes to Wonder Woman then learns with her lasso that Donalsen was behind it. She compares notes with John Key of the city government, who's all-too-familiar with Donalsen's maneuvering to own the town. Key then receives an explosive package.

Diana tries unsuccessfully to meet with the Beach Club's owner, Howard Ketchum, realizing the venue is on Donalsen's hit list. She uses her alter-ego to gain access, encountering one of Donalsen's thugs in Ketchum's office.

Jamie and Duane head into the gambling hall (after Duane supplies a slinky dress to make her look older). She realizes, though, what a creep he is and scoots out of there. She goes to the hotel room where Diana is staying, telling her about the gambling hall. On the way out, they run into Skye, telling him what they know. Ooops. By the time Diana goes to the Beach Club with a search warrant, the back door leads only to an innocent storage room. Di realizes that Skye is sly.

The skateboard contest begins, and Donalsen sends thugs after Jamie, since she has seen too much. Wonder Woman goes to Skye and learns that Jamie's in danger. She dons her helmet, gloves, and elbow and knee pads, and then skateboards to the crooks to stop them in their tracks!

Diana seems to have developed an affinity for hats, wearing stylish wide-brims this episode and last. This one would also seem, years later, to be a bit of a tribute to "Charlie's Angels," airing two years after the well-known "Consenting Adults" episode that featured a skateboarding Farrah. When Duane compliments Jamie in her slinky dress for looking like one of those pretty gals on TV, she quips, "I don't think Farrah Fawcett is losing any sleep." Story editor Anne Collins-Ludwick tells BRBTV the episode wasn't designed to pay tribute to that other landmark chick show, however.

"The Deadly Dolphin"
December 1, 1978
Written by Jackson Gillis; directed by Sigmund Neufeld Jr.
At a marine exhibit, Gladys the dolphin is upset when her dolphin friend Bluebeard is tranquilized and loaded into a truck to be taken to San Diego. Her concern is for good reason; Bluebeard is then promptly dolphin-napped! The animal is part of a Navy research project and was missing from the Caribbean until just a couple days ago, when he was spotted following a boat off the California coast. Bluebeard's service record is also now missing. His 'nappers are the same ones who took him the first time, a real estate developer named Silas Lockhart and his cronies. Lockhart is anxious to get the bottlenosed dolphin back, but why?

Bluebeard's caretaker, Dr. Sylvia Stubbs, was abducted along with the animal. Diana follows her nose to the nearest fresh fish market in nearby Mountain Junction, where she encounters a suspicious lawman, Billy, loaded down with fish, insisting he has "a lot of cats." Diana then locates Dr. Stubbs, who tells her the thieves dropped Bluebeard into the ocean.

Nicolas Coster, that dolphin-napper! Photo courtesy of Nicolas Coster.

Lockhart is working some development deals on coastal property. He's upset that his latest prospect, Ira, won't sell.

Dr. Stubbs and her assistant Darrell send Gladys out to the ocean to look for Bluebeard. Sharks threaten, though, so Diana dons her Wonder Woman diving suit (spinning directly into it this time) and uses a special signal to send the beasts away.

Lockhart has Bluebeard taken to a Pacific Naval testing facility. There, the dolphin is strapped down with an explosive and sent over to a ship to attach the explosive to its hull. It's a "dress rehearsal"; Lockhart is really targeting a huge crude-oil tanker, planning to cause an oil spill that will threaten the nearby coastland. Of course, he's unconcerned that even Bluebeard won't be able to escape the spill's effects.

Wonder Woman tracks one of Bluebeard's thieves, Gaffer, formerly known as Melvin Schultz, Bluebeard's trainer. Diana learns through IRAC that Gaffer just bought a boat, so she finds the vessel at the dock. Lockhart's men find her, however, and Lockhart orders her brought aboard as a prisoner. When Gaffer realizes what Lockhart plans to do, he tries to stop Bluebeard. Diana is able to change into Wonder Woman and dive into the drink. She finds Gladys, too, and enlists her aid to locate Bluebeard, get the explosive and throw it to a safer place.

Nicolas Coster of '80s soap "Santa Barbara" plays Silas Lockhart. We've talked to Coster off and on over the years, and we asked him what he remembers about this role, and how much contact he had with Carter on the set. "I did not have much to do with her, actually," *he tells BRBTV.* "It was one of a host of quick jobs I did at that time. I had my two kids and had to make living, no excuses or apologies. We do what we have to do. I have tried though, through the years, to do my work with a degree of excellence," *he adds glibly,* "sometimes succeeding."

Stuntwoman Jeannie Epper, however, remembers this episode vividly! See her story of the dolphin saving her life in our interview with her.

"Stolen Faces"
December 15, 1978
Written by Richard Carr and Anne Collins; directed by Leslie H. Martinson.
A caped Wonder Woman saves a boy from being hit by a car, but she appears to be badly injured and is taken to the hospital. What gives? Diana Prince is called to the hospital to see this imposter. A big thug then sneaks into this Mary Doe's room to try to harm her, and Wonder Woman chases him down. He escapes from a rooftop.

The unconscious patient then receives another caller, this time a friendlier one. He tells Diana his name is Todd Daniels, and he's been worried about this gal, whose name is Nancy Clark. She's an inspiring actress, it seems.

The men who were pulling her strings as "Wonder Woman" want to make sure Nancy keeps her mouth shut. The ringleader, Edgar Percy, is supplying the models and entertainment for an upcoming charity benefit. The event planner for that high-profile event, John Austin, just happens to be a friend of Steve Trevor. Austin has been receiving threatening anonymous phone calls (which are really from Percy) and is concerned about security for the event.

At the hospital, Nancy awakens and doesn't want to listen to Todd and his concerns. On the roof of a parking garage, Diana is then almost hit by a car. She falls over the edge of the roof, transforming into Wonder Woman as she spins through the air *(the first usage of that technique!)*.

Percy, it turns out, is a master crafter of masks, and the next mask he's making is of Steve Trevor. He plans a huge heist at the charity event, which will be attended by D.C.'s wealthiest.

Steve consults with Austin about security for the benefit. Todd, meanwhile, does some poking around at the event's rehearsals, still curious as to why Nancy was involved with these people.

At the event, Percy moves his Steve Trevor impersonator into position. Todd attends the event, as well, and Diana shows up. She and Todd are quickly apprehended by Percy's thug Fred Roman, however.

The show begins, and the stage is set with models in a scene from the

Roaring '20s — complete with guns. The scene takes a nefarious turn, though, as the models point their guns at the audience members and demand their valuables. "Wonder Woman" then bursts in and takes control, along with the fake Steve. Diana, watching from the sidelines at gunpoint, can take it no more. She breaks away, changes into the real Wonder Woman and brings the whole thing to a theatrical halt.

Stuntwoman Jeannie Epper gets to show her face in this one as the imposter Wonder Woman.

"Pot of Gold"
December 22, 1978
Written by Michael McGreevey; directed by Gordon Hessler.
The place is London, the time is Christmas, and Diana Prince reports in from a parked car, noting that she's outside the office of a man named Thackery. Inside, the man in question is readying the transportation of plates for counterfeit 100-dollar bills, introducing his associate to his not-so-friendly dog, Rasputin.

In the U.S., an Irish shoe-repairman is abducted, but he disappears from his two captors. Diana tails Thackery's associate Charlie, meanwhile, to Heathrow Airport, where he tries to shake her but cannot escape Wonder Woman and her golden lasso. The counterfeit plates, though, are already on a plane en route to D.C., carried by Thackery's attack dog.

The shoe-repairman, Pat O'Hanlan, arrives home and has a surprise visitor — the neighbor girl, Lisa, who knows about his secret pot of gold. Diana has Steve meet the dog's flight when it lands in the U.S., but this vicious dog manages to escape.

Thackery then arrives in the U.S., himself, consulting with the buyer for his counterfeit plates, Vincent Bonelli. O'Hanlan gets another visit from his kidnappers, Bonelli and his two thugs, who want his gold. He's forced to take them to the basement of his shop, where the pot of gold is hidden beneath the floorboards.

Diana checks in with Steve, who tells her some recent gold robberies point to the buyer for Thackery's plates. They set a decoy for the thief. Diana poses as an armored truck driver but is intercepted by the gold thieves and locked in the back of one of the trucks. She changes to Wonder Woman, jumps atop the armored truck as it makes its getaway but then jumps back off to save O'Hanlan from being run over.

Diana manages to get some information about this wily little O'Hanlan from Lisa, who says that she thinks her neighbor is a Leprecaun. Diana then tries to follow the Irishman but loses him. He goes to the airport to retrieve his pot of gold. The thieves find him and lock him into a wooden crate. Wonder Woman arrives at the airport and finds him. He gives her the slip again as she tries to figure out where the gold-for-plates exchange is going to take place.

Diana and Steve bring other IADC agents to the airport. Thackery is inside, pulling a double-cross on Bonelli. Steve and Diana interrupt the scene. The armed Thackery flees with both O'Hanlan and his pot of gold, loading them into a helicopter, then throwing O'Hanlan out once they're in the air! Luckily for this Leprecaun, Wonder Woman is there to catch him. And her golden lasso proves just as precious as his pot of gold, helping her pull Thackery's copter to the ground.

"Gault's Brain"
December 29, 1978
Written by Arthur Weingarten and John Gaynor; directed by Gordon Hessler.
Diana suspects sabotage when fires are destroying the properties of a company with a lot of government contracts, Gault Industries. The chairman of the board, Harlow Gault, just died. Or did he? Watching secretly over his own funeral is the brain (and eyeball!) of Gault! A scientist, Dr. Crippin, has assisted him in this amazing transformation, and he plans to assist him in getting a new body, too.

When Gault's bodyguard Turk learns that Diana Prince of the IADC has been assigned the case of the mysterious fires, Gault *(voiced by John Carradine)* plans a little accident for her.

Gault's assistant / girlfriend, Tara Landon, scopes out a talented athlete and Olympic hopeful named Morton Danzig. She suggests Morton come work at her "uncle's" estate.

Diana gets gassed during a taxi ride, and these guys waste no time —

they dump her into the river in a barrel. But when the barrel hits the bottom of the river and starts rolling — you guessed it!

Diana and Steve trace the fingerprints found in the taxi to a certain George P. Turk. Diana then pays a visit to the Gault estate. While she's making her case to Tara in the drawing room, the weapon-wielding suit of armor behind her chair almost slices her in two. She also spots Morton Danzig at the estate, which proves a new lead in this mystery.

Wonder Woman has a chat with Stryker, who has taken over as the chairman of the board of Gault Industries, and gets some information out of him with her lasso.

Dr. Crippin does an analysis of Morton's physical condition, which is excellent. IRAC informs Steve, meanwhile, that Morton's college records are being altered to make him appear to be a whole lot smarter than he is. Come to find out, Gault is behind a secret takeover bid of his company, under the fake name of Thomas J. Craddack.

Steve goes to the Gault estate to talk to Morton about his college records. Morton is oblivious to the alteration. After his departure, Steve encounters Stryker's associate Daniel Berger, who sheds a little more light on the case. Back at the Gault estate, Crippin tries to prepare Morton for surgery, but the athlete slips away from him, fleeing to the drawing room to come face-to-brain with Gault.

The surgery gets underway. Wonder Woman arrives on the grounds, sneaking away from the guards and Turk then rushing into the operating room. Gault, who has developed telekinetic powers, tries to fend her off by flinging objects at her. Crippin and Tara escape, along with Gault's brain.

Peter Mark Richman. Photo courtesy of Peter Mark Richman.

Classic TV actor Peter Mark Richman is Dr. Crippin. In the scene where Diana is dumped into the river in a barrel, Wonder Woman flips right out of the river in her diving suit. It's a pretty nifty trick, especially since her suit isn't at all wet! And really, can a "Star Trek" fan watch this episode without thinking of the shark-jumping episode "Spock's Brain," also in that show's final season of three?

"Going, Going, Gone"
January 12, 1979
Written by Anne Collins and Patrick Mathews; directed by Alan Crosland.
A Russian aircraft has a run-in with a UFO off Catalina Island and must eject its cargo — then it must eject its pilot, too. After he parachutes down, he's picked up by the U.S. military. Steve is informed of it.

On another case regarding some stolen laser equipment, Diana encounters a martial-arts fighter at a warehouse, and Wonder Woman takes over for her. Diana then joins Steve at the place where the Russian pilot is being held as he recuperates. She and Steve meet Vladmir Zukov, who defends the pilot and won't reveal the cargo the plane was carrying. When Steve and Diana leave the room, the pilot, Yuri Grovka, tells Zukov the current coordinates of this mysterious cargo.

But that cargo is now aboard a submarine and in the hands of new owners. It's a nuclear warhead, and there's some bidding about to take place for it. The bidders represent various backers interested in an edge in the arms race.

Diana returns to her other case and is being followed. At the warehouse, she changes to Wonder Woman and does some fancy gymnastic moves when she meets some bad guys. Zukov also appears, wielding a gun, presumably to "help" Wonder Woman.

Diana and Steve surmise that a certain atomic weapon up for bids is their missing Russian cargo, so they go undercover to learn more. Diana poses as one of the bidders, Mrs. Fox. The other bidders are so amusingly named Brown, Jones and Smith. Steve, meanwhile, plays the owner of a Long Beach nautical goods shop who is Mrs. Fox's supplier of a cash down payment. When her backing is verified, Mrs. Fox is introduced to the black-market auction by organizer Sheldon Como.

Steve keeps one of Como's men at gunpoint while he sends the other back to the auction with Mrs. Fox's down payment, which has a tracer in the briefcase. Unfortunately, Zukov then arrives at the auction and blows Diana's cover. Zukov orders her killed, but Como realizes they need to move the sub out in a hurry instead. Diana learns that Como created the hologram of the UFO to cause the Russian pilot to jettison the warhead right into their hands. They try to jettison Diana from the sub next, but from within her jettison tube she is able to change to Wonder Woman and get back aboard and end this mess.

"Spaced Out"
January 26, 1979
Written by Bill Taylor; directed by Ivan Dixon.
A thief breaks into the Torrance Observatory in L.A. and steals three crystals from a telescope. The alarm goes off, and he ditches them in a crate marked for a Sylvester Grogan before meeting with his "buyer," the sinister Simon Rohan.

Diana checks into a hotel that's hosting guests of a nearby sci-fi convention, much to her dismay, and runs into an old pal — Sly Grogan. He's there for the convention. Diana also sees the thief, whose name is Kimball and who is familiar to her, coming into the hotel. Diana tails him outside, where he scales the building. Wonder Woman approaches him on the rooftop, but he gives her the slip.

At the con area at Paragon Studios, Sly shows Di his starlit (and highly spacey) moonrock display for the event, and Kimball soon comes in looking for Sly. He's being followed by Rohan's thug, because Rohan suspects Kimball is looking for a higher bidder for the crystals. Kimball decides to don the costume of the popular Black Avenger to get into the con unrecognized. Rohan's man realizes this, though, along with the fact that IADC agent Diana Prince is at the event tailing Kimball.

Kimball in the Black Avenger costume finds Sly and asks for a tour of his moonrock display, looking, of course, for the crystals. Rohan's man tries to abduct Diana, but she tosses him into the pool, changes to Wonder Woman, and uses her lasso on him. Rohan then arrives at the con with two other "associates." He finds Kimball breaking into Sly's exhibit room and demands the crystals at gunpoint.

The con officially opens with a costume contest. Rohan has Sly brought in to Sly's exhibit room. Kimball goes to Diana at the contest and tells her that Sly is in danger. He and Wonder Woman then realize that the crystals are in plain view — on the contest winner's scepter. Sly had given them to show organizer Janet, thinking they were worthless plastic and could be used as decoration.

Sly gets away from Rohan by turning on his distracting lighted space display, and Wonder Woman finds the scepter. Kimball, however, escapes her grasp again — this time in a Robby the Robot costume.

Rene Auberjonois of "Benson" and "Star Trek: Deep Space Nine" is Kimball. Besides the tribute to classic sci-fi icon Robby the Robot (billed as playing "himself"), this episode features send-ups of several other greats such as "Star Trek," "Planet of the Apes," "Logan's Run" and "Star Wars." At the costume contest, Diana wears her hair down and wavy, a rarity. Between this and the absence of her glasses, she looks so much like Wonder Woman that the viewer's disbelief certainly is suspended — especially since Kimball sees her in this moment as Diana immediately before seeing her as Wonder Woman.

"The Starships Are Coming"
February 2, 1979
Written by Glen Olsen, Rod Baker and Anne Collins; directed by Alan Crosland.
In Berryville, Pennsylvania, Henry Wilson and his girlfriend, Mary Lou Thompkins, are out "parking" *(you remember that term, right?)* when a UFO appears in the sky. Henry, a budding photojournalist, goes to investigate, but he doesn't return. The next day, his mother makes an appeal on the TV news. Mary Lou, who was meeting Henry on the sly, keeps quiet until she sees IADC agent Diana Prince. She comes clean with Diana and gives her the tape recorder Henry was using when he was "abducted."

At the IADC offices, Steve and his colleagues are watching a real "War of the Worlds"-type moment: an apparent live feed of an alien invasion. Col. Robert Elliot, the Air Force's leading expert on UFOs, arrives to consult with Steve and doesn't think the broadcast, which they've traced to Berryville, is a hoax.

In the tiny town, Wonder Woman inspects some spikes in the road that blew out the tires on Diana's car, then she turns around and sees what appear to be two small alien men. They quickly scurry off. Col. Elliot arrives in Berryville to survey the aftermath of the alien battle.

Henry is then shown alone in a paneled cell, begging his unseen captors to be set free.

Col. Elliot is approached by the "aliens," who tell him that their superiors plan to kill all people on Earth and mine its natural resources. They tell Elliot that in order to stop this assault, he must launch nuclear warheads secretly, and aim them at the People's Republic of China.

Diana looks for the location of the Berryville broadcast transmitter. She finds a secluded old barn, then spies Henry managing to escape through one of its windows, followed by the two alien creatures. She is apprehended at gunpoint. The man behind all of this is right-wing activist Mason Steele. He's been filming this whole invasion hoax, scrambling the transmission to make it appear to be live. He's on a quest to destroy what he sees as the enemies of the U.S., beginning with Red China.

Steele has Diana bound and gagged and left with a bomb. Henry returns to the barn and finds her and slowly disarms the explosives as Diana tensely watches. They compare notes, and Diana learns where Steele's transmitter is in this otherwise-sleepy little town. Wonder Woman goes there to disrupt the signal, so to speak, just in time to stop Elliot from launching the warheads.

There's a little plug in this one for CBS, which originally aired the second and third seasons of "Wonder Woman." As the agents are watching the apparent alien-invasion broadcast at the IADC offices, one explains that the live feed at first "was only on CBS," but then the other networks picked it up.

"Amazon Hot Wax"
February 16, 1979
Written by Alan Brennert; directed by Ray Austin.
That Cathy Meadows is a real songbird, we see *(and in this one we get to hear Lynda Carter sing two tracks from her "Portrait" album of this era, "Next to You" and "Toto")*. Diana, it turns out, is investigating an extortion case involving Phoenix Records. The extortionists, Adelle Kobler and her flunky Marty, have the master tape of the last album of popular deceased singer Billy Dero, and they are pressing Eric Landau, majority owner of Phoenix, for payment.

We learn that the extortionists got their hands on Dero's last tape via one of Phoenix's other acts, Jeff and Barbi Gordon *(Judge Reinhold and Sarah Purcell)*.

One of Phoenix's acts, a trio of guys calling themselves Antimatter *(featuring a young Rick Springfield in his second "Wonder Woman" episode)*, discovers a hidden message in one of Dero's tracks. Antimatter decides to investigate, suspecting Dero is still alive. Indeed, the guys do find him. He's been hiding out for a few weeks hoping his "death" would liven up his career.

Antimatter shows Dero to Cathy / Diana, and they all rush to stop Landau from paying the million-dollar fee for the master tape. Diana changes to Wonder Woman to head off Marty as he flees the scene of the blackmail exchange. He still escapes, however.

Kobler and Co. are miffed that Dero is back and their master tape is now worthless. Unless ... they get their hands on Dero, as well! The Gordons seem just right for this job.

Landau wants to go public "with this whole sleazy story." He demands Dero get into the studio and recut that last album. The Gordons arrive in ski masks and turn up some ear-splitting feedback to distract and abduct. Wonder Woman breaks it up, though. But Dero is still gone, led out by the Gordons and ushered quickly into a car. Wonder Woman is able to nab Marty, lassoing him for some information.

Wonder Woman goes to where the Gordons took Dero and tosses a couple of the resident thugs into the pool. The Antimatter guys, meanwhile, once again prove their worth by helping bring in this case. This only leaves "Cathy" to come clean with Landau, who became quite enamored with this promising young artist.

In her interview on Live Miami (NBCMiami.com) in 2011, Carter said, "When I first started in Hollywood, I was informed I shouldn't tell anyone I was a singer. The days of the musicals were long past." Here, she certainly gets her due. She plays it bubbly as Cathy, at first, before Diana really starts digging into this case and dispenses with the ingénue routine. There's an amusing John Travolta reference, as Kobler, upset that Dero has resurfaced alive and well and the master tape is worthless, says she "couldn't trade it in for a crummy John Travolta poster."

"The Richest Man in the World"
February 19, 1979
Written by Jackson Gillis and Anne Collins; directed by Don MacDougall.
The reclusive, Howard Hughes-like "richest man in the world," Marshall Henshaw, sells his invention, "Missy" — a missile scrambler — to the prime minister of a foreign nation. But Missy is just a little misplaced, then Henshaw is kidnapped. Steve assumes Missy is being transported per the secretary of state's plan to keep the invention safe.

Henshaw wakes up alone out in the woods and encounters a poor runaway kid named Barney. He realizes his employee Dunfield is behind his abduction.

Diana is following the van supposedly carrying Missy, but she then changes to Wonder Woman when the van begins driving erratically. When it stops, she realizes that some explosives were planted under the vehicle's bumper. She then sees that Missy ... is missing.

Henshaw has no ID, cash or credit cards, so he goes with Barney to his ... barn! Steve is trying to find Henshaw, meanwhile, and Diana takes a closer look at Henshaw's factory, where Missy was stolen, speaking with Henshaw's lady friend, Lucy DeWitt.

Henshaw and Barney scrape together cab fare via some bottles to return, and they head downtown. Henshaw has trouble convincing people who he is, since no one has ever really seen the mogul. He and Barney drop in on Lucy, and Marshall quickly realizes that Lucy and Dunfield have been conspiring against him.

Barney lifts the keys to Lucy's Camaro, so Henshaw drives them to his factory to find the only other person in the state of California who knows who he is. But Henshaw — so accustomed to being chauffeured — runs the car into a vegetable stand. Then Diana happens upon them, thinking they're simply two strangers who need a ride. The trio is followed by Lucy's sinister employee as Diana drives them to a pay phone.

Barney is abducted, and a threatening note is left for Henshaw, who then ditches Diana and takes her car. Wonder Woman meets him at the factory and intercepts Lucy and Dunfield, as well.

This is a sweet little story, as a wealthy industrialist gets a taste of being homeless. Carmen Zapata of daytime soap "Santa Barbara" is the prime minister.

"A Date with Doomsday"
March 10, 1979
Written by Roland Starke and Dennis Landa; directed by Curtis Harrington. Diana is consulting with Dr. Roberts about potential germ warfare, when the researcher discovers a deadly virus is missing. His lab worker George *(Bob Hastings)* makes his way out of the building with it. Wonder Woman dons her motorcycle outfit to chase George *(love how she always just steals the nearest motorbike!)*, but he gives her the slip. She finds the lifelike mask he was wearing, however. Steve, Diana and Dr. Roberts realize the "George" they saw was an imposter.

Dr. Roberts has the cranky Prof. Zander working on an antidote to the virus. The professor's lonely and unappreciated housekeeper, Mary Jane Thrip, responds to a free offer to visit the Data-Date Compu-Cupid dating service. As she's sitting in the chair being videotaped for her perfect matchup, she doesn't realize she's being fitted for her own imposter's mask just as George was, with the help of a special computer sensory device.

The real George surfaces, insisting he's been to Florida, but he's really been brainwashed by the perps. Wonder Woman must save him from jumping off a building, since that's what the perps programmed him to do at the mention of truth serum.

Prof. Zander accidentally discovers the antidote to the virus — from a moldy soufflé of Mrs. Thrip's — and he's excited to tell her. But she pulls a gun on him! This gruff imposter Mrs. Thrip then steals the antidote. Wonder Woman chases "her," getting a tip from a white dove, but only encounters the real, and quite harmless, Mrs. Thrip.

Dr. Roberts' other lab worker Dede has been behind the theft of the virus and the antidote, working with a partner named Ward Selkirk. Diana is the next one to visit the dating service. She encounters an amorous D.C. tourism pilot, John Blake, who goes by the handle "Snake on the Make." Then, as she gets into the chair, Dede recognizes Diana, and she and Selkirk cook up special plans for her. She's subsequently gassed.

IRAC clues in Steve on Compu-Cupid's simulation process. Dede poses as Snake to take herself and Selkirk on one of the tourist flights over the White House. They plan to unleash the virus on D.C. for revenge of certain Doomsday experiments that killed Dede's mother. But when Selkirk throws the vial of virus out the helicopter window, Wonder Woman has it well in hand on the ground.

We again get to see Wonder Woman's ability to communicate with animals as the Amazon gets a tipoff from a cooing white dove. Just like a couple episodes ago, there's an amusing reference to John Travolta, who was in the midst of his early TV stardom. When Mary Jane Thrip is being videotaped at the dating service and things don't go well, she muses, "There goes my chance with John Travolta."

"The Girl with a Gift for Disaster"
March 17, 1979
Written by Alan Brennert; directed by Alan Crosland.
A young woman named Bonnie Murphy thinks she has a talent for disaster, and her boyfriend's exploding van seems to make her point. Steve and Diana take a look at the rubble and suspect that thief William Mayfield is a part of this, and his target is J&R Electronics, which is developing a weapon — a microwave scrambler — for the Pentagon.

A scientist, Dr. Koren, takes a look at Bonnie's "talent" and finds that the woman can bend probability curves — in other words, she's a jinx. Bonnie's boyfriend, Mark Reuben, approaches Mayfield with the idea of using Bonnie as a diversion to get the microwave scrambler from J&R.

Another vehicle explodes, thanks to Bonnie, and Wonder Woman is on the scene this time. As she uses a fire hydrant to douse the flames and the building is evacuated, Reuben makes off with the goods. Steve and Diana realize the microwave scrambler has been stolen — but what will Mayfield do with it?

Diana runs into Bonnie at the IADC offices; Bonnie is looking for Mark, who told her he was an IADC agent. But Bonnie doesn't want to hear from Diana that her boyfriend lied to her. She searches on and finds Mark, who continues to lie to and sweet-talk her.

Wonder Woman encounters one of Mayfield's flunkies, Neil, and uses her lasso to learn more about the operation, then she makes him think he killed Diana as he was aiming to do.

The bad guys are targeting a valuable cache of U.S. historical documents, planning to use the scrambler to cut off all communications in D.C.

Diana finds Reuben and Bonnie and tails them in her car, then Steve takes over. Reuben's cohorts hijack a military vehicle carrying some other equipment they need, but Steve catches up to them and a big scuffle ensues. Wonder Woman must break it up. Reuben escapes by threatening Bonnie's life. But she has more leverage than Mark; she flattens the tire of their escape vehicle to get away.

Bonnie finds Steve at the IADC. They realize what Mayfield and Reuben are planning to do. The city then blacks out. Steve and Wonder Woman intercept the thieves at the document depository, and Wonder Woman corners Mayfield.

"The Boy Who Knew Her Secret," Part 1
May 28, 1979
Written by Anne Collins; directed by Leslie H. Martinson.
A jogger finds a strange, shimmering, pyramid-shaped object on the ground, and when he picks it up, something happens to him. He seems to be under the control of this pyramid.

Diana is visiting Dr. Eli Jaffe, who has his eye on an asteroid that he believes crashed to earth at Crystal Lake, California. He sends Diana there to investigate, though she thinks this researcher is nuts.

Diana gets held up at gunpoint at her car. The gunman takes the briefcase that Dr. Jaffe gave her. She changes to Wonder Woman and pursues him, finding the briefcase, the man's gun — and a cat that scurries off.

A high-schooler named Skip Keller is struggling with grades and with the disappointment from his parents. At their home, his dad answers the door and receives a strange pyramid just like the one the jogger found.

Dr. Jaffe's assistant, Cameron Michaels, meets Diana in Crystal Lake, and they take a look at Dr. Jaffe's notes indicating some mysterious "tetrahedron" stones. They go on the hunt for the stones.

Skip takes a horseback ride at the local stables and runs into a girl he likes, Melanie. Diana is also wandering these trails, on foot (and every bit the fashion plate in her fringed suede jacket!), when she spots one of the shimmering pyramids on the ground. Before she can walk up to it, though, a man appears, grabs it and runs off. She changes to Wonder Woman to pursue him, but then she is diverted to help Skip, whose horse is out of his control.

When Skip later arrives home safely, he finds his mother in a weird trance, also infected by one of the silver pyramid stones. His dad has one, too, and is acting all spooky. Since Diana Prince just told him to be on the lookout for these stones, he goes to her hotel in town to find her.

Wonder Woman follows up at the Keller residence, finding Skip's parents in the mesmerized state. Mr. Keller puts the tetrahedrons in a bag and gives them to a police officer outside. Skip sees his friend from school, Pete Pearson, who's also been infected. Skip has to flee from Pete on his bicycle. Diana then returns to where she left Skip, finding him gone but spotting a pyramid on the bed. She picks it up, becomes entranced, and cannot put it down. Skip returns and knocks the pyramid out of her hand. Diana realizes that the pyramid "asteroid" that landed in Crystal Lake was really a ship, and that these 99 smaller pyramids each contain an alien life force that needs a human host to survive.

Back in D.C., Steve is irate with Dr. Jaffe because Diana has not checked in.

Diana, Skip and Cameron decide to work together. Skip goes to the stables and finds Melanie and Pete both entranced along with other friends. Diana and Cameron arrive before Skip's friends can "turn" him, but then when Pete flees, Diana decides to change to Wonder Woman to tail him. She doesn't realize she's been seen!

As Skip, Clark Brandon is such a cutie and seems so familiar. It's not just that he reminds us of Michael Gray of "Shazam!", he also appeared in "Facts of Life" and "Mr. Merlin."

"The Boy Who Knew Her Secret," Part 2
May 29, 1979
Written by Anne Collins; directed by Leslie H. Martinson.
It finally happened — someone finally saw Diana Prince turn into Wonder Woman. Skip Keller can scarcely believe his eyes. He watches Wonder Woman hop on a horse to chase down Pete. She lassos Pete to question his alien abductor, who explains that they came to Earth in pursuit of a dangerous shapeshifting killer. She then returns to Skip as Diana and tells him the plan: pretend to be infected by the aliens as they continue to unravel this mystery.

At a remote barn in Crystal Lake, the human-hosted aliens are meeting, assembling their pyramid rocks back into the larger pyramid shape. Only a few pieces are missing. But the shapeshifter has infiltrated their ranks, then he is discovered and must flee the barn.

At the IADC in Washington, D.C., Cameron Michaels turns up in Steve's office, but we know it's really the shapeshifter, since Cameron is back in Crystal Lake with Diana. This alien is certainly on the move, because later he impersonates Melanie, eludes Wonder Woman, causes a car crash, then surmises the fact that Wonder Woman is Diana Prince.

Skip tries to keep up the alien-abducted act at school. The shapeshifter then poses as Cameron again to drug Diana's water glass. She realizes it and sees, in her haze, his changing forms before her as he explains that he plans to get the pyramid piece Skip has secreted away from the aliens. This shapeshifter also plans to make Diana forget that she's Wonder Woman.

Skip later finds Diana packing to return to D.C., figuring the case is over, which doesn't seem to make sense. The shapeshifter knocks on the door, posing as Skip's dad, causing the suspicious Skip to skip out. He encounters his mesmerized friends again, but he escapes them after revealing that he has the missing pyramid piece. He meets up with Wonder Woman, who asks for the rock rather insistently. Then he sees Diana and knows that something's wrong. The world has gone mad, he thinks. He decides to just give in, since nothing makes sense, anyway, and touch the pyramid himself. But he's interrupted by the shapeshifter, who tries to nab the pyramid, then by Dr. Jaffe, just arrived from D.C. to help sort out this mess.

Diana is still fighting her drugged haze, and she realizes what Skip told her is true, that she is Wonder Woman, just as Dr. Jaffe approaches the larger pyramid at the barn and places the final piece. The real Wonder Woman arrives as the shapeshifter is holding the aliens at gunpoint. She dukes it out with the creature, imprisoning it in the large pyramid, then the townspeople are returned to normal.

And Skip's knowledge of Wonder Woman's secret identity? Nothing that a golden lasso can't fix. Except... what about all those diary tape recordings Skip likes to make?

BRBTV has to wonder, given Wonder Woman's reference at the end of the episode of Diana's reassignment to L.A., and the reinforced mention of Skip's tape recordings, if Skip might have turned up again, had the show progressed to a fourth season with the foundation laid in the next episode.

"The Man Who Could Not Die"
August 28, 1979
Written by Anne Collins; directed by John Newland.
It's moving day in L.A., and amid the boxes and the moving men on this typical suburban street, Diana Prince gets a visit from a frisky chimp. He's chased into the street, where he's struck by a car but is mysteriously unharmed.

Diana then reports to her new IADC field office in downtown L.A., and is able to find the chimp's owner, Dr. Akers, who was researching the aging process with Dr. Joseph Reichman, another molecular biologist. Akers cautions that Reichman may use their research on a human subject.

At a local gym, an athlete named Bryce is telling a friend how he's been participating in research with Reichman. He seems impervious to injury and doesn't even need to eat or drink.

Diana gets a visitor at her new office, the young, precocious T. Burton Phipps III, who's selling snacks from inside his jacket. Diana's boss Dale Hawthorn is not amused, just before telling Diana that Reichman is missing. She goes to the lab he shared with Akers and is greeted by an explosion, changing to Wonder Woman and tending to the shaken Akers.

Reichman, consulting with a man named Dupris, is after Akers' research notes. Diana visits the university looking for the man she saw running away from the explosion. She learns he's Prof. Bryce Candall, whom we now see complaining to Reichman that he wants to feel more human again. Diana visits Bryce's home, but he runs from her, having been warned by Reichman to never talk to the IADC. She changes to Wonder Woman and tries her lasso on him, but it doesn't work. He tells her he doesn't want to be invincible anymore.

Diana finds a gun-toting Dupris at her new house, and he ties her up in the garage then starts her car and leaves. Bryce drops in on her and saves her. Bryce tells Diana he stole Akers' notes for Reichman. They go to where Reichman is hiding out in Topanga Canyon. Diana must change to Wonder Woman when Bryce encounters the estate's guard dogs, then inside Bryce meets with Reichman's lion, again resisting any injury. He tries to get Reichman's notes so he can be returned to normal, but Reichman escapes.

When the dust settles, Diana hires Bryce at the IADC, under the name Bret Cassiday.

This episode was the last one produced, reflecting a new direction for the show, though it aired before the two-part series finale, "Phantom of the Roller Coaster." We have to wonder how the show would've shaped up with no Steve, even no IRAC or Rover (especially Rover — we love Rover). Diana did take that nice little powder-blue Mercedes with her to L.A., however!

Diana's appearance comes even closer to Wonder Woman's in this new direction: Not only is she sans glasses, but her hair (when she's not wearing a hat, which is often now) is styled long and wavy, and the only thing really missing now is her tiara. We learn her new residence is 409 S. Vine, which she leaves in a note for Bryce. There's a reference to a fellow WB / DC property as Diana tells Bryce, when he's trying to figure out what he's going to do at the end of the episode, that he could always join the circus and bill himself as the "Man of Steel."

Since the overall tone of this final episode is so different, and so far removed from the show's first season, it's perhaps a bit ironic that the blond Dr. Reichman is so Nazi-like in his desire to create an "army of invincibles."

"Phantom of the Roller Coaster," Part 1
September 4, 1979
Written by Anne Collins; directed by John Newland.
There seems to be a phantom haunting the Fun Universe theme park. Diana, meanwhile, is posing as a double agent, meeting with an unsavory type. He sabotages her car, so she changes into her Wonder Woman biker outfit and chases him on two wheels. With her lasso, she learns the buyer for her double-agent-provided info is spy Harrison Fynch.

Fynch, it turns out, is also trying to buy the amusement park from owner Leon Gurney, who built the park with his brother, David. Fynch leaves a bug at Gurney's office, and he hears one of the park employees tell Gurney about the strange hauntings at the park. Fynch gets an idea.

A teen named Randy, who loves roller coasters, begs a teacher to go along on a kids' field trip to Fun Universe.

Diana, carrying a listening device in the shape of a 50-cent piece, meets her next contact, Pierce, to sell some information. She makes sure he leaves the diner with his "change."

At Fun Universe, Randy wanders off and is sighted by the park's "phantom" — whom we learn is really the assumed-dead David Gurney. As Steve and Diana listen in on Pierce talking to Fynch, they realize Fynch wants to use Fun Universe as his D.C. surveillance base.

Leon Gurney authorizes a search for Randy at the park, afraid of any possible PR backlash over the teen's disappearance.

Pierce goes to the theme park to plant a bomb as Fynch has instructed. He runs into David Gurney and flees, leaving the bomb behind. David picks it up, then is seen by Wonder Woman, who chases him. He eludes her, returning to where Randy is trapped underground, telling the boy not to be afraid of him. Randy follows David to a computer lab underneath the park. David tells him he was badly disfigured in an explosion in Vietnam and decided to let everyone think he was dead.

Fynch orders a firm hit on Diana, then she promptly has some trouble on the road.

Jared Martin of "Dallas" does double duty as the Gurney brothers, which seems to suggest they are twins, though it's clarified by David in the second part that Leon is a couple years older. Ike Eisenmann of Disney's "Witch Mountain" movies, cute as a button and one of BRBTV's faves, is Randy.

"Phantom of the Roller Coaster," Part 2
September 11, 1979
Written by Anne Collins; directed by John Newland.
As Diana's car gets smashed, Wonder Woman lassos the perps and learns only that they were hired by a mysterious voice on the phone.

In the tunnels below Fun Universe, David Gurney tells Randy the history of the theme park and its popular roller coasters. He has a computer system set up in this underground lab that monitors the park's key ride, the Super Loop, and he has also been designing more rides here. Randy is excited about everything he's learning from David, deciding that he wants to design roller coasters someday, too.

Diana reports back to Steve at the IADC. Leon Gurney gets flak over both the missing teen at his park and the reports of a park "phantom." He pays a visit to his brother in the tunnels — turns out, he's known all along about his little bro David's greatly exaggerated demise. Leon suspects Randy is there with him and tells David to stop hiding out underground.

Since Steve and Diana have realized that Leon's office is bugged, Steve visits Leon in disguise, bringing a script for him to read and signaling that they're being overheard. Together they plant the idea for Fynch that the Super Loop may have vulnerabilities.

Fynch and Pierce take the bait, plotting how they'll sabotage the Super Loop. They employ a park worker to place a device on the ride that will weaken the steel.

David carefully examines the bomb he found, and Randy disappears, returning topside to get David some more coffee. He's spotted by Diana, though, and she chases him back into the tunnels. Now David realizes he's got another problem on his hands, worried that Diana will reveal his secret existence. Then his computer monitoring system sounds an alarm on the Super Loop. David and Randy rush above ground to try to stop the ride, leaving Diana behind. She changes to Wonder Woman and follows.

Wonder Woman manages to plant herself inside the steel structure of the coaster, holding it together, quite literally.

Later, back in the tunnels, Wonder Woman tries to convince David to leave his underground exile. She also asks to take the bomb with her for the IADC's analysis. She uses her lasso to make Randy forget about David and his secret lab. Then she sets her sights on nabbing Fynch.

BRBTV's favorite line: "What do grades have to do with dreams?" David tells aspiring roller coaster designer Randy.

By the Numbers

60 Episodes (pilot + 13 in Season 1; 22 in Season 2; 24 in Season 3)

5 Two-parters (2 in Season 1; 1 in Season 2; 2 in Season 3)

153 Spins (including Wonder Girl's)

45 Bullets and bracelets routines (including the alien beams in "Mind Stealers from Outer Space")

58 Usages of lasso for compelling truth or erasing memory (not always by Wonder Woman)

10 Tiara throws (7 circular, 3 in straight boomerang shape)

5 Voice impersonations by Wonder Woman (all in first season)

10 Costume variations (in order of appearance: standard with skirt, standard, standard with cape, standard with cape and skirt, Western, redesigned standard, redesigned standard with cape, diving, motorcycle, skateboarding)

11 Notable double guest appearances (Roddy McDowall, Rick Springfield, Ted Shackelford, Kurt Kreuger, Eric Braeden, Henry Darrow, Ed Begley Jr., Henry Gibson, Robert Sampson, Bob Hastings, Kenneth Tigar)

3 Queen Hippolytas (Cloris Leachman, Carolyn Jones, Beatrice Straight)

5½ Paradise Island appearances (pilot, "The Feminum Mystique" 1 and 2, "Wonder Woman in Hollywood," "The Return of Wonder Woman," "The Bermuda Triangle Crisis" — considered a "half" because Paradise Island factors into the plot, and Queen Hippolyta is shown, though there aren't actual scenes on the island)

13 Invisible plane appearances

Another one of BRBTV's many Wonder Woman dolls, this one a Barbie by Mattel, circa '90s. That luscious satin cape really makes the figure. The golden lasso is pretty good, too. One drawback is that her boots are fabric instead of plastic as in other Wonder Woman dolls.

> **❝** Women did things they had never done before. They made planes, and they flew the planes. And they became superheroines. But as soon as the war ended, all of the guys wanted their jobs back and the women were sent back to the kitchen. And suddenly there was a mass amnesia, and no one remembered that women had ever been strong. **❞**
> — *Trina Robbins, comic writer and historian,*
> *"Wonder Women: the Untold Story of America's Superheroines," March 2012*

Credits

The names behind it all

Wonder Woman creator	**William Moulton Marston**
Executive producer	**Douglas S. Cramer**
Supervising producers	**Charles B. Fitzsimons, Bruce Lansbury**
Associate producers	**Peter J. Elkington, John Gaynor, Rod Holcomb, Arnold Turner**
Producers	**Wilfred Lloyd Baumes, Mark Rodgers**
Directors	**Jack Arnold, Ray Austin, Bruce Bilson, Michael Caffey, Barry Crane, Alan Crosland, Ivan Dixon, Curtis Harrington, Gordon Hessler, Leonard Horn, Bob Kelljan, Richard Kinon, Don MacDougall, Stuart Margolin, Leslie H. Martinson, Dick Moder, Sigmund Neufeld Jr., John Newland, Seymour Robbie, Charles Rondeau, Alex Singer, Herb Wallerstein**
Assistant directors	**Kurt Baker, Craig Beaudine, John G. Behm, John D. Benson, Ray DeCamp, William Derwin, Bud Grace, Buck Hall, Nat Holt, Victor Hsu, Ed Ledding, Britt**

	Lomond, Kelly Manners, Morry Marks, G.C. Rusty Meek, Jon Paré, Robert Scrivner, Roger Slager, Rowe Wallerstein
Executive story consultants	Anne Collins, Robert Hamner, Brian McKay, Frank Telford
Writers	Margaret Armen, Barbara Avedon, Gwen Bagni, Rod Baker, Kathleen Barnes, Herbert Bermann, Alan Brennert, Judy Burns, Richard Carr, Calvin Clements Jr., Anne Collins, Barbara Corday, Wilton Denmark, Anthony DiMarco, Paul Dubov, Ron Friedman, John Gaynor, Jackson Gillis, Stephen Kandel, David Ketchum, Dennis Landa, Patrick Mathews, Michael McGreevey, Brian McKay, Dick Nelson, Glen Olsen, Katharyn Michaelian Powers, Mark Rodgers, Stanley Ralph Ross, Jimmy Sangster, Tom Sawyer, Elroy Schwartz, S.S. Schweitzer, Bruce Shelly, Roland Starke, Bill Taylor, Dan Ullman, Skip Webster, Arthur Weingarten, Carey Wilbur, David Wise
Music	Charles Fox, Johnny Harris, Artie Kane, Richard LaSalle, Angela Morley, Robert Prince, Roland O. Raglund
Directors of photography	Dennis Dalzell, Robert Hoffman, Joe Jackman, Ted Landon, Bri Murphy, Ric Wait
Film editors	Jamie Caylor, Axel Hubert Sr., William Neel, Barbara Pokras, Tony Radecki, Carroll Sax, Phil Tucker, Richard L. Van Enger, Stanley Wohlberg, Dick Wormell
Casting	Shelley Ellison, Mary Goldberg, Millie Gusse, Caro Jones, Barbara Miller, Alan Shayne, Victoria Tarazi
Art directors	Philip Barber, Michael Baugh, Stephen M. Berger, Fred Hope, James G. Hulsey, Patricia Van Ryker
Set decorators	Sal Blydenburgh, Solomon Brewer, Robert Checchi, James Hassinger, Bill McLaughlin, R. Chris Westlund

Costume designers	**Donfeld, Lennie Barin**
Hair and makeup	**John Elliott, Pat Miller, Shirley Padgett, Cheri Ruff, Karl Silvera, Edward Ternes**
Unit production managers	**Robert J. Anderson, John Burrows, Norman Cook, William Derwin, Mitch Gamson, Wes McAfee, Max Stein**
Property masters	**Jack E. Ackerman, Joe Falcetti, Douglas Forsmith**
Sound	**Alex Bamattre, Al Cavigga, Buzz Cooper, John Delong, Nicholas Eliopoulos, Hy Friedman, Pete Kelly, Jack C. May, Al Overton Sr., Billie Owens, Monty Pearce, Bob Post, Richard Raguse, W.M. Rivol, Don Rush, Evelyn Rutledge, Edwin Scheid, Richard Taylor, Ron Tinsley, Gary Vaughan, Joe von Stroheim**
Special effects	**Robert L. Peterson**
Stunts	**Paul Baxley, Jeannie Epper, Debbie Evans, Sandi Gross, George Robotham, Ron Stein, Dick Ziker**
Animation / titles	**Phill Norman**
Music editors	**Jay Alfred Smith, Nicholas C. Washington**
Assistants to producers	**Medora Heilbron, Hudson Hickman, James Lansbury**
Consideration / vehicles	**American Motors Corp., Kawasaki Motors Corp., Mercedes-Benz of North America**
Lyle Waggoner's wardrobe	**Botany 500**

A Wonder Woman tiara and bracelets set on display at the C2E2 con in Chicago in spring 2011.

> " They had me dumb-down the alter ego in the first few episodes. And I just couldn't do that. ... I worked it around so that she was a pretty cool lady. "
> — Lynda Carter, on Live Miami (NBC affiliate, NBCMiami.com) in 2011

A Comic Comparison

How closely did the screen follow the page, and vice-versa?

The comic books, from which Wonder Woman sprung in the first place, attempted to mirror — at least somewhat — the TV show after it began airing in the 1970s. But as the TV show was just hitting, here's a snapshot of what was going on in the Wonder Woman comic in 1976:

- Wonder Woman was undergoing 12 trials for the Justice League of America to determine if she would be readmitted to the group.
- Steve Trevor was resurrected from the dead and having a love affair with Wonder Woman / Diana Prince, knowing her secret identity.
- Diana worked for the United Nations, but then she was transferred to another area.
- Steve was a high-ranking intelligence officer.
- Paradise Island was just established as being in the Bermuda Triangle, an editorial decision that was made before it was realized that the folks at the TV show were doing it, too, editor Bob Rozakis tells a letter writer in Wonder Woman issue 226.
- Diana was using her lasso, not a spin, to transform to Wonder Woman.

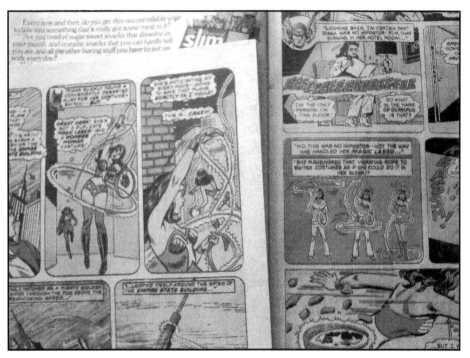

Issue 222 (February-March 1976), left, and 221 (December-January 1975/1976) of Wonder Woman show Diana using her lasso to transform into our hero.

- Diana was able to carry her lasso all the time — its vibrations made it invisible.
- And speaking of invisible, the term Wonder Woman was using for her plane was the "robot plane."

The TV show, meanwhile, premiered in November 1975 with the two-hour pilot setting the Amazon princess in World War II times. Time passed between "specials," as the first few were called, though new episodes for what is now considered Season 1 continued to air through February 1977. The comics responded. Issue 229 of Wonder Woman, from March 1977 (sold in December 1976), took the comic book back in time to the 1940s. A snapshot:
- Diana Prince was Steve Trevor's secretary at the War Department.
- Their work uniforms generally matched the TV show.
- Diana was now executing a spin to transform to Wonder Woman.
- The Wonder Woman costume changed a bit: Her red boots now had the white trim (which would remain, whatever era). Her bracelets

were made of Amazonium (noted in issue 235), though the TV show called it Feminum.
- Wonder Woman still referred to her plane as the "robot plane," shown in issue 235.
- The Nazis figured into the storylines, but this was still the comic book, so Wonder Woman battled juicy villains like Cheetah.

Flash-forward to the future, so to speak (of course, it's all past to us!). In September 1977, the TV show made the jump to modern times with its 90-minute Season 2 premiere. The following spring, with issue 243 in May 1978, the Wonder Woman comic jumped back to the 1970s. Perhaps the writers breathed a sigh of relief. Here's where we were:
- Steve Trevor was just resurrected from the dead and using the name Steve Howard.
- Steve had brown hair, whereas before he was blond.
- Steve knew Wonder Woman's secret identity, and the two were in love.
- Diana resumed working for the UN.

By issue 230 (April 1977), above, Diana was spinning into Wonder Woman.

The invisible plane was referred to as the "robot plane" in the comics, as shown here in issue 222 of Wonder Woman.

- Diana was back to using her lasso to transform to Wonder Woman, surprisingly.
- Her boots kept the white trim.
- Her "robot plane" kept its nickname, and it was noted in the comics that it responded to her telepathic commands.
- Diana was living in New York City.

Some notes on character continuity between the series and the comics:
- Baroness von Gunther first appeared in Sensation issue 4 (April 1942). She was Wonder Woman's first recurring arch-nemesis.
- Fausta Grables first appeared in Comic Cavalcade issue 2, Spring 1943, in a story entitled "Wanted by Hitler, Dead or Alive."
- Remember an Amazon named Dalma in "The Feminum Mystique"? Dalma, first appearing in Comic Cavalcade issue 12 (Fall 1945), was a rebellious Amazon who left Paradise Island, lost her intelligence and became an angry brute. Wonder Woman restored her spirit.
- Formicida never appeared in the comics; neither did the Falcon, Gault or Count Cagliostro.

But what about now? What's Wonder Woman up to these days?

In August 2010 (issue 600), DC Comics replaced her iconic stars-and-stripes outfit with a blue jacket (later discarded), red and gold top and dark pants, retaining only her tiara and lasso. Wonder Woman went street! This new outfit made news everywhere, of course.

In 2011, DC Comics relaunched its entire line of publications to attract a new generation of readers. In this new continuity, Wonder Woman wears a costume similar to her original costume. Also, her origin is significantly changed and she is no longer a clay figure brought to life by the magic of the gods. Instead, she is a demigod, the natural-born daughter of Hippolyta and Zeus, according to Wikipedia.

In more recent history, our hero has ditched her tough-girl pants and returned to her roots in costume, though with some variations, such as the metal choker and bicep bands.

BRBTV's copy of "TV Time '78," which we fondly remember buying as a kid. In the chapter on "Wonder Woman," Lynda Carter does an interview in the Beverly Hills Brown Derby, sipping only water because of the diet she was on at the time and talking about once being a "gangly" teen with "big feet and freckles." Yea, right. Don't all gorgeous celebs say that?

> " I want to sing, act, write music and direct. Maybe I won't do it all, but I can try! I hope my success in 'Wonder Woman' leads everywhere! Somebody has to be everywhere — why not me? "
> — Lynda Carter, interviewed for "TV Time '78" by Peggy Herz

Fun & Useless Information

Some "did ya know" tidbits about the stars associated with the show

Lynda Carter ...

- Appeared on "The Muppet Show" in 1980 singing a tune with the Muppets while items from the set exploded around her, joking later with Kermit that it was one of the "worst experiences" she'd had.
- Appeared on "The RuPaul Show" in 1998, saying, among other things, that though she has probably come around since then, Debra Winger did not enjoy playing "second fiddle" on "Wonder Woman."
- Portrayed Rita Hayworth in a 1983 movie.
- Is 5-foot-9 and a half.
- Played Chloe Sullivan's mother on a 2007 episode of "Smallville."
- Owns an original Wonder Woman 12" Mego doll, along with a lot of other memorabilia.
- Was voted Most Talented Student at Arcadia-Titans High School in Phoenix.
- Told Starlog magazine in 1977 she never really worried about being stereotyped as the Amazon type or being identified too closely with the Wonder Woman role. "Wonder Woman is part of my life right now and I see it as a step in my career," she said.

> **Fine Western Art Collections**
> **West Lives On Gallery**
>
> *Lyle Waggoner*
>
>
> Although born in Kansas City, KS and raised in St. Louis, MS, Lyle Waggoner gained national recognition for his acting abilities in Hollywood. Lyle was a regular on television programs "The Carol Burnett Show" and "Wonder Woman." Lyle has since retired from acting but still is very active in Hollywood with his company Star Waggons. Star Waggons is the largest supplier of studio location rental trailers in the entertainment industry.
>
> Lyle also has had a presence for many years in the valley of Jackson Hole, Wyoming. In Jackson Hole, Lyle has artistically expressed himself again through sculpting bronzes. His talent is apparent in his bronzes, which display elegance and humor simultaneously.

Lyle Waggoner ...

- Screen-tested for the "Batman" role that went to Adam West in 1965 (you can catch a clip on YouTube).
- Was dubbed "The Golden Boy" by Carol Burnett on an anniversary special for "The Carol Burnett Show."
- Starred in a 1968 Dodge Adventurer TV commercial clad in a cowboy hat, then a top hat and mask.
- Middle name is Wesley.
- Was the first Playgirl centerfold in June 1973.
- Has two sons, Jason and Beau.
- Was elected mayor of Encino, California, in 1976.
- Is a sculptor whose works can be seen at Galleries West Fine Art in Jackson Hole, Wyoming (see the web screenshot above), and are usually humorous renditions of lovely ladies, some of which are cast at Eagle Bronze in Lander, Wyoming, according to Wikipedia.
- Doesn't exactly freely grant interviews — BRBTV tried, for this book, and it's been attempted by other writers over the years, too! Waggoner is absent from the "Wonder Woman" DVD interviews, and web searches for interviews come up empty. *Alack and alas* ... It's really too bad ...

Richard Eastham ...

- Went on to play Frank Hilson on "Dallas" in 1991.
- Performed with the St. Louis Grand Opera in the days before World War II.

- Was married to his wife, Betty Jean, for 60 years until her death in 2002.
- First screen acting credit: "There's No Business Like Show Business" in 1954.

Beatrice Colen ...

- Played a rehab counselor in the 1994 TV movie "Roseanne and Tom: Behind the Scenes."
- Appeared in 22 episodes of "Happy Days," portraying a waitress and Marsha Sims.
- Was born in New York and died at only age 51.
- Was the granddaughter of playwright George S. Kaufman.
- Had two sons, James Cronin and Charlie Cronin.
- Played a customer on "Alice" after her "Wonder Woman" year.

Normann Burton ...

- Most often had his first name spelled as "Norman."
- Was reportedly a graduate of The Actor's Studio in New York.
- Died in a car crash on the California/Arizona border while returning to his home in Mexico.
- Along with Roddy McDowall, Woodrow Parfrey and Eldon Burke, was one of only four actors to appear in both the "Planet of the Apes" movie (1968) and "Planet of the Apes" TV series (1974).

S. Pearl (Saundra) Sharp ...

- Portrayed Nurse Peggy Shotwell on "St. Elsewhere," as well as Nurse Carolee Wilson on "Knots Landing" and Nurse Denning and Nurse Powell on "Barnaby Jones."
- Appeared in two "Charlie's Angels" episodes.
- Website: www.spearlsharp.com.
- Wrote "Black Women For Beginners" for the popular Writers and Readers' For Beginners documentary comic book series.
- Has recorded two poetry w/jazz CDs, "Higher Ground" and "On the Sharp Side."

Cathy Lee Crosby entertains U.S. Marines during a United Service Organizations tour in the early '80s. Photo from Wikimedia Commons; public domain.

Cathy Lee Crosby ...

- Wrote the book "Let the Magic Begin" in 2001.
- Didn't want to host the show "That's Incredible!" at first, thinking it was a stupid idea.
- Father was a radio / television announcer.
- Told Jeff Sutherland, host of Jeff's Star Talk, "That's Incredible" stands out in her mind as her most memorable work.
- First acting credit: A 1968 episode of "It Takes a Thief."
- In 1982, attended the 54th Academy Awards with future Princess Diana paramour, Dodi Fayed, according to the IMDb.

And Now a Word From . . .

A cast member, a writer and a stunt gal all offer their perspectives

S. Pearl Sharp:
Death by sliding door? Not when he's around!

Somebody had to step in and keep Steve Trevor organized and on track when Diana Prince got a promotion as an "associate" and colleague in the 1970s timeframe. That fell to the graceful, understated Eve, Steve's secretary in that second season. In the role was Saundra Sharp, lending some diversity to the cast. Nowadays, she goes by S. Pearl Sharp, and she's an accomplished poet, screenwriter and filmmaker. She took some time to chat with BRBTV via phone in 2011.

In your acting career, you went by the name Saundra, but you go by S. Pearl Sharp now, correct?
"Yes. Pearl is my middle name, so my first initial, middle name."

How did you first hear about the role on "Wonder Woman"?
"I was sent by my agent to audition for it."

Had you watched the show before that?
"No."

What was it like being on the set of "Wonder Woman"?
"It was good. It was a good show to work on. It got interesting because of the politics. There was a period when sometimes she wouldn't show up, and then they would have to figure out something else to shoot for the day. At one time I had an inkling of what that was about, but I'll censor that."

How is the character of Eve similar to you?
"She was gorgeous and bright!" (Laughs.) "It was an interesting time, because along with a number of my colleagues that came out here from New York, we had done a lot of theater. Because of shows like 'Good Times' and 'The Jeffersons,' we felt there was going to be a lot of work for us. There was a sort of exodus here at the time. The unique thing about Eve is that she was a black woman but it was not referenced on the show. That was important. There was also the wonderful episode where Judyann Elder and I played the same person. So she's playing me, and the point where she's playing me, then I pull the mask off."

What was Lynda Carter like to work with?
"She was kinda regular, when she was there. There was no drama on the set, where I was concerned, or they were concerned. People were very professional. They did their lines. They were lovely. Once in a while with her not showing up, people were getting stressed out."

How about Lyle Waggoner?
"He's lovely. A gentleman. I did have one incident on the set when I was going through the automatic doors one day, and I don't know whether I wasn't paying attention, or the guy operating them wasn't, but the door came right down on my head. I was still walking through, and the door came down. And when I came to, Lyle was holding me in his arms with this worried look on his face, hoping that I was OK. He was a gentleman. It was interesting, nobody was … Sometimes you're on sets where people are 'on' all the time, you know, when they're always in character, but that didn't seem to be the way on that set. People were sort of doing the job, getting the show done."

You did six episodes of the show, correct? Which was your favorite?
"I think the favorite one was the one with Judyann Elder when we did the face exchange. It was very interesting, I had never done anything like that before. In terms of the interest level, and preparing for the role, and how they figured that out physically.

"Her late husband is Lonne Elder the playright. She's still performing. She's also directing. She directed one of the NPR series. And she directed one of her husband's plays, which they do in front of a live audience, then it's broadcast on the radio."

Do you have any mementos from the show or the set?
"Not really. I have a couple photos, I think, and that's about it. I think at that time, people weren't looking at it as this great history piece. When you're doing this stuff, you're not thinking about that. You're thinking, thank God I have a job!"

Any funny memories from the show that you can share with me?
"I really don't. I wish I could be more entertaining!"

Do you keep in contact with any of the cast or crew?
"No. I remember running into Lyle at something quite a few years ago. We just kinda said hi and all that. That was it. I've never been in Lynda's presence again. Once I did those episodes, I wasn't back.

"Whatever it was that was causing Lynda to not show up, I think after that season there was a bit of a break. I don't know if there was a change in channels. I remember that."

You had recurring roles as a nurse on both "Knots Landing" and "St. Elsewhere" in the '80s — any fear of being typecast?
"Probably, because I had also been a nurse on 'As the World Turns.' My first extra job. My first five-up job. And then I was a nurse on 'Marcus Welby.'" (Laughs.) "I was very experienced by the time I got to 'St. Elsewhere.' Then I was a doctor on one episode of 'The Bold and the Beautiful.'"

So a little bit of soaps work.
"'Yes, back when it was live!'"

Artist Alex Ross and writer Paul Dini collaborated on the oversized graphic novel, "Wonder Woman: Spirit of Truth," released in 2001 as part of a set focusing on DC's higher-profile heroes.

When you were a little girl, what did you want to be when you grew up?
"I was destined to be a dancer. That's why I was on this planet."

But then you ended up being a poet.
"Yes. Writer, actor, director, poet. Which is all in the creative pot."

Looks like "The Healing Passage: Voices from the Water" is a very important project for you. Tell me about it.
"That is a feature-length documentary film currently on the documentary channel. It came out in 2004. I started making films around '80, '81. But this is my big swan song. A 90-minute feature piece. Took 10 and a half years to finish. The slave trade, and using their art for healing."

You served as a director, producer, writer and actress for this film. Are there more documentary projects like that in your future?
"I did several hour-long documentaries for the city of Los Angeles and

several shorter ones for their channel 35. Then I did an hour documentary called 'Life is a Saxophone.' Hopefully by the end of the year I'll have the anniversary reissue of that. So yes, I've been doing the documentaries since the '80s. Kinda went into film initially as I'm going to take these classes. ... Then it was, I can't audition, I've got a class! I'm much happier on the other side of the camera than in front of the camera. I do have a new piece that's out, 'Redeemer,' in which I play a grandmother. That came out in March."

What do you feel is your most important life's work?
"I think my most important work is connected to the last documentary, and the poetry, and that is using the art of poetry to help people heal and create health. So being able to use the film to do that is important. I was one of four women who were in the very first breast cancer self-exam commercial. There was an Asian female, me, a Chicano, and a white woman. We were completely covered; we had on these leotards. They had this doctor come in, and he showed us what to do. And nobody would run the commercial. It took about five years from when nobody would run it, until it would show after the late-night Johnny Carson show. I remember I saw it then. And it took about six to seven years to get it to soap opera / middle of the day, which is what it was designed for."

When was the commercial made?
"It was in the early '70s; I think I was in New York when I did it. We all had on black leotards, and we're all doing the same thing, and the doctor is standing off to the side, with a voiceover. He wasn't in the scene with us, but he was there making sure we didn't do anything medically incorrect. Things have changed."

On "Wonder Woman" you shared a scene with Rover where you were giving him an oil lube job. What was Rover made of? How did he work?
"I don't know! I don't remember how that was happening. This is pre-special effects, so whatever it was, they had to make it happen right now."

What do you feel was the most important message of the show?
"Hmmm. I think probably to the extent that Superman had the message of doing good and righting wrongs, Wonder Woman was the female

counterpart of that. The idea that women had that power, and that authority. Again, it has to be transferred to the magical. The rest of us were sort of supporting pawns in that agenda."

Anne Collins-Ludwick:
Scripting an Amazon princess

She was Anne Collins back then, and she was there for the second and third seasons of "Wonder Woman," though her career has also included work on "Matlock," Vega$, "Fantasy Island" and "Buck Rogers in the 25th Century." Collins-Ludwick gave us some very interesting insight into the "Wonder Woman" series and her part in it, via email in 2011.

How did you get this writing work for the "Wonder Woman" TV series?
"There were very few women writing for hour-long episodic TV shows in the mid-'70s. Since I had done a couple of scripts for 'Hawaii Five-O,' and since the producers thought it would be a good idea to fill the story editor vacancy that had arisen on the show with a woman, my agent got me the gig. I was living in Denver at the time, so I packed up my VW Rabbit and moved to L.A. Ah, to be in my 20s again ..."

You are credited on the IMDb as executive story consultant for 24 episodes, and story editor for 14 episodes. Does that sound about right?
"Yes, that sounds about right, since some of the scripts for that second season had already been written by the time I came aboard."

What's the difference between an executive story consultant and a story editor?
"The difference between the two titles is negligible; in both cases I worked with freelance writers to develop stories and scripts which, invariably, I rewrote. The story consultant gets paid more than the story editor and oversees the story editor/s."

You came along in the second season, after the show changed from the '40s to the '70s. Would you have liked to have written for the Nazi / WWII storyline, also?
"As I recall, the first season of 'Wonder Woman' was very tongue-in-

cheek and cartoonish and probably, because of its WWII background, hard for the show's young, Friday night audience to relate to. The network and/or studio hoped to boost the show's ratings by modernizing the stories and changing the tone to be more fun and adventure/fantasy-oriented in a 'Wild Wild West' type of way, which was right up exec producer Bruce Lansbury's alley. In short, no, I would not've liked to have written for the first iteration of 'WW' — I'm not sure I would've 'gotten' it."

Do you have a favorite episode among those you worked on?
"Guess I liked the 'Phantom of the Roller Coaster' the best. Deformities usually make for interesting characters and relationships."

Watching Wonder Woman's physical feats on these episodes is so cool, even decades later. How much did you draw from the comics for her various demos of prowess?
"The comics provided us with parameters for WW — the lasso, tiara, bracelets, her strength, speed, etc. — but for the more physical 'feats' a great deal depended on what could actually be produced and what would look cool on camera. As I recall, I think the first time WW saved a falling person's life by catching them was in an episode I wrote (we did that stunt to death in the episodes that followed). In any case, I don't recall ever referring to the comics to come up with stunts for show — the stories, and our imaginations, usually dictated them."

Were you responsible for the naming of the episodes? (I'm amused that there seems to be a lot of "The Man Who ..." and "The Boy Who ..." and "The Girl ..." going on here!)
"The writers usually came up with the names for the episodes they wrote. Sometimes the network or studio would 'beef them up' but nobody really agonized over them. As for all the 'Man Who ...' 'Girl Who ...' titles, we just thought it would be fun to utilize a convention like that. Plus those titles kind of emphasized the human element of the stories we were telling."

How much direction were you given by the producers or the network for the episode stories? Or was it really a blank slate for you?
"I cannot over-stress how much of a collaborative effort it was (and no doubt still is) to come up with ideas and plots for 'WW' and all the other

series I worked on afterwards. Everyone had a say, from the producers to the stars to the studio to the network, whether it was as simple as, 'Let's do a show we can shoot at Magic Mountain,' or so-and-so is willing to do a guest spot — let's do a show that exploits his/her assets. I'm not sure there's such a thing as a totally blank slate when it comes to TV writing, but it never bothered me — I always considered collaboration to come with the territory. And on 'WW,' I was fortunate to be working with Bruce Lansbury, who had a wonderful imagination and was always full of great ideas."

Is it true that the "Girl From Ilandia" episode was designed to be a pilot for a spinoff? Why didn't it get off the ground?
"Yes, I think 'Ilandia' was created as a possible spinoff at the request of probably the studio (Warner Bros). The network may not've been interested in pursuing it for any number of reasons. I don't recall its being a big deal, or that anyone was really banking on its success."

Am I right in thinking that the episode "Skateboard Wiz" seems to be a bit of a tribute to "Charlie's Angels," airing two years after the landmark "Consenting Adults" episode that featured a skateboarding Farrah? Plus, when Duane compliments Jamie for looking like one of those gals on TV, she quips, "I don't think Farrah Fawcett is losing any sleep."
"I remember 'Skateboard Wiz' because it's one of the scripts Alan Brennert wrote for the show and to this day I think Alan is one of the most talented TV writers ever. As far as I know, it was in no way related to 'Charlie's Angels'; skateboards were huge back then (and our main audience was mostly comprised of kids, after all) and skateboarding was very visual so it was a natural for an action-oriented show. As far as I know, the reference to Farrah Fawcett is coincidental — she was pretty darn huge back then, too!"

I talked to Saundra Sharp, who played Eve, this past weekend, and she said her favorite episode was "Light-Fingered Lady" because she liked the little trick that was played when another actress portrayed her, disguised as an ex-con former cellmate of Diana's disguised character, pulling off a mask (I know, confusing!!!! and I'm really taxing your memory banks now!!!). Were you encouraged to try more inventive techniques like this?
"Again, we tried our best to come up with stuff that was story-driven

and fit in with the fun, fantasy tone of the show without going overboard into campy cartoon-land."

The episode "The Man Who Could Not Die" is a real bummer. Lyle Waggoner is gone. The IRAC and Rover interplay is also gone. Dale Hawthorn is established as Diana's new boss in L.A., it's implied that Bret Cassiday will have a hand in the future action, and the spunky T. Burton Phipps III seems to have the makings of a sidekick. So what gives, with all of that? Were you-all setting it up for a very different fourth season that didn't happen? What did we miss?!!!
"Sorry, but I really don't recall the precise genesis of the 'Man Who Could Not Die' episode, though it was obviously an attempt to retool the show and save it from cancellation. I do remember that either Lyle Waggoner wanted off the show or the powers-that-be wanted him off, but in any case, this was an attempt (no doubt spearheaded by the studio) to show the network what the series might be like if Steve Trevor left and Diana got to interact with some new, fresh characters. But the network didn't go for it and 'WW' became history."

Did you get to spend any time on the set? What was that like?
"I loved going down to the set! I was totally new to the business and it was always a thrill to watch them shoot and to chat with the stars and guests stars and production people. Rarely was it absolutely necessary that I go down to the set, but if I had an excuse to do so, I'd go down."

Do you have any keepsakes or mementos from the "WW" set or from your involvement in the show?
"I have copies of all the scripts I wrote for the show tucked away in a trunk in storage. I also have a couple of photos made from outtakes from the show. One was of Diana Prince making a funny, cross-eyed face, which Lynda was kind enough to autograph. I also have (somewhere — geez, I hope I didn't pitch it when we moved!) one of the small silver pyramids that supposedly made up a big silver pyramid that served some bad guy's nefarious purposes, but I can't recall the exact episode in which it appeared."

Was there any input on potential storylines, or proposed storylines, from the cast, particularly from Lynda Carter or Lyle Waggoner? Did they ever give feedback on the scripts?
"Lyle was just happy to be doing the show and rarely had any kind of feedback for the writers, either positive or negative. Lynda would have suggestions and concerns every now and then, but she was never overbearing about it and never caused any problems."

How much did you feel influenced by the actors' own nuances as you were working on these scripts, and, perhaps, how many episodes did it take you to get used to the particular actors' mannerisms and ways of presenting themselves?
"The main characters weren't exactly what you would call complex and they were cast accordingly. Lynda, bless her heart, was extremely new to acting, and I quickly learned it was wise not to give her huge speeches to memorize or long sentences to say. She tried her best but my gosh, she was young and inexperienced and under tremendous scrutiny and pressure and the whole situation was tough for her. She and I got along fine and I liked her — she had (and no doubt still has) a very good and kind heart."

The notable guest stars on this show are so fun, such as Gary Burghoff of "M*A*S*H" on "The Man Who Wouldn't Tell." Did you have any input into casting?
"I could make suggestions when it came to casting, but I had no real input. Nor frankly did I really want any. My job was to write the script; casting it was up to someone else."

Are you in contact these days with any of the cast members?
"I am not in contact with any of the cast members. I did, however, have the pleasure of having dinner with Bruce Lansbury down in the Palm Springs area this past February. He's older (ain't we all) but he still has that twinkle in his eye and possesses a wicked sense of humor. Again, getting to work with him (on 'WW' and later on 'Buck Rogers') was truly a great privilege. And I'm still in contact with Alan Brennert, who is now mostly writing novels."

Have you followed the progress of the attempted "WW" remake with actress Adrienne Palicki? What do you think of all of that (especially the much-talked-about costume!)?
"Don't know anything about the attempted 'WW' remake. Don't really care."

What do you think is the most important message of this '70s "Wonder Woman" series, so many years later?
"Like most '70s TV, 'Wonder Woman' was just mindless, innocent escapism, far different from the hour-long, somber, in-your-face shock fests so rampant on TV today. Maybe its message today would be, 'Hey, it's okay that tonight's episode wasn't ripped from the headlines — this is your chance to just sit back, empty your mind, and enjoy.'"

Jeannie Epper:
This daughter of a stunt dynasty carves her own niche

Jeannie Epper comes from a very successful Hollywood stunt family spanning four generations, and her resume certainly extends far beyond "Wonder Woman." Take "Charlie's Angels," for instance, or "The Bionic Woman," "Logan's Run," "The Rockford Files," "Beverly Hills Cop III," "Con Air," "Blade," and a ton more. And this gal, in her 70s, shows no signs of slowing down. On the day we talked to her in July 2011, she had just done an explosion scene for CBS' "Criminal Minds." Epper, who was profiled in the 2004 documentary "Double Dare," gave us the scoop via phone on doubling "Wonder Woman."

Do you recall how many episodes of "WW" you were involved in? And did it include the first season?
"Yes. We did a pilot, and then we did three or four specials, and then it turned into a series. The very first year, I missed a few episodes because I was down with 'Close Encounters of the Third Kind.' I took the job because it was offered to me by Steven Spielberg, and I thought, hmmm, maybe this would be a good connection. ... I ended up probably pretty

much on the rest of the seasons. Although I didn't do the motorcycle stuff. That was done by a girl named Debbie Evans. We had 22 episodes a season, so that would be three years; I probably worked on at least 50 or 60 of them.

"Debbie Evans, she's probably among the top stunt drivers in Hollywood. She's one of those girls we kinda took a chance on, and lo and behold, she did an amazing job. She's like 5 foot 2. It was kinda a funny story. We were looking for a girl who could do anything, driving, jumping, etc., and we couldn't find anyone Lynda's height who could do all those things. My brother knew someone. We hired her even though she was so small."

What memorable stunts did we see you do on the show? What stands out to you now?
"Probably the one where I was running down the airplane; I think it was a 747. Almost everything. Her flight work. Any jumps through windows or jumps down through skylights. Every high jump was a challenge for me, because I didn't like high work. I wouldn't recommend it for anyone who doesn't like high work. Keeping the costume on gave us a time, too. We had to figure out how to keep that costume on. They made the costumes with satin, and those stays; it was like a bustier, so when you jumped or moved, it would fold out. So it took a while for the wardrobe department to figure that out."

Did you do the skateboarding in the episode "Skateboard Wiz"?
"No. I'm not a skateboarder."

What about the gymnastics in "Going, Going, Gone" and "Screaming Javelins"?
"Nope. That was not me, either. That was a girl named Sandi Gross. I was her (Carter's) main double, and anytime they needed someone who had a speciality, we searched for someone who was good in that field. Sandi was a world-class gymnast."

The dives in "The Deadly Dolphin"?
"I did that. I swam with the dolphins, I guess it was! The funny thing about that episode is that the major camera work was done at the water park down there — I think it was Sea World or Marineland. I don't even think it's there anymore. People used to come and watch the dolphins swim, and the sharks swim. I got a chance to ride a dolphin. They're kind of slippery. But when we filmed that, I started to lose my direction

underwater. I don't know anything about drowning; I'd have to read about it. I think you get kind of lethargic, and you don't know where you are. The dolphin grabbed me by the arm and pulled me to the surface. That's a true story. He or she sensed I was in danger and actually took a hold of me and pulled me up, and the crew came and got me. They found that my body temperature had dropped dramatically. So that's the lesson to be learned — listen to your body."

There was a two-part episode called "The Boy Who Knew Her Secret" that featured horseback riding. Was that you?
"That was me. It was pretty fun riding. Riding in that costume wasn't challenging for me because I'm a really good horsewoman. But we wore panty hose back in those days, and they were slippery. But it was really fun."

Do you still have any of the "Wonder Woman" costumes you wore?
"The only thing they allowed me to have is they had the bands, the bracelets, and the earrings. I never got the costumes and the boots. Lynda still has one of hers."

Yes, she's talked about that in interviews. That she's on the lookout for another one.
"Yes. When I did 'Double Dare' with Zoe Bell, we went to San Diego, to the comic book show, and they had some there. One or two of the original outfits. But they were selling them for thousands and thousands and thousands of dollars. ... The difference between hers (Lynda's) and mine was, obviously she had a smaller waist, and she had a piece between the boobs that would give it a little more definition. Hers were selling for 10, 12 grand. Mine were selling for 5 and 6. At the time I should've borrowed the money and bought one.

"Andy Mangels is the one who got a hold of me and got us to come down there and promote 'Double Dare.' We had 8-by-10 photos printed, and they were gone. We could've sold 5,000 of them."

I spoke with Andy Mangels when I worked on my "Isis" report, because he put together the DVD set with all those great features. He's a big Wonder Woman fan.
"Once in a while we shoot a hi to each other. ... They have a Wonder Woman day or something every year, and just before that sometimes he

Jeannie Epper (seated next to Lynda Carter) during a panel discussion at the premiere of the 2004 documentary "Double Dare" in Washington, D.C. Photo courtesy of James R. Green Jr.

asks me to participate. Lynda's not always available now that she's on her singing career. Have you ever heard her sing?"

On the episode of "Wonder Woman" where she sang a couple songs from her album at the time.
"I have her original album that she signed to me and gave to me. Put away. You know it's funny when you're working on a show and you're just working. You're not thinking. I didn't think of 'Wonder Woman' as the iconic thing it is today. And of course, they've been trying to redo it into a TV show or movie."

Yea, and it didn't go anywhere as a TV show. What did you think of the new street outfit?
"The first one, I hated what they did, then they kinda redesigned it. I thought it was a cool costume, but it just wasn't Wonder Woman. They

never changed Spider-Man. They never changed Batman. My gut feeling from the very beginning was that that costume was kinda going to bite them. I heard from her double, Shauna Duggins, that the script was bad and just wasn't directed well."

What was it like to actually get to show your face as Wonder Woman's double in the episode "Stolen Faces"? Do you remember that one?
"No. Not so much. A little bit. They all run together to me now."

You seem taller than Lynda Carter. How tall are you?
"I'm 5'9"."

So you weren't taller than her. I was thinking you were.
"No."

Did you suffer any injuries on the set?
"No. Don't ask me how. But neither one of us got injured on that show. I mean, we would get bruises and stuff. But nothing major."

What was Lynda Carter like to work with?
"She was great. We became really great friends. She actually came to my church and visited all the little kids. She was such a sweetheart. My son was 8 years old and he would go in to school and tell everyone that his mommy doubled Wonder Woman. I would go and talk to them, but I was blond. They weren't convinced. So Lynda invited the class all the way down to where we were working, and allowed them to see Jeannie become Wonder Woman. That transformation. That was all Lynda's doing. Now instead of the little liar boy telling a tale, he became the hero."

And that was while the show was still airing.
"Yes."

What about Lyle Waggoner?
"You know, I loved Lyle. I really liked him. I don't really not get along with anybody. I'm nice to people that are nice to me. I think they had some issues, but I'm not quite sure. But I never step into that arena, because it's not my story to tell. I did have one time where the Enquirer called me. At the time they called her the 'Wonder Bitch.' I had the Enquirer calling me and offering me money if I would tell what really

went on on the set. Of course, I told them they were beautiful and we all got along, and they didn't want to talk to me. It was so mean and hurtful. You know one of the reasons they were that way with her? She was smart. She was too smart to let them do that to her. She knew how the character should be played. She's quite bright. Back in the '70s, I don't know if women were allowed to be that way yet. A lot of them were, but they didn't speak their mind like her. She was very focused on how her character was going to be."

From the research I did, I saw your brother Tony was in the episode "The Fine Art of Crime," and your brother Gary was the courier in the episode "Pot of Gold." Does that sound right? (I try to check what I read online!)
"That's the one where I ran down the top of an airplane and jumped in the back of like the luggage. One of those little carts that pull the luggage across."

"Pot of Gold," the one with the Leprecaun?
"Oh, that was a tricky one. I had to ride on top of that truck. I didn't have anything to tie me down. I had to do that all free. They've come so far with free and special effects and stunt rigging. They really didn't do that much then."

And toward the end there was a scene with a helicopter, where Wonder Woman had to stop the bad guy from getting away with the Leprecaun and his gold. And Wonder Woman caught the Leprecaun as he fell out of the helicopter.
"Oh, yes."

I know you're still working these days, because you mentioned just doing an episode of "Criminal Minds." So what else keeps you occupied, these days?
"I have little grandkids that I love having and doing things with. I do a little training with stuntwomen; if they need me with anything, I come and help them. Right now, I have a new knee replacement, so I'm recovering from that. I love to garden. I like to walk. Normal things. I'm a crafter; I like different crafting things. I made a doll that won a prize. I like to be busy. Since my knee, I've gotten into my computer, because I just sit. I play those games for hours."

Like the stuff on Facebook?
"Yes, the Farmville and Yoville and all that. I'll play for hours, and it may seem like a big waste of time, but I don't consider it that."

Sometimes you just need some mindless entertainment, to clear your head and decompress.
"Yes. Because TV now is just terrible."

Yes, I don't get into all the reality shows. I love the classic stuff like we're talking about now.
"I worked on 'Charlie's Angels' and so many of those shows — they were corny, when you look back at them. But they were such groundbreaking shows for women. 'Wonder Woman,' 'Police Woman.' We don't have any of that today. ... My brother was a stunt coordinator for the last couple years of 'Charlie's Angels.' I doubled for a lot of those girls. ... I worked on a few (episodes of) 'Desperate Housewives.' I've doubled some of those girls. Talk about pencil thin! Teri Hatcher is scary-skinny. But she's very beautiful in person. Her features are still perfect. I know she's in her 40s."

Yes, she is. And I remember there were a couple seasons of "Lois & Clark: The New Adventures of Superman" in the '90s where she was a much more normal weight.
"It's such a battle out there. Jennifer Aniston looks amazing. She keeps herself so fit. She's healthy fit."

What do you feel is the most important message of the "Wonder Woman" TV show now, years later?
"What I got out if it most was what Lynda showed, that whatever character she played, she played it smart. She wasn't just a comic book person. She thought things out. Of course, I knew her magical lasso was magical. But for me it was a turning point in my career. I never thought the photos we took with my camera the last day of the shoot would be the things that traveled around the world and made me the most famous stuntwoman. I had fun. I was tested daily on that show with the stunts. I think it was fun for every girl to have a superhero. She didn't have to punch everyone out; she thought things through. I think, the fact that we had a great relationship and still do. And she came to the 'Double Dare' premiere and she spoke to everybody. We always talked about the couple stunts that she did. She'd had a motorcycle accident, and she talked about the things that I had told her to do when we were working together. We

bonded a lot."

She did do a few of her own stunts on the show, didn't she?
"She could do a lot more than like the fight work. We had to keep her wrangled down, because she was really good at doing the fight work and wanted to do it. She had those beautiful long legs. When you do a fight routine, it's like a dance routine. It's complicated beyond what you would think a fight would be. She always wanted to be a part of that. So we would let her. But not too much, because we couldn't let her get smashed in the face."

Tell me a little about "Bionic Woman."
"Well, the gig on 'Bionic Woman' was because I doubled Lindsay Wagner on a pilot of 'The Rockford Files,' and she continued to request me. Back then there were so many TV shows that just had women guest stars. Then when 'Bionic Woman' happened, she requested me. That's when the boob thing happened." *(On a different phone call, Epper told how when she auditioned to double for Lindsay Wagner, they found she was too well-endowed.)* "They had a couple other girls come in, and they continued having me double them. Back in those days, you weren't a day player like you used to be in the '20s, but you'd be at a studio and you'd work on different shows."

So let's switch gears and talk about "Dynasty." How did you hear about the gig on "Dynasty"?
"I stood in for Linda Evans on 'Big Valley' and did all her stunt work."

So you worked on "Big Valley"? You really have a long resume.
"I was so busy that I could've been 20 Jeannies at one time. There were so many projects."

So you doubled Linda Evans on 'Big Valley' and she remembered you later when 'Dynasty' came along.
"Yes. Because back then they have the right to ask."

The actors?
"Yes."

How many episodes did you do?
"I don't even remember. Every catfight. I did the horseback riding. Remember Rock Hudson, before they knew he had AIDS? He looked like

a really old man. We were doing that horse chase. My brother Andy stunt-doubled him in the horse chase, and I was doubling her. And she rolls down the hill, and he comes down and scoops her up and kisses her. And ..." (pause) "I shouldn't really say it because it's not my story to tell, but yes, I was there that day. She was a little worried."

Yes, I remember the talk at the time, that she was concerned, but it was downplayed, because of course they didn't want to cause hysteria.
"That was before they knew about saliva. They didn't know so much as they know now about that disease."

Do you keep up with Linda Evans now?
"Not so much anymore now. We used to. ... I also did stair falls for her. You remember the episode where she fell down the stairs? I did that. But the catfights were the best. You know of all the episodes, I have in its entirety the one where Linda was fighting herself in the attic. That was a rough fight. That was a really, really rough fight. The pond one was fun."

Jeannie Epper meets her match, so to speak, as Krystle fights Krystle (well, really Rita) in the "Dynasty" episode "The Vigil."

So in the attic scene with the real Krystle and fake Krystle fighting, who was the other stuntwoman?
"Donna Evans was able to come in and be the twin. She dated my son way, way back, in the '80s. She's married now and has a family. She doubles for Anne Hathaway. We worked on 'Princess Diaries' together, and I doubled Julie Andrews, and she doubled Anne. She used to double Sharon Stone and lots of others. Back then, there were a lot of big actresses who were doing action stuff. Her sister Debbie does all the car work for Angelina Jolie."

Did you do all of the "Dynasty" catfights involving Krystle?
"I didn't do the pillow fight. My sister did. I was on another show. I wasn't under contract to them yet. They'd bring me in and use me when they needed me. Later they put me under contract, because they wanted the same people to double the same actresses. But in the pillow fight, it was her and a girl named Regina Parton."

Do you remember how many catfights you were involved in?
"I want to say at least five. Remember the one they had up in the dressmaker's place?"

For the reunion movie.
"Yes. I have to think about it. I'm going to look it up and see if I can remember. For 'Catfights & Caviar,' they sent me everything that had ever been shown on that. Did you ever see that? If you go online and search, you can see all that stuff. I just sit there sometimes and laugh."

What was your most memorable moment on "Dynasty"?
"Wow. There's probably too many. I'd have to think about that one."

What was Linda Evans like to work with?
"Just great. We've known each other since we were 19 years old because of 'Big Valley.' I rode horses for her on that."

What about Joan Collins?
"I loved working with her. I loved to watch her because she was so amazingly old Hollywood, and to get to see that, to see that she was old Hollywood, was great. She was demanding. Linda would always calm her down. But a lot of times she was right about things, too. She would just throw a tizzy and shut the set down. And if she really wanted to

irritate everybody, she'd take two or three hours to get ready. Linda was like me, just getting ready to work. Joan was a glamor queen. She didn't come to the set most of the time without being completely made up.

"There was a certain thing that went on in that period. Joan wasn't that old. She liked me because I understood her as a woman. Things would get rough and they'd make you do what you didn't want to do, and I didn't do that with her. She'd be like, 'Oh thank God, it's Jeannie.'"

Who was it that doubled for Joan in those catfights?
"She had a few, but her main double was Sandy Robertson. ... We would get rehearsal days where we would go in and practice the fights and get them ready. Sandy left the business a long time ago. It's a hard business to stay tough in."

What do you think was the biggest challenge you faced on "Dynasty"?
"We did a lot of fire stuff. Do you remember the one where they didn't remember which one got burned to death? He carried both of us out."

That was a cliffhanger at the end of a season. A cabin fire.
"Yes. Thank God my brother was the one doubling whoever the guy was." *(Geoffrey Scott as Mark Jennings)* "You always have to trust people in a situation like that. Anytime you do fire, other people are there to take care of you. I never got burnt, either.

"I like to critique my own work, and I'll sometimes think, could I have done it better. I think we did a really good job on that episode. They were trying to get it in one take. By the time it was over with, we were like, 'Please say print!' Then they would kinda punch in and get some little pieces. That was probably the hardest one."

And the attic catfight. Which was when George Hamilton was on.
"Yes. He and I had to go through a plate glass window. I loved him. He was the brownest man I ever saw, and he was the nicest man. He's just one of the old toughies, you know. But he kept his looks. Some of them, they change. They don't look like themselves when they were younger."

Do you have any keepsakes from "Dynasty," any prop or something you were able to keep?
"I could go through some of my old jewelry and see if I have any of that. I could have. All of the clothes were made my Nolan Miller. He made my clothes and her clothes, and we weren't allowed to take them. There was one outfit where I said, 'Can I just wear this out Saturday night,' because I knew they were going to rip it off me the next week, and it was a no. ... They made a lot of money on those shows."

And I imagine Nolan Miller was no small expense to have working for the show.
"Oh, yes. But boy, could he fit clothes to your body. Because they fitted me just like they fitted Linda. For somebody like me who could never afford to have someone make them outfits like that, it was something. All those clothes fitted to me. You wonder where they ended up. Probably auctioned off somewhere."

They must have kept a lot of them in storage, because I remember Heather Locklear saying, when she first got the "Dynasty" role, because of course it was another Aaron Spelling production, that she was able to get in to see the outfits from "Charlie's Angels," and she was remarking how tiny they were. For her to say they were tiny, when she's so tiny, that was really saying something!
"Oh, yes. They all were. I stayed on top of it. I still do to some degree. You just get old. It puts a lot of stress on you. You can't go out with everybody and party and sit down and eat a bowl of spaghetti because you might be in a bikini tomorrow. I remember when we shot the last couple seasons of 'Charlie's Angels,' and Tanya Roberts was always the one shown in a bikini. I was always on top of it and not eating stupid foods so I could look like her in a bikini. And I was 40-something and she was like 22."

Our amazing cover artist Dale Cuthbertson offers his interpretation of Lynda Carter in that wonderful, Wonder Woman diving suit. He's a fan, too, ya know! Image courtesy of Dale Cuthbertson.

A Wonder Woman figure that's part of a set of reproductions of the popular Mego "World's Famous Superheroes" figures of the '70s. This updated version is actually much more detailed than the full-body-leotarded '70s Mego Wonder Woman, which, yes, we also own! Unfortunately, the repro line was canceled in 2011, just after this one was released. We seriously wanted an updated Batgirl!!!!

> " Wonder Woman's always been the strongest of the female DC characters, and so her popularity definitely helped pave the way for other female characters. "
> — Lauren Montgomery, in the "Wonder Woman the Amazon Princess" feature of the 2010 "Wonder Woman" animated DVD

Birthdays

A sprinkling of special days of key cast and crew

Beatrice Colen January 10, 1948
(died November 18, 1999)
Dawn Lyn January 11, 1963
Bruce Lansbury January 12, 1930
Leslie H. Martinson January 16, 1915
Eric Braeden April 3, 1941
Lyle Waggoner April 13, 1935
Carolyn Jones April 28, 1930
(died August 3, 1983)
Cloris Leachman April 30, 1926
Charles B. Fitzsimons May 8, 1924
(died February 14, 2001)
William M. Marston May 9, 1893
(died May 2, 1947)
Debra Winger May 16, 1955
Richard Eastham June 22, 1916
(died July 10, 2005)
Ted Shackelford June 23, 1946
Tim O'Connor July 3, 1927

Donfeld July 3, 1934
(died February 3, 2007)
Ike Eisenmann July 21, 1962
Stanley Ralph Ross July 22, 1935
(died March 16, 2000)
Lynda Carter July 24, 1951
Beatrice Straight August 2, 1914
(died April 7, 2001)
John Saxon August 5, 1935
Rick Springfield August 23, 1949
Seymour Robbie August 25, 1919
(died June 17, 2004)
Henry Darrow September 15, 1933
Ed Begley Jr. September 16, 1949
Roddy McDowall September 17, 1928
(died October 3, 1998)
Henry Gibson September 21, 1935
(died September 14, 2009)
Leif Garrett November 8, 1961
Dack Rambo November 13, 1941
(died March 21, 1994)
Herb Wallerstein November 28, 1925
(died September 29, 1985)
Cathy Lee Crosby December 2, 1944
Normann Burton December 5, 1923
(died November 29, 2003)
Dick Moder December 11, 1906
(died April 17, 1994)
Clark Brandon December 13, 1958
Jared Martin December 21, 1941
S. Pearl Sharp December 21, 1942

Merchandise

Collectors, rejoice!

Wonder Woman merchandise itself is vast and varied and has been around for many decades; we illustrate some of our own general WW merchandise throughout this book. This chapter, however, will for the most part stick to items that were specifically tied to the '70s TV show. Some of this information comes from the Wonderland site (thanks, Mia!); visit Wonderland-site.com for color photos of many of these items.

DVD / Video

- "Wonder Woman: The Complete First Season," released June 2004 by Warner Home Video.
- "Wonder Woman: The Complete Second Season," released March 2005 by Warner Home Video.
- "Wonder Woman: The Complete Third Season," released June 2005 by Warner Home Video.
- "Wonder Woman: The Complete Collection," released November 2007 by Warner Home Video.

- Collector's Edition VHS tapes of two episodes each, Columbia House.

Miscellaneous Memorabilia

- Mego dolls: Wonder Woman / Diana Prince, Steve Trevor, Queen Hippolyte, Nubia. 12" high, first released 1977. Second version of Wonder Woman was released with a completely removable cloth outfit (rather than a painted-on top). Mego also designed a prototype for a revolving playset to go with the dolls, spinning from the War Department office to the Paradise Island palace to Wonder Woman's special communication center. It was not released, though it was featured in Mego's 1978 catalog, according to the Mego Museum. (Note the variation from the widely accepted spelling of Queen Hippolyta's name, though the name was never used in the series itself.)

Above and opposite: Catalog pages showing the luscious Mego offerings for the show. Images courtesy of MegoMuseum.com.

WONDER WOMAN™ CAST ASSORTMENT 73501

For amazing World War II adventures, just like the ones on TV's hottest hit, surround Wonder Woman with these fully poseable friends and foes. Here's Major Steve Trevor. Wonder Woman's forever getting him out of tight situations, but she doesn't mind at all.

Handsome Major Steve's her boyfriend. He stands 12½" tall and is dressed in an Army Airforce Uniform. Queen Hippolyte™ is Wonder Woman's Super-Mom—a royal Amazon of major proportions! She has blond hair is 12¼" tall and comes costumed in a flowing toga. Watch out for this lady! Nubia™, arch-mistress of evil is Wonder Woman'[s] possessed of magic po[wers] is Wonder Woman's S[uper] sessed of magic powe[rs] 12¼" high and has bla[ck hair with] a white streak. Both N[ubia and] Hippolyte have rooted styleable hair (wash a[nd set]). Each doll comes with a[...]

WONDER WOMAN'[S ...]

The continued succ[ess of Wonder] Woman's TV adven[tures ...] created right before [your eyes with] her playset. Dresse[d ...] she's in her office r[eady to fight] crime. Then she's W[onder Woman] in her special comm[unications] center, and in her o[ther outfits.] Now there's a Won[der Woman] Wardrobe that you[r ...] 12" Wonder doll (s[...])

© 1977 DC Comics Inc.

- Mego doll fashions for Diana Prince, various.
- Posters, various designs, 24" by 36". In first-season outfit with cape, and in second-season outfit, 1977, Thought Factory, Sherman Oaks, California. Plus British-made posters usually identified as the "Red Poster" and the "Blue Poster," Pyramid Posters Ltd., Leicester, England, UK, Ref. PF 2062 and 2051.
- Jigsaw puzzles in a variety of images by American Publishing Corp., 1977-1978; 121 pieces at 8½" by 8", 200 pieces at 11" by 17", 551 pieces at 18" by 24".
- Wristwatch by Ingraham.
- Iron-on stickers, '70s.
- 8" by 10" color stills from the show, as well as black-and-white publicity shots, to be found on eBay.
- Phone cards, approximately 3 3/8" by 2 1/8", issued by Patco in the USA as collector cards with numbers 23 through 26 on the back. The back also has instructions for use and a toll-free number. Printed on the bottom of the back of the cards is the following information: Card expires 31/03/1997, Cards issued 250 pcs.
- Key chain, 2" by 3" and featuring the image of Lynda Carter in the WW outfit; spotted on eBay in 2012.
- Stamps *(shown above)*, with image of Carter in WW outfit and $1 in right corner, multiple designs, spotted on eBay in 2012.
- Oversize postcard of a painting of Lynda Carter as Wonder Woman by pop surrealist artist Isabel Samaras. The title of the painting is "Spero Melior." (The Latin expression means "I aspire to greater things.") 4¾" by 6½"
- Other postcards published in Europe in the 2000s, various designs, 4" by 6".
- Postcards, 1999, Pyramid Ltd.
- Collector's cards made in Argentina, set of 8, full color. Also, boxes of 25 collector's cards made in Argentina, 3.5" by 2.6", and round collector's cards from Argentina, 3.4".
- Spanish playing cards made in Argentina, featuring Carter in images from the show.
- Matchboxes with images of Carter from the show, made in (again, yes) Argentina, set of 10.

- Sculpted bust *(shown above, snapped by BRBTV at a comic shop in Kalamazoo, Michigan)*, in honor of DC Comics' 75th anniversary, Lynda Carter's portrayal of Wonder Woman in bullets-and-bracelets pose. Hand-painted, cold cast in porcelain, 5.5" tall by 2.5" wide by 2.5" long. Sculpted by Jack Mathews, limited edition of 3,000 pieces. Released 2010, DC Direct.
- Statue: limited-edition, hand-painted cold-cast porcelain, 13" high by 7½" wide. Limited to 5,000 pieces total. DC Direct.
- Wonder Woman fan-designed T-shirts in several styles, 1999, Renroc-Australia.
- Wonder Woman costume replicas, spotted on eBay in 2012.
- Wonder Girl costume replica: one-piece bodysuit of red and blue spandex with cross wrap bodice adorned with red and white star appliques and sequins, gold leather belt with detachable lasso of truth and gold leather tiara with red star, pair of red patent boots,

pair of silver cuffs adorned with center star and five smaller lower stars, GM Design.
- Numerous custom items can be found on eBay, using images of Carter from the series for keychains, necklaces, rings, bracelets, clocks and more.
- Scripts, spotted on eBay and other auction sites. Some scripts are from episodes that never went into production, "The Velvet Touch" and "Wonder Woman and the Watergate Baby," the Wonderland site says. Though they look to be original, no one really knows if they are originals or copies.
- "The Q Guide to Wonder Woman: Stuff You Didn't Even Know You Wanted to Know ... about Lynda Carter, the iconic TV show, and one amazing costume" book by Mike Pingel, Alyson Books, November 2008.
- "Channel Surfing: Wonder Woman" book by Mike Pingel, Amazon CreateSpace, February 2012.
- "What Would Wonder Woman Do?: An Amazon's Guide to the Working World" book by Jennifer Traig and Suzan Colon, Chronicle Books, June 2007.

Albums / Cassettes

- Lynda Carter: "Portrait" LP album, © 1978 Epic Records, U.S. release and U.S. promo release.
- Lynda Carter: "Portrait" Picture Disc LP album, © 1978 Epic Records, US release.
- Lynda Carter: "Portrait" LP album, © 1978 Epic Records, Japanese release with outer strip with Japanese writing.
- Lynda Carter: "Portrait" LP album, © 1978 Epic Records, UK release. This cover was the same one featured in the European and South American release.
- Lynda Carter: "Portrait" LP album, © 1978 Epic Records, Argentinean release.
- Lynda Carter: "It Might As Well Stay Monday / I Believe In Music," 7" Single (45 RPM), © 1972 EMI Records, promotional UK release.
- Lynda Carter: "All Night Song," 7" Single (45 RPM), © 1978 Epic Records, commercial U.S. release and promotional U.S. release.
- Lynda Carter: "Toto (Don't It Feel Like Paradise)," 7" Single (45 RPM), © 1978 Epic Records, promotional U.S. release and promotional Canadian release.

Oversize postcard of a painting of Lynda Carter as Wonder Woman by pop surrealist artist Isabel Samaras.

- Lynda Carter: "The Last Song," 7" Single (45 RPM), © 1980 EMI Records, commercial UK release.
- "The Willie Burgundy Five," LP album featuring Lynda Carter as a model on the cover, U.S. release.
- CBS promotional LP record for several series of the CBS Fall 1977 lineup. © 1977 CBS-TV.
- "Wonder Woman" Theme by The New World Symphony, 7" single (45 RPM), © 1977 Shadybrook Records.
- "Wonder Woman" Theme by Carol Medina, CD single.
- Lynda Carter: "Portrait" cassette, Argentinean release, © 1978 CBS / Epic Records.
- Lynda Carter: "Portrait" 8-track, U.S. release, © 1978 Epic Records.
- Rare Korean cassette featuring Wonder Woman stories and music.
- "Tema de la Mujer Maravilla," Uruguayan single featuring the Wonder Woman Theme.
- "Los Superheroes de Los Chicos," Argentinean single featuring the "Wonder Woman" Theme.
- "Wonder Woman" Theme remixed by The Wonderland Band.

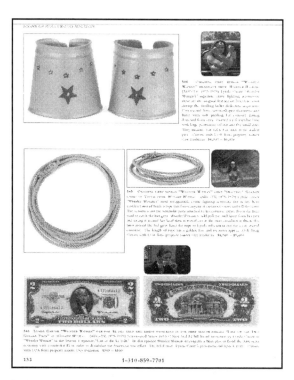

In 2011, an Icons of Hollywood auction of memorabilia included several items from the first season's production: a set of bracelets, a lasso, and a two-dollar bill.

For other Wonder Woman merchandise, as well as a list of websites celebrating our hero, see Andy Mangels' WonderWomanMuseum.com.

Special snapshot: Some other Amazonirific merchandise

Have we mentioned we loved those Warner Bros. Studio Stores they used to have at the malls? Of course we have. This author was on a tour of every Warner Bros. Studio Store branch in the nation, actually, during her travel schedule of covering cons back in the early days of her work for ComicsContinuum.com. Here are two of those nifty finds, both dated 1999: a big, solid black mug with images of not only Wonder Woman but also Superman, Batman, Flash and Green Lantern; and a thick tumbler that was part of a set including Batgirl, Superman, Batman and more.

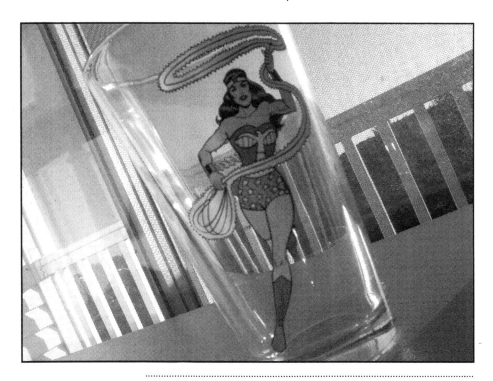

The Wonder Woman straw from the set of animated "Justice League" kids' meal toys from Subway.

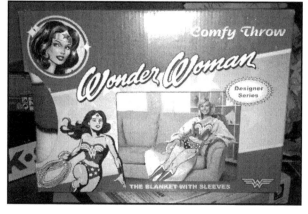

When the "Snuggie" craze first hit a few years back, this author swore she'd never own one. Then, when she saw this one in a local store's sale circular, she thought ... oh no, that wonderful bro of mine and his family, who are always on the lookout for cool superhero stuff for me, are going to see this ... I just know it. Just a few weeks later, Christmas 2011 ... Yup, you guessed it.

On this page and the next spread: Items spotted while this author was out shooting interviews for the Washington, D.C.-based TV show, "Fantastic Forum," at a comic shop in Silver Spring, Maryland. It was Free Comic Book Day, May 2012, and oh, what a delight to see so many Wonder Woman goodies.

"The Essential Wonder Woman Encyclopedia" by Phil Jimenez and John Wells, released in April 2010 by Del Ray, is about 500 pages of an A-to-Z guide on our hero from her 1940s comic-book roots.

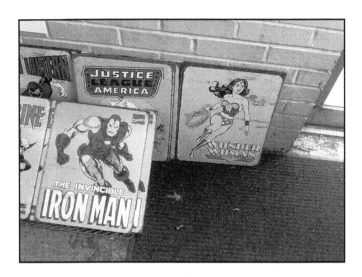

The superhero tin signs perched near the shop's door look vintage. They're from Desperate.com — and they were only $10 each! Our girl sure seems to be in a '70s-era pose!

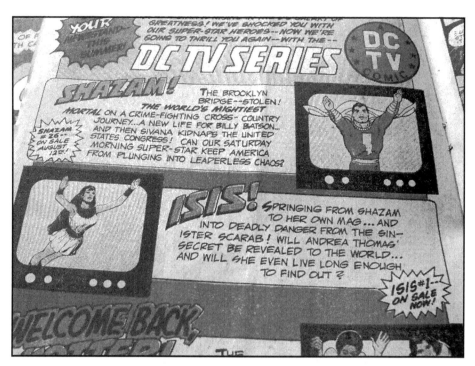

This was the era when Saturday morning just rocked. An ad from issue 226 of Wonder Woman, October-November 1976.

THE SECRETS OF ISIS

> " I got into the business a year or two after Jackie, Kate and Farrah (Jaclyn Smith, Kate Jackson and Farrah Fawcett), so between the three of them, they really opened up the business for women who weren't six feet tall. You didn't have to be like Lauren Hutton anymore to be successful as a commercial model. "
> — Joanna Cameron, explaining her time before "Isis,"
> in a 2002-2003 interview on "The Unofficial Isis Appreciation Page,"
> http://www.angelfire.com/tv2/isis/cameron2.html

ISIS

Blazing a trail for little girls everywhere

Actress Lynda Carter will forever be remembered as Wonder Woman, a female superhero sprung from the comic books into live-action TV to enthrall girls everywhere in the mid-'70s. But two months before she debuted in her "satin tights," as the theme song goes, someone else beat her to the punch to become the first ever female superhero to star in her own weekly live-action American TV series. She was a hero created specifically for television but making the hop to the comic-book page just a year later — ironically, to join Wonder Woman in the DC family.

She was the mighty Isis. And she still endures today.

As us former little girls of the '70s look back on our heroes of that time, we know Isis arrived on television first of them all, even before what BRBTV affectionately terms The Great Chick Triumvirate: the aforementioned "Wonder Woman" (November 1975), "The Bionic Woman" (January 1976) and "Charlie's Angels" (September 1976). Ooooh ... it was a beautiful era, indeed, wasn't it?

Isis seemed to have it all, as a female idol. Cute little white minidress with a cheerleader flair in the skirt. Exotic Egyptian touches, hearkening to the allure of Cleopatra and so finely applied to waist, collar and forehead. And those brown platform go-go boots. Wow, did it all come together. That was one rockin' outfit. We all wanted one. I swear we did. This author is still tempted to make one — it's the one female costume you really never see parading around at comic cons. Are you with me, gals o' my age?

But it wasn't just about how feminine and pretty Joanna Cameron's Isis was from our vantage point, over our bowl of cereal on Saturday morning. It had to be about the power, the strength, the smarts, the goodness, the honesty, the values, the desire to help others. The answering to no one. The equal footing with — or even *higher* footing than — the men around her (especially in the case of poor Rick Mason!). She made us feel like we could grow up to be *that*.

She surely helped take a lot of us girls-of-the-'70s far in our lives, inspiring us at such a young age. A true perspective of empowerment. It was an important message in that era.

Isis debuted on CBS-TV on Saturday, September 6, 1975, in a series produced by Filmation and designed to be the female counterpart to its already-popular half-hour "Shazam!" series for kids, which had been on the air for a year. "Isis" joined "Shazam" for "The Shazam! / Isis Hour" for two seasons, then syndicated out solo as "The Secrets of Isis."

"Living in a household full of ladies, you've got to think about doing shows that really relate to them, too," executive producer Lou Scheimer reminisces in the extras for the "Isis" series' 2007 DVD set. Scheimer had already seen a string of successes in not only the "Shazam!" series but numerous other projects for Filmation, including the animated "Star Trek" and various Batman, Superman and Archie series. For "Isis" to succeed was no surprise for the veteran, even though this live-action platform was a departure for the famed animation studio. "It really roared. It was an incredibly successful show," he says.

The character of Isis was based on a goddess named Isis in ancient Egyptian mythology. This Isis was the matron of nature and magic and the friend to the downtrodden, Wikipedia says. On the show, the young, pretty, brunette schoolteacher Andrea Thomas discovers the amulet of

Isis during an archaeological dig in Egypt, and she soon learns that the amulet has the power to transform her into a modern-day incarnation of the Egyptian goddess, with powers over nature, super-strength and the ability of flight. With these amazing abilities, Isis saves those in trouble and rights wrongs everywhere, reciting enchanting, rhyming mantras as she does it.

"O mighty storm that roams so free, now hold back and calm the sea ..."

"Wind that carries me afar, now be a cushion for this car ..."

True-life, everyday scenarios dominate the action, which most often takes place at the school where Andrea teaches. And often, amid such scenes as the demonstration of a scientific concept or a consultation with a troubled student, Andrea gets whisked away to a secret place to command a transformation into her other identity with one swift "Oh, mighty Isis!"

And, as a reinforcement of the concept of her power over nature, Andrea / Isis has a pet crow named Tut that often lends a wing, so to speak, in the action.

"We were creating a character from the ground up," says assistant director Henry J. Lange Jr. "This was a character that didn't exist in the comic-book lore. So everything was new. How the character transformed from the civilian to the superhero. All of that stuff, we totally came up with, the writers and the directors. So it was pretty exciting in that sense."

And there was certainly no short supply of sweet allure — as well as distinctness — in this brand-new character. Bob Kline, a designer for the series, explains in his own DVD interview, "In designing Isis' costume, we wanted to give her a short skirt so we could see her legs, and the medallion on her head became the symbol of her character, and we also designed the lettering that would appear in the main title, to fit within that medallion. The medallion that represents Isis is based on an actual Egyptian symbol that's associated with the historical Isis."

That blending of fresh elements with age-old mythology worked well for both the true audience, the kids, as well as the more educated viewers who might actually be able to recognize the difference. "We used a lot of

Capturing a pop-cultural icon: An interior shot of the DVD set.

stock photos and still photos for the main title sequence to get an authentic Egyptian look," Kline says. "The hieroglyphics seen in the main title are a drawing that I did as a layout, that were painted in the background department, so what looks like actual Egyptian hieroglyphics in the main title were actually created in the studio."

Cameron, the show's producers have said more than once, was hired for her legs, plain and simple. But the value of this actress, who already had several years of small roles under her belt at that point, went beyond that, for sure. The industrious star, who by all accounts of fellow cast and crew members kept largely to herself during filming, did her own stunts.

"Joanna Cameron was a delightful change from the all-male cast of 'Shazam!'," Lange says. "Joanna was really great at that. She was a teacher, but she was also a superhero. One of the great things about Joanna, and I do hear this from many people, as much as she was a role model for young girls, she was also a model for young boys. She was cute. We had her in that nice little tennis dress-length tunic, and she had great legs and was very athletic. I think there were a lot of fathers that, if their son or daughter were going to switch to something else, would say, no, I think we're watching 'Isis' this morning."

Joining Andrea as regular characters on "Isis" are fellow schoolteacher Rick Mason (the lamented "Lois Lane" of the series who seems oblivious to the similarities between the beautiful superhero and his coworker), played by Brian Cutler, and student Cindy Lee (Joanna Pang) in the first season, replaced by Rennie Carol (Ronalda Douglas) in the second season, as well as the school's principal, Dr. Joshua Barnes (Albert Reed). It was Cutler who was chosen first, actually.

"They were casting the show. A whole bunch of guys auditioned for it," he tells BRBTV. "Norm Prescott and Lou Scheimer liked me. I was the first person cast for the show, and then I was there for the rest of the casting. It was the normal audition process. I was cast, and then we went from there."

What was the audition like, we asked him. "They had some sides from the script. You know, some pages of dialogue. I just had to cold-read them with Norm and Lou. They were very hands-on because they'd been in animation for a long time, and this was their second attempt at live action."

Two episodes of the series were shot per week. Shooting happened in the summer, beginning in July and August 1975 for the first season, with available California daylight, starting at 7 a.m. There were no night scenes.

"On 'Isis,' we shot the shows in two and a half days," Lange says, "so what we'd do is we'd prep two shows and shoot two shows. The elements that took place at the high school we usually shot on Wednesday, the midday between the two episodes. It was actually the one day that Dick Rosenbloom, who was the producer, would give us the camera dolly." He laughs. "The rest of the time we were pretty much hand-held or on sticks. And it was one day we'd get a lot of extras in and we'd shoot that one day for both episodes. The rest of the time it was on location, wherever it was. We used a lot of locations in the valley, and it was deep in the valley where we were in Canoga Park, which was really pretty virgin territory then, and they hadn't been overshot by film companies. Since it was a Saturday morning show,

Brian Cutler runs his own acting studio these days. Photo courtesy of Brian Cutler.

everybody was pretty excited to see us. ... We also shot some in downtown L.A., and up in the park areas."

Cutler echoes the view of the hectic schedule in his own DVD interview, "We were on a six-day shooting schedule, which was a horrendous thing for anyone to do. Anybody who does episodic television knows what that's like. We shot two episodes a week, which is really cooking. We would start bright and early in the morning. ... The majority of the stuff was done on location. ... The school we shot at was closed during the summer, so if we needed to shoot on the campus or in one of the school rooms, we had the availability of doing that without any of the students being there."

The flight shots for Isis were all done on one day, with wires, then used where needed throughout the episodes. Footage of Cameron saying "Oh mighty Isis" and her incantation for flying was also shot once then used repeatedly where needed (hence, Andrea often wears the same fun '70s shirt and skirt combo in the episodes).

"Joanna really did all of her own stunts," Lange affirms. "We didn't have any doubles on 'Isis.' We spent a day flying her on wires. Now you do it against green screen. ... We flew her on wires for a day, so all of those flying shots in various versions were her with the wind machine blowing and her on wires. And then when she would rise up, we would either put her on a crane or the camera dolly, and we would just raise that up in the shot. And use smoke behind her for the transition of when she changed."

"I think everybody had to get used to the idea of live action being made for Saturday morning," says producer Richard M. Rosenbloom, who worked on both "Isis" and "Shazam!" "Budgets were extremely low compared to what was being done in primetime television and in other places in terms of shooting film. We shot in summer, and in California, days were very long. We shot always until the sun went down, to get everything we possibly could."

David Wise, who with his girlfriend at the time, Kathleen Barnes, wrote for the series, furthers the lament about budget in his DVD interview. "The hardest thing to do on 'Isis' was the stunts, because the budget of this show would not pay for the corned beef sandwiches of a low-budget film in Hollywood today. It was infinitesimal. So actually coming up with stunts that looked like anything remotely impressive was very, very difficult, because they had no special effects, they had no budget for anything."

But budget notwithstanding, the show made an impact. Suddenly, little kids everywhere were taking note of this action-packed Saturday morning series, which seemed — for its lack of cartoon panels — to treat them more like grown-ups. Fan mail rolled in.

"I think the show was very timely," Cutler says on the DVD extras. "It had a great appeal because it had a message and a moral in every single episode. ... During the running of the show, we got tons of fan mail all the time." Cutler says he still receives positive email about his role as Rick Mason. "It's interesting and unique to see the impact the show had on people and still has on people. My wife watched 'Isis' as a young girl, and she remembers all the episodes."

"Most of the letters asked for an autographed picture," Joanna Pang Atkins tells BRBTV of the response she received in her first-season role as Cindy Lee. "Some of the girls would tell me they wore their hair in pigtails like Cindy, and one young fan asked me to marry him and he sent me a ring. I think he told me it was his grandmother's, so of course I had to send it back!"

"As each episode aired, I found myself being recognized everywhere I went," says Ronalda Douglas Lombardo. "It was adults, it was children, it was parents. I got fan mail, and I enjoyed that. I enjoyed signing autographs. ... A lot of them were teenagers, so the messages were getting out there to people of all ages." For Lombardo, it was a debut that no doubt helped lead her to roles on other shows such as "The Jeffersons," "What's Happening!!" and "Good Times."

The series broke ground not only where the portrayal of strong females was concerned, but also in its racial diversity, putting front and center an authoritative school leader who was African-American and a key student who was Asian, then another who was an African-American female. "They hired across all sorts of color lines," Lombardo says in the DVD extras. "Albert Reed was the principal; he was a black man. Joanna Pang, obviously, she was Oriental. ... We had a lot of different ethnic backgrounds. Lou Scheimer was really good at making sure that the shows we did represented all of the ethnicities you will find in any area you live in. Everyone was represented. And the stories were such that whatever race you were, you could identify."

BRBTV asked Atkins how aware she was at the time, as a young woman, that the show was ahead of its time where diversity was concerned. "All the actors were just happy to be working, and I don't know that we were thinking so much in terms of diversity then (at least among the actors)," she says. "My fan mail was from boys and girls that loved the show."

And here at BRBTV we have to wonder, particularly in watching Atkins in the episode "Fool's Dare," if there were any of her own experiences, growing up, that helped inform her portrayal of the girl who could do anything those silly boys could do!

"'The Secrets of Isis' was created so that girls could have a superhero to look up to," Atkins tells us. "I did like that Cindy Lee was always interested and trying to do things — including what the boys did — even if not always making the smartest decisions ... but how else would she need Isis to come to the rescue?!"

She adds, "My mother instilled a lot of confidence in my brother and me. I think we both believed that we could do anything we set our minds to."

So how much of Joanna Pang did we see in Cindy Lee? "Cindy Lee was always positive, active and enthusiastic," the actress tells us. "She always wanted to help others and be involved. It was easy for me to play Cindy Lee because I had many of those same traits."

And as long as we're on the subject of Cindy Lee, BRBTV also posed the question to Atkins, is there anything you would have changed about her character, if you could have?

"I was wishing Cindy would have a superpower, too, and she could be the sidekick to Isis. That way I could've stayed out of trouble situations."

Soooooo .... If Cindy were a superhero, too, what powers would she have? "I think Cindy would want to fly, because she admired Isis, and then she could keep up!"

Despite all the fun Atkins was having as the "sidekick" student assistant to Andrea Thomas, she was not asked back for the second season. Atkins treaded carefully with this issue in her interview for the DVD set:

"A lot of people have asked me over the years what happened during the second season and what happened to the character of Cindy Lee, and honestly I don't have a really good answer for that. I know that the first season was very well-received, and from all the personal appearances and the people I met, I know that the character of Cindy Lee was also really well-received. We did 15 shows, and again I say, I hear that we were the number one show in the nation. So when we finished the first season, of course we had a period of time off, and it was time to get ready to go back for the second season. And I was back living in New York, and I kept waiting for a call, you know, 'get ready to come back, we're going to be filming on such-and-such a date, we're going into our second season.' And I never got a call, and it was getting close to the time when we would be filming, and I called my agent in California ... He didn't have any answers, either. It took him a couple days to finally get some answers, which were really not answers. It's kind of the standard answer that you'll always hear. We're not going to use the character of Cindy Lee this year; we're going in a different direction. Yes, I was disappointed, of course. I had loved doing the show. But again, being in show business, you go from job to job. And 'Isis' was one of many really great jobs that I've had. I've really had a wonderful career."

Atkins, who now teaches dance to children in New Jersey, followed up that thought with BRBTV:

"I started performing when I was very young. You go to hundreds of auditions, and sometimes you get the job and sometimes you don't. When you don't get the job, you just have to move on to the next one. As an actress your fate is decided by casting people, producers, directors and often network executives, so you don't have a lot of control as to whether or not you get the job. You have to go to auditions and do the best that you can, and have a thick skin about it. Of course I was disappointed that I was not asked back for the second season of 'Isis.' I'd had a lot of great jobs and opportunities before 'Isis,' so I had to be ready to move forward to the next great jobs after 'Isis'!"

So the likable Rennie Carol filled that teacher's assistant spot with aplomb, though this fresh new actress, whose debut was marked in the September 1976 episode "The Seeing Eye Horse," had a bit of a time adjusting.

"My first day on the set, I threw up all day," Lombardo says in her DVD interview. "I was so nervous. That first day was so nerve-wracking for me, and (director) Earl Bellamy made me feel so comfortable. Although I did throw up." She laughs.

Nevertheless, the show rolled on. And it became evident, through the episodes, that this superhero tale had some classic elements. Namely, its own, unique "Lois Lane" character.

"'Superman' always looked the same to me," Cutler jokes. "Andrea would take her hair down and become Isis, and so by doing that, I never knew the difference. You have to justify this by looking at what we call the suspension of disbelief in acting."

We asked Cutler in our own interview with him if that was difficult for him, as an actor. "No. It wasn't hard at all," he says. "You just live the moment. It was kinda fun, actually."

He elaborated in the DVD interview: "For me, it was a good role to play because unlike some of the other superhero shows that came after us, and of course Isis was the first live-action female heroine on TV, for me, it was that thing where I never had to be rescued or saved or anything. I was usually part of the rescue and had some difficulty maybe on my own doing it, which was why Isis came in and saved the day, if you will. I didn't have any problems with it. It was a fun, fun show. I've been getting emails and letters from people since the show was on the air. ... People surf the web and they find you. ... 'Lois Lane' is fine."

Joanna Cameron at a 2006 con. Photo from Wikipedia user Mojojojo7777769, in the public domain.

But the Lois Lane thing wasn't the only amusing aspect of schoolteacher Rick Mason's character.

"The clothes were mine," Cutler says. "Basically I wore slacks and a sport coat and a tie. Lou and Norm wanted to stay away from anything that was too outlandish or too outrageous. ... I always wanted to look very presentable (and respectable). ... I think a lot of the clothes I wore were very much in style at the time, and you have to remember that that time was the '70s. ... I think overall it's a pretty straight, standard kind of look."

Yea, yea. OK. You get a pass on that one, Mr. Mason. But we couldn't help but ask Cutler ... right after we inquired if he has any keepsakes from the "Isis" set (he doesn't — even his scripts might be lost in storage somewhere) ... if those clothes are still somewhere perhaps in the back of his closet ...

"Oh, God, no," he asserts. "No, no, no. They're all gone. They're gone to another universe, I think. Where they belong."

Well, then how about bloopers from the set? Any foibles we'll probably never see on an "Isis" blooper reel?

"Oh, I'm sure there were," Cutler tells us. "I don't know that I can remember any in particular. There are two episodes where I'm wearing sunglasses. I never wore sunglasses in any other episode. Right between the eyes I had been stung by a bee or wasp, and it showed. But we had to keep shooting, so I said just give me some sunglasses, and we went right on shooting."

This Filmation-created character of Isis, along with Rick Mason and the rest of the crew, made the journey to the comic book page a year after debuting on TV, appearing first in Shazam! No. 25 in September 1976, then launching into a separate DC comic, The Mighty Isis, the following month. The stakes were certainly much higher on the printed page and ancient Egyptian lore was relied upon heavily, with the heroine battling the 3,000-year-old magician Scarab, the fiery Creature from Dimension X, the evil, narcissistic Set, Aten, and Serpenotep the serpent king. The

The first-ever comic book appearance for Isis was in Shazam's regular title, before she branched out on her own in the issues shown on the next page.

Rick Mason character showed a bolder romantic interest in Andrea Thomas, and the concept of identity was explored: After the establishment of two distinct identities for Andrea and Isis, rather than one being the alter ego of the other, the comic took Isis in the direction of actually abandoning Andrea the schoolteacher.

The original comic series only lasted for eight issues, however. Decades later, in 2007, Bluewater Productions launched a Legend of Isis comic book series. Though the character bears little resemblance to the Isis of the TV series, there was coordination between the two entities: The comics contain ads for the "Isis" DVD release, and the DVD set contains a look at the comic.

An Isis character has also sprung up in DC Comics more recently. In the weekly 52 series from 2006, she's an Egyptian woman named Adrianna Tomaz, a refugee who is enslaved and brought to the Shazam villain Black Adam. Adrianna has an amulet that changes her into the goddess Isis. DC / Warner Bros. also employed a variation of Isis in a 2010 episode of the CW show "Smallville," where Lois Lane is transformed into the goddess after examining some ancient Egyptian artifacts. *Hmmm* ... Kinda makes you wonder what other plans there might be for this female superhero property ...

It's been reported that actor Kelsey Grammer's production company Grammnet has obtained the rights to do an Isis movie. The film, set up at

A couple issues of Bluewater Productions' comic-book take on Isis.

Paramount Pictures where Grammer had a first-look deal, was announced in December 2004, with a script by Ali Russell. The movie was supposedly based on Bluewater Productions' comic. And indeed, MovieInsider.com's page for the film credits Darren Davis of Bluewater as a writer alongside Russell, with the synopsis, "A young girl finds the bracelet of the ancient god Isis and inherits her powers in addition to awakening a dark force."

"The Secrets of Isis" series got a sprinkling of other merchandise besides comics back in the day, namely a hard-to-find Mego doll (or action figure, perhaps? it's a girl, you know, and girls are often "dolls"!), a Golden Book, some View-Master reels, a Halloween costume, a Magic Slate, at least one sticker book and coloring book, plus jigsaw puzzles. It's enough to make us drool as we surf eBay.

The DVD set for the series is no disappointment, by any means. The collection brims with cast and crew interviews, still shots from the show, a brief episode guide, and even the scripts of the episodes. And hey, it's certainly not easy to find something like episode scripts on a TV show's DVD set. BRBTV applauds Andy Mangels, who put together all these goodies.

"Knowing that this was likely to be the only DVD set the series would ever have, I wanted to put as much on the set as possible," Mangels tells BRBTV. "The only real issues that came up were space and budget. Every time you put something onto a DVD, even if it's as simple as a PDF of a script, it costs the company money, so I had to justify every choice."

He continues, "I would have liked to have the isolated music and effects tracks for more episodes, but since the music was really repetitive anyhow, it would have mostly ended up sounding the same. I did make sure, though, that we did that with the 'Shazam!' cross-over episodes, so that we could get all of his themes put in."

Was there anything he planned to include but wasn't able to?

"I wanted to put in the original series bible and some other material that was used in the development of the show, but it just wasn't feasible," he tells us. *Oooohhh* — we would've loved to have seen the series bible!

"I also wish that we had gotten all of the morals and better versions of the bumpers and alternate credits, but we went with the material we could get. A lot of that material just doesn't exist any longer. When Filmation was sold in 1989, to L'Oreal and later Hallmark, much of the material that wasn't useful for syndication markets was just thrown out. The original film and music, any bloopers, etc., were all just gone! Thankfully, series co-star Joanna Pang had a video collection she had put together, and I had some older materials, and between the two of us, we were able to get as much rare footage as possible."

He adds, "I wish that Bob Kline had been able to find his original presentation and opening credits art that he had created for Isis, but alas, he wasn't able to. We discussed having some packed-in exclusive comic art postcards in the set, similar to those we did for 'He-Man,' 'She-Ra,' 'Flash Gordon' and 'Defenders of the Earth.' We were going to go with Alex Ross and Matt Haley, both of whom are Isis fans, but those didn't work for the budget."

Also: "We discussed doing an 'on-pack exclusive' for Best Buy or another retailer, which would have included a sculpted version of the Isis amulet, and even provided reference for a sculptor, but the costs were deemed too high, and the retailer exclusive market was too small to justify the

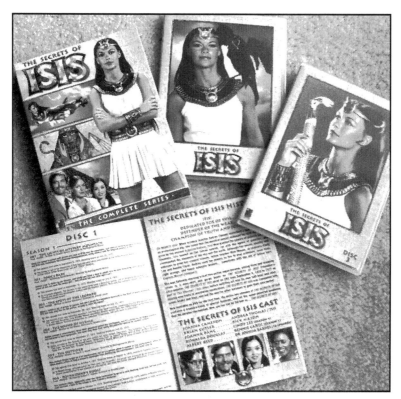

BRBTV told Andy Mangels that this is the most downright loaded DVD set we've ever seen for a television show.

expense." I told Mangels that would've gone just great with the Isis costume I've always wanted to make! But speaking of costumes ...

"We also talked about having a live model as Isis for Comic-Con 2007, and were talking with a costumer about that, but it didn't happen," Mangels says. "We did give out temporary tattoos of the logo, and had some Isis T-shirts printed for Comic-Con, though!"

One question I posed to Mangels regards the absence of the lead actress herself among the interviewees.

"I pursued Joanna fervently for quite some time," he says. "The status in Hollywood is that 99 percent of DVD companies do NOT pay anyone for interviews or commentary tracks, and most stars and production personnel are fine with that. They consider it a part of PR, or furthering their legacy, or a gift to their fans. Joanna lives in Hawaii now and works at a hotel. We offered to fly her to Los Angeles for two to three days, and put her up at a nice hotel, and give her a reasonable fee for coming in; we also talked to her about appearing at Comic-Con. She would have filmed all of her material in about a two- to three-hour time, and then been able to enjoy L.A. on the company.

"Unfortunately, Joanna felt that our offer was not enough. I begged the company to do more, and we made a second offer, which was also rebuffed. Then, using the idea I had from the interviews with Brian Cutler and Joanna Pang, I went on Craigslist for Hawaii. I found a film crew there who were very close to Joanna. The woman who ran it was an award-winning documentary director, and, it turned out, was an Isis fan. They were willing to go to Joanna's house or the hotel she worked at, at her convenience, to do the interview by speakerphone, as I had done the others. Additionally, we did offer Joanna a fee to do this.

"So, for a few hours' work, she'd get a good fee, did not have to leave home, got to work with a female-run crew, and got a chance to speak to her fans. Joanna chose not to do it. It's her choice, but it's the biggest regret that I have with the DVD set. I know how much Lynda Carter and Lindsay Wagner have appreciated their fans, and both of them appeared on their DVD sets. It would have been wonderful for Joanna to do the same. Unfortunately, she chose not to, so we have to respect that."

For how comprehensive it is, the DVD set has another missing item: The morals aren't actually attached to the episodes, though many are included separately in the set.

"When the shows went into syndication, especially in the British market, the morals were removed from the episodes," Mangels tells us of "Isis" and "Shazam!" "Since the digital prints we were provided by Entertainment Rights (now Classic Media), the current owners of the Filmation library, were for the British runs, the morals had not been digitized. Whether those film elements even still exist in a warehouse somewhere in Europe is unknown, but we found as many as we could, in the best quality that we could, and put them on the discs."

So what are they all doing these days?

Through the years, the cast members of the show have moved on to other careers — a range of occupations as diverse as hotel manager, dance instructor, acting coach and church choir singer.

As mentioned, the star of the show, Joanna Cameron (whose first name is often credited as JoAnna) now lives in Hawaii. She has progressed through a decade in home health care work to a marketing degree. She was kind enough to call me for this story on a Sunday night from her island paradise, where she juggles two jobs managing a hotel and working in a PR capacity for "Island Lifestyle" clothing maker Tommy Bahama.

Cameron, who walked away from show business in the early '80s after a respectable career that even, beyond "Isis," included a proliferation of TV commercials putting her in the Guinness Book of World Records three years in a row, is very happy these days. That much is evident, as you talk with her. There's a lilt in her voice, a softness reminiscent of when her superhero alter-ego once delivered the moral messages to the teens she shared scenes with. Cameron will answer a question or two, but she'll definitely ask them, too. In our conversation, she was interested in where I was originally from, where I am living now, if I am married, if I have kids, how I met a mutual friend of ours, and more. And she encouraged me several times to come visit her in Hawaii, where she would, I'm sure, be a congenial hostess. It was a human compassion beyond mere conversational politeness.

And these days, as in the days of filming "Isis" by all accounts of her fellow cast and crew, she values her privacy.

"I live an extremely private lifestyle on purpose. I'm not one of these super-young people like, I would give you an example, Halle Berry? She's a superstar of this generation," Cameron tells me. "I live pretty quiet. I cycle. That's what I do. I still ride long-distance bicycles. That's part of why I live here."

She rarely gets recognized as Isis in her work these days. She joked during the call that she was at that moment wearing Ray-Bans and a hat that said "Tommy Bahama." She says if people do recognize her these days, "it's because of my voice and my walk. I don't look like a 19- or 20-year-old Egyptian princess anymore. Who does?"

Still, the fans do, indeed, find her, at least through mail — both traditional and electronic, though she's not an avid Internet user. Her P.O. box is listed on sites such as the Unofficial Isis Appreciation Page at http://www.angelfire.com/tv2/isis/home.html. "I get mail from all over the world. I just look at it and shake my head," she says. "The only reason I don't use my email is that it becomes so overloaded I can't handle it. My honey looks at me and goes, what are you going to do with these people? I say, I've got an idea, honey, I've got an idea."

That idea is a project, of which she speaks sparingly, but which is obviously close to her heart. "I have some people who have approached me about doing something. It's called 'Razor Sharp.' I'm very proud of it. I had to go into Washington to get approval to do it. ... It's one of the rare opportunities for a woman to direct."

The original "Blue Angels in Razor Sharp" is a 1982 documentary film, hosted by Cameron, focusing on the U.S. Navy's flight demonstration team, the Blue Angels. Cameron says she has been involved in directing a couple other DVD projects. As for the DVD set of "Isis," Cameron gave me her perspective on not being a part of the interviews. Suffice it to say she is disappointed over the issue and would've loved to have been a part of the project.

Her co-star Cutler, meanwhile, has his own acting studio these days, the Commercial Actors Studio in Kansas City, which he started up in 1994.

"I came to Missouri to do 'The Unsinkable Molly Brown,' he explains to BRBTV. "The woman who started the Missouri Repertory Theatre came to see the show and came backstage after the show and said, 'I really love your work. Would you be interested in working in the Missouri Repertory Theatre?' I said sure. Because what does an actor want to do? An actor wants to act. I was going through a difficult time. I thought this would be a nice change. That contract, which was a two-year contract with the Missouri Repertory Theatre, turned into a 14-year contract."

So one thing led to another, there in Missouri. "Theatre and film are two totally different areas," he says. "I thought I would see if there was any interest in the area in film, and I saw that there was. We're known as one of the best acting studios in the country."

The man who trained Cutler served as his inspiration to then coach other prospective actors. "There are a lot of people that say they were trained by Charles Conrad, but Charles was a very reclusive man," he tells us. "I can say that I was close friends with him, and he would help a lot of people become big stars, and somehow they would say that they made it on their own. They would forget Charles. So I wanted to carry on his legacy. I wanted him to have someone he knew and trusted carrying on his legacy."

There's been no shortage of work for the company. "We've done three feature films in the past few years. 'My One and Only,' 'Ambrose Bierce: Civil War Stories,' 'Hope.' We stay busy, production-wise. I like directing. I like coaching. My wife is the unit production manager. We get very involved in what we do; we have a great team that we work with."

Atkins has created a robust career of the activity she enjoyed long before taking on the role of Cindy Lee: dancing.

"I am very involved in arts education," she tells BRBTV. "I am a teaching artist that is placed in schools for multicultural dance residencies. The residencies are very rewarding because I see children blossom and become more confident. I also want them to learn about the culture and traditions of other countries and become more accepting of differences between people and places. I've just put up a new website with lots of that information at www.JoannaPangAtkins.com."

What's her preferred style of dance, we wondered? "I enjoy all styles of dance. I started in ballet when I was very young, and with that training and technique, you can move more easily into other areas of dance. I toured the world with an Asian dance company, which eventually led to my world dance residencies. Recently I started taking Nia classes. Nia is a class that combines movements and concepts from yoga, Tai-Chi, Tae Kwon Do, Aikido, jazz and modern dance."

BRBTV was also curious (how could we not be?) if there's any chance Atkins will make a return to acting. "I really enjoy the teaching, so I haven't thought about acting in a while. But my husband, Dick Atkins, is a producer, so maybe he'll cast me in something!"

Lombardo, as she mentioned in her interview for the "Isis" DVD set, is doing something she loves, too, in L.A. And it's something she also got to do in "Isis," in the two-parter, "Now You See It ..." / "... And Now You Don't."

"I actually started off as a singer, and I sing today," she says. "I sing at the Cathedral of Our Lady of Lourdes downtown. I work with the Cardinal. And also once a month I go to East Lake Detention Center, and I sing a Mass, a service for the teenagers. I think I get the most out of that. The kids applaud after everything I sing, every song I sing during the Mass, they applaud. They're so hungry. I think I love doing that more than anything else I do right now. ... I sing weddings, I sing funerals, you name it, I sing it."

The Isis lore and the love live on

And even as these actors enjoy their post-"Isis" lives, the legacy of the show lives on. We now-grown-up viewers will gladly attest that this series carried an important, serious message, beyond the moral presented in each half-hour. Lisa Everetts of Pennsylvania, a lifelong fan of "The Secrets of Isis" and member of the show's Facebook group, believes that this era of television — the age where Saturday morning was a real event for kids — is gone. Gone with it, even, are any real quality TV shows for kids.

"Back in the '70s and early '80s, even if kids didn't have the best parents on the planet, they were not bombarded with negativity on TV like they are now," Everetts tells BRBTV. "They could go to the TV and adults were doing shows for kids, like 'Captain Kangaroo,' 'The Magic Garden,' 'Mr. Rogers,' 'Romper Room,' and 'The Electric Company,' 'The Big Blue Marble,' and there was great stuff on for teens. Today, boys have nothing, where they use to have 'Happy Days' (The Fonz), 'MacGyver,' 'The A-Team,' 'Riptide,' 'Knight Rider,' 'The Dukes of Hazzard,' and 'The Hardy Boys,' and 'Grizzly Adams' and lots more. Nobody killed anyone in those shows. Even shows like the old 'Tarzan,' 'The Lone Ranger,' 'F-Troop,' 'Lassie,' 'Rin Tin Tin,' and 'The Little Rascals' were so great for kids."

She continues, "There was such variety. Look how different 'The Munsters' was from 'Nanny and the Professor' or 'The Beverly Hillbillies.' But they all dealt with 'families.' It seems today, there is no such thing as a 'functional' family. It's dysfunctional every which way you look. I think it's a shame. Probably the most 'dysfunctional' was once 'The Partridge Family,' with a single mom."

You sing it, sister. BRBTV knows so many other people of our era — the now 30- and 40-somethings — who are frustrated that any sense of great television has now been lost in the quagmire of reality TV. Mangels, also part of our generation, does his own reminiscing:

"I was a fan of both 'Shazam!' and 'Isis.' I grew up in a small town in Montana, and we only got one channel on our black-and-white TV (KCFW, an NBC channel from Kalispell). However, if you moved the antennas just right, you could get signals for the ABC and CBS stations

Where did Saturday morning go? A center spread ad from the first issue of The Super Friends comic, November 1976.

from Spokane, Washington. 'Shazam!' aired on CBS and I loved it, and in September 1975, they debuted the new 'The Shazam! / Isis Hour,' with a female heroine. I had always loved Wonder Woman in the comics and animated on ABC's 'Super Friends,' but the Lynda Carter TV series wouldn't debut until November 1975, so Isis became a new live-action favorite."

He says, "I loved the rhyming verses that she did to cast her magical spells, and actually used to have a big piece of butcher paper that I would write the spells on as quickly as possible so I could remember them. Then, when I was outside playing, I would use Isis' spells in my 'pretend time.' When 'Wonder Woman,' 'Isis,' and then 'Bionic Woman' were on the air in 1976, I was in heaven. I loved superheroes of any type, but particularly enjoyed the super-heroines."

"When I was a kid," Everett says, "we raised six raccoons, a red fox, a groundhog, a gray squirrel, a skunk, and I rescued a sparrow hawk from some kids who were trying to stone it to death at summer camp, and I taught it how to fly, and then released it into the wild (which was always my grandparents' property). I think that's why I loved 'Isis' so much. You could use your imagination as a kid, to go outside and play. I can remember racing my brother through the yard — pretending we were bionic, and we'd jump off the front porch, or off a stone wall, and pretend we were in slow motion. Everything was geared toward children."

Everything on TV for kids is violent these days, Everetts says. "You know that in the first season of 'CHiPs,' they never drew a gun on anyone ever. They showed them helping people, just like the show 'Emergency!' There's a huge difference. When I watch shows like 'The Greatest American Hero' or 'The Incredible Hulk,' the alter-egos of the heroes are always great people. They are doctors or teachers, and you see them doing good things. Like David Banner in the TV show — he made science seem really interesting. Jaime Sommers was a teacher, Andrea Thomas was a science teacher, and they incorporated it into the show."

Everetts got the rare opportunity to spend the day with Joanna Cameron, actually, during a con in Baltimore in 2004. For this owner of a bed-and-breakfast, it was a chance to meet a true hero of an era gone by.

*Joanna Cameron and Lisa Everetts.
Photos courtesy of Lisa Everetts.*

"You'd watch Saturday morning TV," Everett says of the '70s, "then you'd run outside to play the rest of the day. I loved 'Land of the Lost.' I have met Kathy Coleman, who played Holly. We are lucky that we had that. That's the time period that it was great to pack your lunch in a lunchbox — and the lunchboxes were so cool back then. I can remember me and my brother packing our lunch, and going for a walk up the railroad tracks by my house, and we'd just sit in the sun and eat our peanut-butter and jelly sandwich and drink Kool-Aid out of a Thermos. Poor kids today have nothing. I get so sick of seeing kids hunched over texting each other, instead of playing a board game or putting a puzzle together. It's really sad."

Robert Gillis of Massachusetts is also a fervent "Isis" fan who watched the show as a kid and got to meet the show's star as an adult. For him, it was the late-2004 Boston Super Megafest con, and it was the moment of a lifetime.

"To see Joanna in person and actually have the opportunity to speak with her, one on one, for me, still has a dreamlike quality," he wrote for the Foxboro (Mass.) Reporter in 2006. "She is such a wonderful role model, such a gifted person, such a giving, kind woman, and my hero."

Gillis got to chat with Cameron, learn about her life and what she did in her career after leaving the show. It only made him appreciate her all the more.

"I know that Joanna Cameron is just a person, an actor in a TV show," he says, "but she was always such a special part of my childhood, and such a wonderful role model. To finally meet her, give her hug, and talk to her, well, it's just a dream come true. I admire her for her philosophy of taking care of people. She did that as a fictional character on a TV show and gave lessons and morality tales. As a nurse, she provided one-on-one care to dying people and gave them love and dignity, and now she helps people to learn to relax and relieve their stress. What an inspiration."

He continues, "Sometimes our role models disappoint us when we meet them or get to know them better. Meeting mine was just the opposite. Thirty years after 'Isis,' I admire and respect Joanna Cameron more than ever for all she's done and continues to do, and of course, there's still that 11-year-old in me that gets to say, 'Oh, my God! I met Isis! I met Isis!'"

Joanna Cameron and Robert Gillis. Photo courtesy of Robert Gillis.

Colleen Corrigan is a friend of Robert Gillis and also a big "Isis" fan. Corrigan has actually done what this author has always wanted to do: make an Isis costume. The northeast Pennsylvania resident took several months to put it together. And yes, she also watched the show when it originally aired. "Relentlessly," she quips, "every Saturday. I didn't care what was going on. I didn't care if the world was coming to an end."

The idea of creating a costume, however, came only recently for her.

"I have no idea what made me start thinking of the show," she says. "I hadn't thought about it in decades, even though I was obsessed about it as a little kid. All of a sudden last year, around March, I started thinking about it." So Corrigan went online and found her friend Robert's "Isis" story and started finding the episodes to watch. She set out to put together the pieces with the idea of wearing the costume to Salem, Massachusetts, for Halloween 2011.

"I got this idea in my head, and it was not going to leave. It took me six solid months. I even said to my husband the week before Halloween, do you realize we were still putting together the final touches of this costume this time last year?"

For sure, it wasn't easy. "I wanted it to look as identical as possible," Corrigan says, "which was a challenge. The first challenge was I wanted to find somebody who could actually make the whole tennis dress part of it."

She found a seamstress, whom she contacted in July 2011. She showed her photos of Joanna

Robert Gillis added a background of the Sphinx to a photo of Colleen Corrigan in her Isis costume. Photo courtesy of Colleen Corrigan.

Cameron as Isis, and the seamstress said she could make the dress. But six weeks later, what Corrigan got looked like a nurse's outfit. "Needless to say, I never called her back. ... I was upset about that, I cannot even tell you."

It was only one step in this uphill battle, it turned out. "There were so many disappointments involved in the planning of this costume, it was unbelievable."

Corrigan decided to instead begin with a knit tank top, then she ordered a white cheerleader's skirt online. She found dark, short go-go boots in Tennessee. But then finding the wig was a toughie. She looked at various shops around her area, and some wanted $500 or more. "I got to the point that I didn't know what I was going to do." Finally she found a little costume shop that had one last wig of long, straight black hair (first season, not second, you'll note!). "How I got that at the 11th hour was truly a miracle," Corrigan says.

"The other parts, all the decorative parts of the costume, I was racking my brain," she says. "I went to a flea market that used to be not too far from me, and I thought, they have to have stuff that resembles it. I went to every booth and picked up belts and bracelets. I went to the Walmart and got a big piece of black belt and thought I'm going to glue everything on there. I used gorilla glue to keep everything on there, and then when I tried to bend it, it wouldn't bend. So we were spending every night the week before Halloween trying to unglue it."

For the amulet, a metalworker stepped in. But all the metalworker made were the horns. "I said where is the disc?!"

The center part of the headband is a drawer knob. The horns alongside it were cut out of a piece of wood by one of her friends. She ended up using felt for the waistband and wristbands, though parts had to be redone. "Thank God I got a big piece of felt."

But alas would come the biggest letdown of all her work: The stormy weather in Salem that Halloween. "I was all bundled up," she laments. "The only thing you could see was the skirt." Plus the wig got messed up in the 11-hour drive in the blizzard. "It was quite the adventure. I have to tell you!"

True fandom, for sure. We know the show inspired it.

So now, many years later, Brian Cutler tells BRBTV what he feels is the message of "The Secrets of Isis":

"To be good to your fellow man. To understand each other. To listen. To not judge. It covered all those things, you know. In every episode they covered a piece of all of that."

Andy Mangels also voices his view to us:

"I think that Andrea Thomas being a schoolteacher was an integral part of the character, and made it a much stronger show than if she had investigated crimes, as the original concept would have been. In both identities, Andrea and Isis were strong, caring, and independent, qualities that were amazing to see on television at the time. She really was a feminist heroine, and like Wonder Woman, someone you'd want as a big sister to protect you if you were a kid. And the morals and messages of the show were very important, not just to the producers, but to the viewers themselves."

Joanna Cameron stated it well in her interview for VH-1's "Where Are They Now?": "It was a new concept for women to have powers of their own, be independent, so I think it gave little girls growing up a concept that they could become empowered, that they could have superpowers."

As this author spoke to her, though, and asked what she feels is the most important message of "Isis" now, she voiced it so softly and succinctly across the Pacific Ocean:

"This is all about personal self-respect, dignity, education."

CAST

Who else was in on the action?

Ann Taylor ("The Cheerleader") ... **Laurette Spang**
Art Byron ("The Lights of Mystery Mountain") ... **Ken Wolger**
Bigfoot / Richard ("Bigfoot") ... **Bill Engesser**
Bill Cady ("The Sound of Silence") ... **Leigh McCloskey**
Bill Sherwood ("Dreams of Flight") ... **Tom Williams**
Billie Miller ("To Find a Friend") ... **Buddy Foster**
B.J. Tanker ("The Sound of Silence") ... **James Canning**
Captain Marvel ... **John Davey**
Carrie Anson ("Funny Gal") ... **Sandra Vacey**
Charlie ("The Hitchhiker") ... **Barry Miller**
Charlie Michaels ("The Outsider") ... **Wirt Morton**
Chela Montoya ("Dreams of Flight") ... **Cynthia Avila**
Chick Jeffers ("The Lights of Mystery Mountain") ... **Mike Maitland**
Chuck Nelson ("The Spots of the Leopard") ... **Lou Frizzell**
Cindy Lee ... **Joanna Pang**
C.J. Howe ("Now You See It ...") ... **Evan Kim**
Cy Kahn ("Fool's Dare") ... **Frank Whiteman**
Dave Parker ("Year of the Dragon") ... **Roger Kern**
Dorothy Bieder ("No Drums, No Trumpets") ... **Christopher Norris**

Dr. Gerry Blankfort ("The Seeing Eye Horse") ... **James Griffith**
Dr. Herb Rogers ("Lucky") ... **Robert Forward**
Dr. Joshua Barnes ... **Albert Reed**
Ernie Rothchild ("Fool's Dare") ... **Joshua Albee**
Fabian ("Rockhound's Roost") ... **Thomas Carter**
Feather Robbins ("Now You See It ...") ... **Craig Wasson**
Frank Iverson ("Fool's Dare") ... **Jeffrey Tyler**
Fred Wieting ("No Drums, No Trumpets") ... **Mark Lambert**
Freddie Charleton ("Girl Driver") ... **Susan Lawrence**
Glenn ("Lucky") ... **Brian Nash**
Gregg Aley ("Funny Gal") ... **Jonas Agee**
Har Winstead ("The Outsider") ... **Harry Hickox**
Hope Carswell ("The Hitchhiker") ... **Jewel Blanch**
Inspector Bryce ("Now You See It ...") ... **Jerry Douglas**
Isis / Andrea Thomas ... **Joanna Cameron**
Jack Evans ("The Sound of Silence") ... **Philip Bruns**
Jenny Nelson ("The Spots of the Leopard") ... **Debralee Scott**
Jim Danch ("No Drums, No Trumpets") ... **Michael Greene**
Joann Clayton ("The Hitchhiker") ... **Lynn Tufeld**
Jocko ("The Sound of Silence") ... **Wayne Storm**
Joe ("To Find a Friend") ... **Tommy Norden**
Joel Moss ("The Lights of Mystery Mountain") ... **Kelly Thordsen**
Julie Chen ("Year of the Dragon") ... **Jeanne Joe**
Kevin McCauley ("Rockhound's Roost") ... **Steven Paul**
Larry ("Now You See It ...") ... **Ben Frank**
Lee Webster ("Bigfoot") ... **Scott Colomby**
Mac Lennard ("Girl Driver") ... **Steve Doubet**
Mark Dawson ("Dreams of Flight") ... **Paul Hinckley**
Mickey Moses ("Bigfoot") ... **Neil J. Schwartz**
Mr. Anderson ("To Find a Friend") ... **Russ Marin**
Mr. Chen ("Year of the Dragon") ... **Victor Sen Yung**
Mr. McCauley ("Rockhound's Roost") ... **Bill DeLand**
Mr. Tilden ("The Outsider") ... **Morgan Jones**
Mrs. Schuster ("The Seeing Eye Horse") ... **Kathleen O'Malley**
Nancy ("Scuba Duba") ... **Eileen Chesis**
Noah Schuster ("The Seeing Eye Horse") ... **Gregory Elliot**
Phil Hobbs ("The Outsider") ... **Anson Downes**
Professor ("Now You See It ...") ... **Paul Hampton**
Randy Martin ("Lucky") ... **John Doran**
Ranji ("Now You See It ...") ... **Ranji**

Raul Montoya ("Dreams of Flight") ... **Fabian Gregory**
Rennie Carol ... **Ronalda Douglas**
Rick Mason ... **Brian Cutler**
Roger Buck ("The Show-Off") ... **Meegan King**
Rudy Horton ("The Class Clown") ... **Alvin Kupperman**
Sam Niles ("Fool's Dare") ... **Charles Cyphers**
Sgt. Connors ("The Spots of the Leopard") ... **Ed. Cross** *(yes, with the period after his first name!)*
Sheriff Harley ("The Lights of Mystery Mountain") ... **Hank Brandt**
Stanley Crane ("The Class Clown") ... **David Cole**
Steve ("The Hitchhiker") ... **Brad David**
Steve Conrad ("Scuba Duba") ... **Brian Byers**
Steve Elwood ("The Show-Off") ... **Harry Gold**
Tom ("The Cheerleader") ... **Danil Torppe**
Tom Anderson ("To Find a Friend") ... **Mike Lookinland**
Tom Jenkins ("The Spots of the Leopard") ... **Paul Jenkins**
Wayne Moss ("The Outsider") ... **Mitch Vogel**
Wynn ("The Cheerleader") ... **Colleen Camp**
Zookeeper ("The Show-Off") ... **Harlan Warde**

Bobby Brady in an "Isis" episode? Believe it, and see the synopses for "To Find a Friend" in the chapter that follows. Here, actor Mike Lookinland is at the Big Apple Convention in Manhattan on October 1, 2010. Photo by Luigi Novi, from Wikimedia Commons.

CHARACTERS

Step inside the classroom of Miss Thomas

Isis / Andrea Thomas

Andrea Thomas is a high school science teacher in Mid-City who, while on an archaeological dig in Egypt, dug up a box containing the amulet of Isis. With this amulet, she's able to transform into the goddess Isis, having magical powers over animals and the elements. As Andrea, she's smart, pretty and compassionate toward her students. Probably in her 20s. Wears glasses and often wears her long dark hair in a ponytail tied with a ribbon (then as Isis, wears her hair free). Drives a Camaro that was red at first then repainted yellow.

Rick Mason

Science teacher at the high school in Mid-City, and friend and colleague of Andrea Thomas. Tall and handsome, with a kind spirit and good sense of humor, as he is frequently the butt of jokes. Probably in his late 20s or early 30s. Rather enthralled with Isis, but cannot see that she is actually the alter ego of Andrea Thomas. Drives a white jalopy. Owns a boat called the Star Tracker. Teaches scuba diving to the kids. Skeptical of UFOs and science fiction.

Cindy Lee
High school student and good friend of Andrea Thomas and Rick Mason. Friendly, kind, often smiling. Wears her hair in pigtails, and often wears bib overalls.

Dr. Joshua Barnes
Administrator at the high school and boss of sorts to Andrea Thomas and Rick Mason. Gentlemanly, middle-aged, intelligent and levelheaded.

Rennie Carol
Student assistant to Andrea Thomas at the high school. Has a high-pitched voice. Likes to sing. Knows something about car mechanics (from her brothers). Drives a convertible.

Tut
Pet crow / myna bird (referred to as both, between the episodes and the accompanying comic books) of Andrea Thomas and of Isis that helps out occasionally when needed. Has a perch in Andrea's classroom, as well as in her Camaro. Likes sweets.

Colleen Corrigan as Isis flying over the pyramids with a little help from Robert Gillis and his photo-editing program! An avid fan, she even took a trip to California to visit Reseda High School, the school used for the show (more on that later!). "I ran around every part of that school that I could possibly get near or close to," she says. Photo courtesy of Colleen Corrigan.

New York City freelance artist Liza Biggers has crafted her own interpretation of our hero, as shown here in an appearance Biggers made at Meadowlands, New Jersey, in July 2005. Photo courtesy of James R. Green Jr.

Oh, mighty Isis! Schoolteacher Andrea Thomas transforms into the amazing, ancient figure in issue 3 of the original comic book series.

> “I still think that the real beauty a woman has comes from the inside out. She can be given all the bones, structure, and the education money can buy. And if she's not a beautiful person, I don't think she's a beautiful woman.”
> — Joanna Cameron, on the "Merv Griffin Show," 1977-78

EPISODES

Your guide to the action of "Isis"

The show begins with the rousing, "Oh, my queen, said the royal sorcerer to Hatshepsut, with this amulet, you and your descendants are endowed by the goddess Isis with the powers of the animals and the elements ... You will soar as the falcon soars, run with the speed of gazelles and command the elements of sky and earth ..." Now science teacher Andrea Thomas has dug up the treasured amulet 3,000 years after those words were spoken, to be endowed with the magical powers of Isis.

"The Lights of Mystery Mountain"
Production #82003
September 6, 1975
Shooting: July 23, 1975
Written by Russell Bates; directed by Hollingsworth Morse.
In Andrea Thomas' classroom, student Cindy Lee has returned from a hike on Mystery Mountain with photos of what appear to be flying saucers, and she tells about the disappearances of campers as well as burned spots of earth in the area. Andrea and fellow teacher Rick Mason take Cindy back up to Mountain Park to show the sheriff her photos, but

The DVD set includes the scripts from the episodes, such as this one from the pilot. The scripts were followed pretty closely in what ended up on screen, but it's fun to note little deviations.

he's skeptical. Andrea decides to run some tests on a burned area. But then Andrea, Rick, Cindy and Sheriff Harley get called to an abandoned vehicle found at the park, and they hear strange sounds and see the moving lights in the sky, themselves. Cindy runs to the car for her camera, then gets picked up by her convertible-driving friends Art Byron and Chick Jeffers, whom we suspect are up to no good! Rick and Andrea think Cindy is missing, and the fact that a fresh burned spot has shown up on the ground doesn't help. While Cindy is distracted, Art and Chick show her photos to a businessman named Joel Moss, who wants the negatives. The three students flee Moss then find the sheriff and point him toward Moss, who tries to get away. Not if Andrea has anything to do with it: For the first time ever, we see her call to "Oh, mighty Isis" and transform into the powerful ancient goddess, then commanding, "Oh zephyr winds which blow on high, lift me now so I can fly." She then commands the sun to overheat his car, stranding him. She calls on the ancient sphinx to torment him with the same flying lights he's been faking at the park. Turns out, he had discovered gold on the land and was trying to coerce people to sell their property to him. He, of course, is apprehended, and Art and Chick show proper remorse for agreeing to play the UFO pranks for him, confessing all.

Moral: Having a little fun or playing a joke is never an excuse to do what you know is the wrong thing. "Before you play a joke on someone," Isis says in the moral segment at the end of the episode, "ask yourself, how would you like it if they were playing the joke on you?"

This episode, though the first to air, was actually the second one shot, with "Fool's Dare" being the first in the can. In an amusing moment, Cindy wonders why Andrea is never around when Isis is, and Rick comments that perhaps all the excitement would be too much for the science teacher. Hatshepsut was a real Egyptian monarch, ruling from 1479 to 1458 B.C. as the fifth pharaoh of the 18th dynasty.

"Fool's Dare"
Production #82007
September 13, 1975
Shooting: July 8, 1975
Written by David Dworski; directed by Hollingsworth Morse.
Dr. Barnes tells Andrea and Rick how nine cars have been stolen in the area in the past couple weeks. Andrea parks at the public library, and the two thieves promptly hot-wire her hot red Camaro. Cindy is biking with her pals Ernie and Frank, meanwhile, when they come up to the junkyard. The two boys explain how they once snuck into the place and that girls could never do such a daring thing *(furthering the women's lib hintings begun in the show's pilot)*. Cindy takes their dare, though. The boys then take off and leave her there alone. Andrea, meanwhile, emerges from the library to find a big empty parking space where her car used to be. She hikes it back to the school and tells Rick what happened, bringing with her a soiled rag she found on the ground to examine under the microscope. She finds evidence of paint and recalls a newspaper story of two years earlier about car thieves, one of whom, Sam Niles, got away. At the junkyard, Cindy, who fell and hurt her ankle, spies Andrea's Camaro being brought in. She secretly watches as they begin painting the

car right then and there. She's almost discovered when she accidentally knocks over a spare hood. Frank and Ernie, worried about Cindy, return to the junkyard, in time to meet up with Rick and Andrea, who've been checking junkyards looking for Niles. Knowing Cindy could be in danger, Andrea summons the power of her amulet to transform to Isis. She tracks down the perps, hurling some tires to detain them.

Moral: When someone tries to convince you to do something that seems wrong, listen to your own voice and heart about the matter. "Doing anything that you know is wrong is dumb, because you're the one who'll pay for it," Isis says.

"I remember that episode really well," Joanna Pang Atkins says in her interview for the DVD set. "It was the first day. I had to ride a bike, and I hadn't ridden a bike for years and years. ... We had to go to this junkyard, and I had to climb this fence and jump into the junkyard, and I was thinking it's a good thing I had a dance background because you had to be athletic to do this part."

Isis' black bird Tut — sometimes referred to as a crow and sometimes as a myna bird — is introduced in Andrea's classroom, then helps Isis at the junkyard in her search for the car thieves. The amulet in Isis' tiara shows her that the thieves are in the junkyard; it's an occasionally used device for the superhero.

In the scripts for both of the first two episodes, Cindy refers to Andrea as Miss Mason rather than Miss Thomas, though it was, of course, corrected in filming. The script for this episode called for Andrea's car to be painted blue by the thieves, adjusted to yellow in the filming. Another discrepancy: In the script, Tut speaks, greeting Dr. Barnes by name when he first enters the classroom at the beginning and commenting on the new color of Andrea's car at the end.

"The Spots of the Leopard"
Production #82005
September 20, 1975
Shooting: July 28, 1975
Written by James Schmerer; directed by Arnold Laven.
Jenny Nelson is coming out of the grocery store with her dad when they witness a kid stealing her friend Jimmie's bicycle. Jenny's dad Chuck does nothing to stop it, leery because he just got out of prison. In Andrea's classroom, she, Rick and Cindy (and Tut) are discussing recent burglaries in the area. Back at Jenny's home, insurance investigator Tom Jenkins drops by to talk with Chuck. Jenkins, who helped send Chuck to prison, thinks the ex-con may be involved in the recent burglaries, though he denies it. Jenny is worried because her dad lied about being home last night. She confides in Miss Thomas, who expresses to Rick later her positive impression of the ex-con despite this new suspicion cast on him. Jenny's dad ushers her off on an impromptu camping trip, right after she spies his wallet full of fresh cash. When Jenny doesn't show up to school, Andrea, Rick and Cindy go to the Nelson home and learn from the neighbors that the Nelsons have evidently gone camping. But Andrea suspects trouble, changing to Isis and flying in just in time to free Jenny from a log that has trapped her after a fall. She encourages the girl to have faith in her father and trust that things are not always as they seem. But Jenkins comes around again to see Jenny's dad, this time enlisting his expertise in setting a trap for the thief. Chuck decides on a deviation from the plan — he wants to catch the thief himself and clear his name once and for all. As the thief loads the beautiful diamonds into a briefcase, the witnessing Chuck comes face to face with ... Jenkins! And this insurance investigator has a not-so-nice turn-about planned — claiming he just caught Chuck red-handed with the jewels. But Isis has arrived, and she heard otherwise. She lifts the getaway car so it can't get away, in time for the police to arrive. So Jenny learns that "having faith in someone you love is worth all the effort," as Andrea says.

Moral: Sometimes things aren't as they appear to be, and faith in your loved ones is worth all the effort if they're accused of doing something wrong. "If they have," Isis says, "it'll come out soon enough, but if they haven't, they need someone who'll believe in them when others won't. That's what being a true friend really means."

Andrea's car has kept the pale yellow paint job the car thieves gave it in the previous episode, since Andrea had quipped that she didn't really like red anyway. Tut speaks in this episode. There are hints of a "close" friendship between Andrea and Rick as she pledges to cook him dinner in exchange for his help painting her apartment. This is the first episode featuring more than one Isis appearance. Though Andrea is described as a science teacher in the show's opening, she mentions in this episode that she teaches chemistry.

"The Sound of Silence"
Production #82008
September 27, 1975
Shooting: July 30, 1975
Written by Sid Morse; directed by Arnold Laven.
Andrea has been experimenting with a device that emits a force field, which she calls a Circlegard, and she demonstrates it to Rick, Dr. Barnes, Cindy and fellow student Bill Cady. The highly intelligent Bill has some anger issues over losing the science contest and its prize money, which would have enabled him to get a car. He hits up his friend B.J. Tanker, who recently went clean, for the location of a sinister former contact, Jack Evans. Later, the Circlegard is missing from Andrea's classroom. Andrea suspects Bill, but she and her colleagues also realize the Circlegard is emitting some dangerous radiation. Bill has gone off to demo the device to Evans and his flunky Jocko, hoping to sell it to them. Andrea learns from B.J. just who it is Bill has gone to see, and she transforms to Isis and takes to the sky. Evans, meanwhile, wants a "more practical" demo of the device, planning a bank robbery with this new tool — with the reluctant help of Bill. They then see Andrea approaching the gate of Evans' plush pad. Jocko "detains" her inside the house. Dr. Barnes, Rick and Cindy learn from B.J. that Andrea went to see Evans. Andrea, meanwhile, is able to communicate with Tut, outside the window. The bird then provides a distraction by ringing the doorbell, and Andrea gets away. She changes to Isis and flies off in pursuit of Evans and Jocko, who have fled by car, with Bill their captive. She commands lightning to fell a tree in the path of their car. When Evans and Jocko try to flee on foot, Isis uses trees again, this time enclosing them in a wall of trees. The two perps try to entice Bill to use the Circlegard against Isis, but our powerful hero pauses and allows him to do the right thing.

Moral: Stealing is never right, even if it's for desperate or noble reasons. "We all know that two wrongs don't make a right," Isis says. "They only make things worse."

A young and fluffy-haired Leigh McCloskey plays Bill, just a few short years before he would enchant Lucy Ewing as Mitch Cooper on "Dallas." Here he's high-strung and a bit dark, quite a departure from the young doc on Southfork. The script for this episode called for a deviation from Isis' "Oh, zephyr winds ..." mantra for flying, though it was not used in filming: "Sister goddess RoHaLind, let me ride thy mighty wind!"

"The Outsider"
Production #82016
October 4, 1975
Shooting: August 4, 1975 in Franklin Canyon
Written by David and Susan Dworski; directed by Hollingsworth Morse. The new student in town, Wayne Moss, is extremely talented where knowledge of the environment is concerned, but he's catching a lot of flak from fellow students who think he's a hick. Andrea is trying to encourage him, but two football players, Charlie Michaels and Phil Hobbs, are plotting to frame him for the theft of rival Westside High's mascot, a raccoon. Cindy catches up to Wayne at a local pond and sees the way he has with plants and animals. Rick and Andrea hear that Westside High's mascot has been stolen and wonder if Wayne was involved. Back at the pond, Wayne is upset to see that a housing development will soon go up on the land, so he takes to the nearby bulldozer to rip down the sign. The machine is out of his control, though. Andrea arrives on the scene and changes to Isis. She commands the force of gravity to allow her to roll a rock uphill in the path of the bulldozer. The irate construction foreman, Mr. Tilden, then arrives and chastises Wayne. Andrea also arrives and suggests a more legal way to stop this housing development, but the operation has already been cleared by the local government. Rick also arrives, and together they decide to appeal to the land's owner, Har Winstead. The "ecology study" Rick shows to Winstead is Wayne's book of notes on the pond, which shows the landowner just how much wildlife his holding supports. With Winstead's approval, they then must race to stop the construction worker from setting the initial blast. Isis steps in to handle that one quite handily. And wouldn't you know — Charlie and Phil are at a loss as to

how to care for the ailing raccoon they stole, needing the help of the fellow student they bullied.

Moral: Don't ridicule others because they're different — embrace and learn from the differences.

This author hasn't heard that mean label "dink" — uttered by Charlie and Phil in reference to Wayne — since her big brother used to say it around this same time period, the mid-'70s. A costuming change was made for Wayne from the script, which called for him to wear bib overalls. A bit too much of the stereotype, perhaps? Or maybe it would've been too similar to Cindy Lee's own outfit of overalls, since Wayne shares so many scenes with her in this episode. And that little pause Wayne gives as he watches Isis leave the scene after stopping the explosion at the end was meant to imply he knows her secret, reinforced a bit more by the actor when he playfully asks Andrea if she got "lost" in the woods while all this action was taking place.

"Rockhound's Roost"
Production #82010
October 11, 1975
Shooting: August 13, 1975 in Malibu Canyon
Written by Robert F. Joseph; directed by Arnold Laven.
Kevin McCauley collides on his bike with new foreign student Fabian, copping a big attitude all the while. Fabian arrives to school late, bringing his rock collection for Andrea's lesson on rocks and minerals. Andrea is working it out so Fabian can go on the class field trip to Rockhound's Roost, but Kevin is still flinging the 'tude, especially when Fabian says he talked to his dad. Kevin wants to get out of his chores at home, so he fakes his dad's sig on the trip's permission slip. On the field trip, Andrea witnesses Kevin throwing the dishes he was supposed to wash into the river and decides to teach him a lesson in responsibility, changing to Isis to restore the dishes to where they belong. As Andrea, she then asks Kevin about the dishes and baits him into his lie. She wonders why Kevin changed his mind about this field trip he didn't want to go on. Kevin goes with Fabian to gather firewood for the group. Rick learns that Mr. McCauley never really signed the permission slip for the trip. In the woods, as Fabian tries to stop Kevin from skipping out on the field trip as he is planning, a menacing bear is nearby. The two walk and

BEHIND THE SCENES: MALIBU CANYON FRANKLIN CANYON

The setting of Malibu Canyon was used for "Rockhound's Roost." Malibu Canyon is a chief pass through the Santa Monica Mountains, where the Malibu Creek flows, and Malibu Canyon Road is a major north-south route connecting the coast to the inland valley, Wikipedia says. Numerous movies and TV shows have been filmed in the area, such as "Planet of the Apes" and "M*A*S*H."

Franklin Canyon was used for shooting "The Outsider," and appropriately so, since it is home to a diverse array of plant life and indigenous wildlife. Franklin Canyon Park is a public park near Benedict Canyon at the eastern end of the Santa Monica Mountains, Wikipedia says. The 605-acre park features a three-acre lake, a duck pond and five miles of hiking trails. The park was used for the opening credits of "The Andy Griffith Show," for one thing, but also for a wealth of other filming over the years. We're talking "Bonanza," "The Brady Bunch," "Murder She Wrote," "Criminal Minds," "Twin Peaks," even our fave "Dynasty." The duck pond was used in "On Golden Pond."

Malibu Canyon, looking north (upstream), in Los Angeles County. Photo by user IngerAlHaosului from Wikimedia Commons.

Franklin Canyon Pond, California. Photo from the U.S. National Park Service, public domain.

talk, and Kevin learns that though Fabian will someday be a ruler in his native country, he still embraces the responsibilities of more servantly work. The bear approaches them, and Kevin steps in to divert the creature from Fabian, whose foot is trapped by a rock. Isis arrives and commands the sun to enclose the bear in a circle of fire. Rick also arrives. The bear retreats when the circle of fire does. Back at the class' campsite, Andrea is treated to Rick's tale of his daring exploits with the bear.

Moral: Don't shirk your responsibilities; they build character. "Being responsible means knowing the right thing to do, and doing it," our hero says.

Andrea gets a little variety in her wardrobe in this one, veering from the denim skirt she has been wearing thus far to khaki slacks.

"Lucky"
Production #82011
October 18, 1975
Shooting: August 18, 1975
Written by Ann Udell; directed by Hollingsworth Morse.
The young, freckle-faced Randy Martin, about to begin high school, loves his smart dog, Lucky. Randy aspires to be a veterinarian, he tells Andrea. The 10-year-old Lucky is also the school's mascot, and he seems to be a lucky charm for the baseball team, which has been winning every game. At the beach, Cindy and Randy run into students from a rival school, Central, who do some trash-talking about the upcoming game. Lucky dives into the water for a ball and is in danger of drowning in an undertow. But not when Isis is around. She first retrieves Randy, who went in after the dog, then charges back in for the canine. Afterward, she must take the terribly weakened Lucky to Dr. Rogers at the animal hospital. Back at her classroom, Andrea gets the downer of a call from Dr. Rogers: The unexpected swim was a bit much for the aged pet. She must break the news to Randy, who is heartbroken. He wanders off to a dangerous, closed-off dam area, where the water pressure is being tested. It's a good thing Isis tracks him down there, because Randy gets injured on the rocks just before the water is going to flow. She rescues the boy then explains to him how precious things like plants and animals must live and die in a cycle of life. And to further the lesson, Glenn, one of the students from Central, has a special gift for Randy.

Moral: Life means living and dying. "Losing something we love is never easy, but it's a part of growing up," Isis says. "The cycle of life is all around us. If you look, you'll see it everywhere, in flowers, animals, people. But remember, every ending is also a beginning."

Kudos to Joanna Cameron for the scene where Andrea is on the phone with Dr. Rogers — she really nails the emotion. This could have been a brutal episode for any young pet-lover, but Isis' gentle instruction for Randy at the end redeems the subject matter to a valuable and touching lesson on life.

In a forgivable continuity error that would certainly be carried on in the "Wonder Woman" series, Isis lands in front of Randy at the dam wearing her high-heel boots, then is shown stepping toward him on the rocks in flat boots.

"Bigfoot"
Production #82012
October 18, 1975
Shooting: September 9, 1975
Written by J. Michael Reaves; directed by Arthur H. Nadel.
On a class trip to the woods, Cindy and fellow student Lee Webster swear they've seen a Bigfoot monster. Isis decides to investigate and finds some oversized footprints. Back at Andrea's class, Dr. Barnes encourages the students to not be quick to believe rumors. Lee, Mickey and some fellow students, though, decide on their own to go on a little expedition for this "fabled" creature. Lee wanders off alone and gets injured, encountering a scruffy, woods-dwelling man, who assists him. Cindy lets Andrea and Rick know that the boys have gone hunting with their cameras. Isis goes looking for them, getting a hand (wing?) from Tut in her search. She finds the other boys and helps them make their way out of the woods before continuing her search for Lee. Lee, meanwhile, has established a rapport with the gigantic woodsman, who explains that he has retreated from people who don't understand him. The hefty man makes an attempt to retrieve Lee's fallen camera, but the rope he's using breaks. Isis to the rescue: She commands the rope to safely encircle and lift him. The goddess then invites this "Bigfoot" of a man, whose name is Richard, to come back to civilization with them. Maybe at some future point he will.

Moral: Don't judge a book by its cover or believe everything you hear; gather the facts. "It's the way a person acts, not the way he looks, that is what counts," Isis says.

When Rick corrals Andrea from the woods, explaining that it's not safe and she's "not Isis," Andrea lifts an eyebrow at the camera. It's not the first time she's done that! Her little play with Rick's collar was ad-libbed from the script, however, as is her comment to Tut on her favorite poem later in her classroom.

This episode reflects the popularity in the '70s of the Bigfoot / Sasquatch lore. Bigfoot also made appearances on the "Six Million Dollar Man" and "Bionic Woman" series and was the topic of movies like "The Legend of Boggy Creek." The man who plays "Bigfoot" in this episode, Bill Engesser, towers over both Scott Colomby and Joanna Cameron, as the three are shown standing together, and you get more of a feel for how this rather-petite superheroine's build differs from the amazon Lynda Carter as Wonder Woman, debuting the following month. Once in a while, Andrea daringly speaks to Rick without her eyeglasses, including at the very beginning of this episode.

In this one we also see the trick of the rope moving on its own to encircle the woodsman and then rising toward the sky to Isis, in flight. Writer J. Michael Reaves says in the DVD extras, "The stunts in 'Isis,' as you can imagine, were always a bit of a hard thing to come up with. ... When you're producing a TV show on a budget of like a dollar ninety-eight, and you don't have access to computer graphics or anything of the cool stuff that we have today, you have to get a little inventive. There were only so many times you could see Isis or Captain Marvel grab a hold of a car bumper and stop the car from driving. You had to come up with other stuff. ... We kept having to come up with stunts that were interesting and original and would take like nothing to do. It was hard."

"To Find a Friend" *(sometimes listed as "How to Find a Friend")*
Production #82013
October 25, 1975
Shooting: August 20, 1975
Written by Henry Colman; directed by Hollingsworth Morse.
The young Tom Anderson really loves mini-bikes and badly wants to ride one. But he has trouble making friends, and the only way he can get on a bike is to trade an item. He gets his dad's gun and shows it to biker Joe, but Joe tests it out, breaks a nearby headlight, then zooms off with the gun before Tom can stop him. It's Andrea's birthday, meanwhile, and Rick and Cindy have a cake for her. Rick also needs her help with Tom, who's been giving him trouble in class. Tom skips class, and Andrea and Rick know something's up. They find him at the motocross track, and he comes clean. Isis decides she must find this Joe guy, so she commands time to replay the scene between Tom and Joe so she can get a look at him. At the Anderson house, Tom's dad tells Andrea and Rick the gun, an old war souvenir, is more dangerous than they realize and could explode. They comb through the yearbooks, but Cindy makes a good point in that this Joe kid might be a dropout(!). They scout around town, unsuccessfully. Andrea uses her amulet to secretly help Tom remember another clue — that Joe made a reference to hunting rabbits. Isis finds him at a popular hunting spot, and she again commands time, now freezing it so she can run up and grab the weapon out of Joe's hands.

Moral: You can't buy friends. "Real friends are those who like you for yourself, not because you give them presents," our hero says. Also, a gun is not a toy. "Play it safe — don't play with a gun."

Mike Lookinland, Bobby of "The Brady Bunch," is lighter-haired as Tom. This episode marks the first time Andrea flashes her amulet to someone, and the first time Isis commands time.

"The Show-Off"
Production #82015
November 1, 1975
Shooting: August 11, 1975
Written by David Wise and Kathleen Barnes; directed by Arnold Laven.
The Science Club Campout is on its way, and Steve Elwood is determined to show off and hang up the promotional banner in a dangerously high place atop the school building. The small-statured Steve has some issues, and he's angry when Isis arrives and lifts him off the edge of the building. Rick warns Andrea later that Steve's showing off could cause more problems. The class is then off on the campout. Steve and Cindy take a walk near the campsite to find firewood. Cindy steps into an animal trap, and Steve tries to play hero. The others arrive, and when Rick is the

The original comic books included a little side element of Cindy Lee hitting on Rick Mason (shown here in Isis' very first appearance, Shazam! issue 25). BRBTV asked Joanna Pang Atkins if she knew about that, and she laughingly said she didn't.

one who is able to release the trap, Steve is irate once again. Andrea talks to Steve, trying to encourage him to just be himself. But Steve thinks the girls will never go for a guy "whose only muscles are between his ears." The class then takes a hike, so to speak, but learns from a zookeeper that a gorilla is on the loose in the hiking area, Craggy Glen. Andrea changes to Isis. On the hiking trail, Rick and the students are in the path of a landslide and must take refuge in a cave on the hillside. And what else is in the cave but ... the gorilla, of course. The opening to the cave is obstructed, but Isis arrives. She holds off a cave-in then commands the gorilla to help clear the cave opening.

Moral: Don't try to show off; just be yourself. "Respect is something that must be earned," Isis says, "and the best way to start is by being honest with yourself. Trying to be someone you're not only makes you look foolish, and sometimes it can be very dangerous."

When both Andrea and Isis tell Rick that his fishing hat might actually frighten the fish away, he begins to wonder if Andrea could be Isis (his, "Hey, she couldn't be --?" was ad-libbed from the script). It's funny, also, that when Isis finds Rick's garish hat by the hillside cave where the group is trapped, she calls out to him, and he answers her back by name — correctly, not as Andrea. Isis has a similarity to Wonder Woman with her "way with animals."

"No Drums, No Trumpets"
Production #82021
November 15, 1975
Shooting: September 12, 1975
Written by Arthur H. Nadel; directed by Hollingsworth Morse.
The science fair is underway in Larkspur, and Fred Wieting gives a demonstration of his ham radio for Dr. Barnes. But Dr. Barnes announces someone else as the winner of the fair, and Fred's very unhappy with being a runner-up. He speeds out of the Larkspur High parking lot. Andrea takes off after him in Rick's car. Fred goes over a hill in his little convertible and is left in a very precarious perch. Along comes Isis, who commands the winds to push the car back up the hill. Rick, Cindy and science fair winner Dorothy Bieder arrive to find Fred safe. As Andrea drives Fred and Dorothy back in Rick's car, they make a little detour to a ghost town near Larkspur, half because they're out of gas and half as a point of curiosity. Strange things start to happen, and Andrea goes inside

one of the buildings to investigate. She falls off some decrepit old stairs. The trio then find the van described in a recently publicized local robbery, realizing this ghost town is a hideout for crooks. But then Andrea realizes something worse after the robbers find them — she lost her Isis amulet in her fall. As the robbers, which include Jim Danch and his cohorts Terry and Drain, are loading up their van, Fred is able to secretly get his ham radio and call for help, a distress signal that is also picked up by Rick and Cindy in Andrea's car. Unaware, the robbers then take Rick's car keys from Andrea and tell the captives to start walking. As one of the perps discovers the car is out of gas, Andrea locates her amulet and changes to Isis. She imprisons the one perp by commanding the spirits of this ghost town to assemble the walls of an old shack around him, then the police arrive. She flies off to intercept the fleeing van, commanding the clouds to surround it.

Moral: Not winning a contest doesn't make you a loser. It's how you handle losing that determines who you are.

A spooky ghost town setting and some dangerous crooks lend a fresh splash of intrigue to this one. It's noted in the DVD set that the scene with the old shack surrounding the perp was shot backward. The name of Andrea's school is rarely mentioned on the show, except, perhaps, for the episode "Lucky," when students from rival school Central call it Mid-City (a name included in the script, as well). Here, we get a shot of the cornerstone of science fair host Larkspur High, built in 1938, which is mentioned in the script as being in the same state as Andrea's school, and the slightly variant dialogue in the script also has Andrea remarking that Larkspur is the area where she grew up.

A young and cherubic Christopher Norris of "Trapper John, M.D." and "Santa Barbara" portrays Dorothy Bieder. The expressive Mark Lambert, who portrays Fred Wieting, however, out-acts everybody in this one. In an amusing twist, Isis plays with Rick once again, saying the same thing that Andrea says, this time telling him he needs to fix the gas gauge in his car.

Voted best episode of the series by BRBTV. Fave quote: "Sometimes you learn more by losing than by winning," Rick tells Cindy.

"Funny Gal"
*Production #82030
November 22, 1975
Shooting: September 2, 1975
Written by Sid Morse; directed by Hollingsworth Morse.
First of three appearances of Captain Marvel.*
The overweight Carrie Anson likes to draw attention to herself with strange outfits and equally strange stunts. But when she's behind the wheel of a car out of control, Isis steps in. After the danger is over, Carrie has no interest in Isis' words of encouragement to feel better about herself. Andrea, Rick and Cindy then have a picnic lunch, where Rick successfully scams some food off the two ladies amid their playfulness. Cindy hatches the idea to start a campaign for Carrie as student body president. Carrie's good friend Gregg Aley is signed on to that. Carrie overhears their plans, and it deflates her further. But Gregg is tired of her constant self-putdowns. Rick invites Andrea and Cindy to his boat, though the Star Tracker never seems to leave the dock — Rick puts the girls to work on the vessel instead. Carrie sees Rick's boat as a potential tool for her campaign and wants to borrow it. Slim chance of that, so she decides to steal it. Out on the water, she radios a fake mayday as part of a campaign publicity stunt. The stunt's on her, though, because there's trouble with the boat's engine and a storm is moving in. Isis tracks her but the job is too much for her; she commands Tut to find Captain Marvel for some assistance. He heads in her direction, and Isis holds off the storm. Captain Marvel arrives at the boat and swims it to shore by rope. Carrie, of course, realizes how silly she's been.

Moral: You can't expect other people to like you unless you like yourself first. "Each of us has many things we can be proud of," Isis says. "So don't put yourself down."

John Davey, the second person to wear the Captain Marvel costume in the companion "Shazam!" series, makes his first of three appearances here. Likewise, Isis makes three appearances on "Shazam!" On the picnic, Rick tells Andrea that he's going to get married as soon as he finds someone who "looks like Isis and cooks like you." As with Steve Trevor in "Wonder Woman," Rick doesn't seem to find the alter-ego beautiful. Silly boy.

"Girl Driver"
Production #82018
November 29, 1975
Shooting: August 25, 1975
Written by David Wise and Kathleen Barnes; directed by Arnold Laven.
Cindy tells Andrea the latest: There's a girl running for Auto Club president, Freddie (Frederica) Charleton. Her chief competition, Mac Lennard, stops by the Charletons' garage and belittles her mechanical skill. "Talk about a chauvinist pig!" she says. Amid their trash-talking, Mac inadvertently starts a gas fire. Isis arrives and commands the fire to disappear. The heroine has some strong words for the rival students. Back in the classroom, Rick hatches the idea of a rally to decide the matter between Mac and Freddie. But Mac decides a drag race on the street would settle things better. Cindy has a tough time but finally talks Freddie down from it, despite the obnoxious Mac's tauntings. At the rally, moderator Dr. Barnes cautions the two that this is not a race; it's a test of skill and attention to details and checkpoints. Mac, since he's such a jerk, cheats in the rally by hiding a sign that Freddie will need for directions. When Freddie falls behind, Andrea is suspicious, changing to Isis and using her amulet to see the moment when Mac stole the sign. She then calls on Mother Earth to block the path of the rally with a fallen lightpole. It forces Mac and Freddie to work together to clear the road — and the air. When they resume their drive, Mac's car goes out of control with a tire blowout and goes off a cliff, and Isis commands the winds to carry it safely to the ground. Mac realizes Freddie is a good sport and he forfeits the rally to her.

Moral: Cheaters never prosper, and males and females should have equal opportunities. "Not too many years ago," Isis explains in the moral shot at the end, "there were a lot of jobs that people thought were just for men. But times are changing, and today there are no jobs that are not open to qualified people whether they be men or women. Each of us should have the chance to do whatever we dream, be it mechanic, astronaut or president of the United States."

We learn there's a Logan City nearby this setting (though it's called Mason City in the script). In her snazziest save yet, Isis lands smack-dab on the hood of Mac's car, in a shot showing only the backs of her legs, just before commanding the wind to float them to the safety of the ground. Though the name doesn't come up in the episodes, the scripts refer to Andrea's pendant as the Thutmose pendant.

"Scuba Duba"
Production #82019
December 6, 1975
Shooting: August 27, 1975 at Hansen Dam
Written by Sid Morse; directed by Arnold Laven.
An eagle's nest has been spotted at Rocky Point, and bird-lovers Steve Conrad and Nancy go investigate. They want to get a photo of the eggs, so Steve foolishly uses a frayed rope to lower himself to the mountain ledge where the nest is. Andrea drives by, in search of the nest herself, and sees him just as the rope breaks. She changes to Isis and commands the rope to come back together to save Steve. Isis lectures Steve on equipment safety. The lesson is lost on him, though, and his eyes glaze over as Rick then discusses safety in the scuba class. Mr. Mason is concerned about this student. At the next scuba class, Steve is careless with checking his equipment and heads out diving alone even though he knows he needs to wait for his partner, Nancy. He gets caught underwater. Andrea changes to Isis and sees through her amulet that Steve is in trouble. She arrives at the dock and dives right in with Rick's tank. She's able to save Steve, but Rick is torqued off at his problem student. Steve's heartfelt apology softens his punishment.

Moral: Rules are there for a reason. "Safety first means nothing is more important than being sure you think before you act," Isis says.

The script called for the nest discovery at the beginning of the episode to be that of a condor, subject to what kind of stock footage could be obtained. Also, when Isis arrives at the eagle's nest and unites the rope's frayed pieces, her original scripted command used the word "hemp."

Though it's been said by multiple people that Joanna Cameron did not use a stunt double as Isis, this episode features a rare time that she did, according to the information on the DVD set — for the underwater scene.

"Dreams of Flight"
Production #82020
December 13, 1975
Written by David and Susan Dworski; directed by Hollingsworth Morse.
Both Chela Montoya and Mark Dawson are skilled at building model airplanes, but Mark's bragging is a big turnoff, particularly to Cindy. Chela's brother Raul doesn't want her building model planes like the

boys. Andrea has a chat with Raul to see if she can convince him to let Chela enter the model design contest for Aeronautics Day. White boy Mark then does some racist trash-talking to the Hispanic Raul. This sways Raul's opinion about Chela's involvement in the contest. An artist, Raul also has been having some difficulty getting started on painting a large mural project. Mark returns to taunt Raul a second time, and Raul chases him through the barrio, then getting trapped in the back of a semi-truck. He soon finds himself in danger when the truck rolls out of control, and Isis must step in and save him. Mark, meanwhile, steals Chela's model plane. Andrea and Rick suspect Mark and visit a hobby store, speaking to Bill Sherwood and learning that Mark bought a part for the plane there. Raul finds Mark at a quarry on the dried-up riverbed and again chases him down. To escape, Mark gets caught in a precarious position, hanging from a catwalk. Isis arrives and commands the winds to lift him gently to the ground. Mark regrets his actions toward Raul and his sister. Raul is able to finish his mural, inspired by Chela — and assisted by Mark.

Moral: It doesn't make sense to put someone down because they have a different background. "What does make sense is treating others just the way we want them to treat us," Isis says.

Writer David Dworski, who credits his wife Susan with this story, says in the DVD extras that the idea came from their driving around in East L.A. and seeing the murals that graced the barrios. They hired local kids as extras, as well. Reseda High School was the real-life setting for Andrea's school, and a quarry in East L.A. was also featured in this episode, through which Raul chases Mark. "The 'Dreams of Flight' mural gave us the whole story," Dworski says, "because in the mural, and you see it at the end of the picture, a couple of times fairly close up, you see the dreams of Latino aspiration in an Aztec god who's winged and flying through air. You see astronauts and rocket ships going to the moon, and you see the moon. You see a little girl sitting in a rubber tire hung from a tree in her backyard and she's got a model airplane in her lap, and she's dreaming of flying. You see a couple of young kids in there also playing with model airplanes in the big mural. And once we had that, we had the story, because this was the dream of youngsters everywhere, to fly, to go to the moon, to fly fast planes, to invent them, to build them and so forth. And all of it was wrapped up in this one mural."

Season 2

"The Seeing Eye Horse"
Production #82022
September 11, 1976
Written by Peter L. Dixon and Sarah Dixon; directed by Earl Bellamy.
The blind Noah Schuster just underwent an operation to regain his sight, but when Dr. Blankfort removes his bandages, the surgery proves to be unsuccessful. He's upset, though Andrea encourages him to still aspire to great dreams. When Noah goes riding, the horse gets spooked. Isis rescues Noah, who's more upset than ever (but who also notes that this heroine sounds just like his teacher Miss Thomas!). Andrea has an idea to get Noah a horse specially trained for the blind — a seeing eye horse. But Noah is hesitant to warm up to this new horse, Sunny. In his frustration, the boy knocks over the glass jug from a water cooler next to the stable, and a fire is started between the glass, the straw and the blazing sun. The horse wanders off, and when Noah goes to look for him, he falls off the dock and into the water, unable to swim. Sunny dutifully goes into the water to bring the boy back out. Noah then tries to lead the horse to the trail back to the stable, where the fire is now blazing. He gets close enough and realizes there's a fire, but he's still afraid to ride the horse. The horse crouches down to the ground to help the boy aboard, then he's able to ride in and try to free the other horses from the barn. Tut, who now has his own perch in Andrea's car, flies to the fire and frets appropriately, then flies off to warn Andrea. She changes to Isis and commands the clouds to send rain and "quench the flame," then rescues Noah from the danger.

Moral: Meet your fears head-on, or they'll beat you.

The new student friend to Andrea and Rick, Rennie Carol, is ushered in with no introduction, and no reference is made to Cindy Lee and her disappearance. The opening sequence is changed to reflect Rennie, with a retaping of the voiceover segment to add Rennie's name. Isis' hair is also changed for this second season: It's now full and wavy and just below her shoulders, rather than arrow-straight and to her waist. In addition, the superheroine's eye makeup is amped up, further differentiating her appearance from that of Andrea. New stock footage of Andrea changing to Isis and calling out to the "zephyr winds" is filmed to accommodate the changes. Special note to any grammarian out there bothered by the use of "which" instead of "that" in the "zephyr winds" mantra: The writers corrected it in the scripts, such as the one for this episode, then it was corrected in later filmed segments!

"The Hitchhiker"
Production #82023
September 18, 1976
Written by Sid Morse; directed by Earl Bellamy.
Joann Clayton and Hope Carswell have been warned about hitchhiking, but they're not paying attention. They get into the wrong car with the wrong guys, though, Charlie and Steve, and their speeding gets them chased by the cops. Andrea and Rick are out horseback riding when they see the car chase. Andrea changes to Isis and heads off after them. She commands molecules to be separated so that the boys run right through a roadblock, then she stops time and reverses it after the car heads right over a cliff. Once rescued, Joann swears off hitchhiking. But Hope? Not so much. Then, in class, Andrea performs a chemistry experiment meant to reinforce the point about danger to Hope and Joann. Rick, who's still sore from the horseback ride, is having car trouble, and Rennie tries to help him out. He instead decides to hitch a ride with Andrea. Hope and Joann have insisted they won't hitchhike again, but when it comes time for that weekend's picnic, Charlie comes by the bus stop and offers them a ride. Hope takes him up on it, against Joann's better judgment. Later, Hope doesn't show up to the picnic, and Andrea smells trouble when Joann finally confesses that Hope hitched a ride with Charlie. After his high-speed antics, Charlie's car stalls on the train tracks. Isis arrives and commands a lightning bolt to come to her so she can fire up the engine, and Charlie moves the car off in time for a train to go whizzing by.

Moral: Don't take anything for granted — thrill-seeking and hitchhiking are not safe.

Barry Miller, who for a young guy is pretty charismatic, plays Charlie here, and also stars as Barney in the "Wonder Woman" episode "The Richest Man in the World."

"The Class Clown"
Production #82026
September 25, 1976
Written by Arthur Nadel and Norman Cameron; directed by Hollingsworth Morse.

Dr. Barnes introduces Rudy Horton, the new student at school. Rudy has quite a warped sense of humor, playing practical jokes on the other students. After a stunt in her class, Andrea has a chat with Rudy, explaining that making people laugh doesn't always mean making friends. But later, in her empty classroom, Rudy can't resist rigging up Stanley Crane's winning science project, a life raft, to inflate — with the help of a car parked outside — and thereby cause chaos and destruction in the lab. Isis arrives to help Rennie, who had gone to the class to feed Tut and got caught in the mess. Isis commands the smoke and fumes to clear and the broken beakers to be restored. The prime suspect: Rudy. They give him a chance to explain but forbid him from going on the class field trip. On the day of the trip, Andrea and Rennie stay behind to finish grading papers while Rick drives the bus of kids. They stop at a cafe, and Rudy secretly arrives behind them in his car. He gets under the hood of the bus for a little sabotage. When Rick starts up the bus, smoke comes bellowing out. Rudy then "arrives" to try to solve the problem and play the hero. But he didn't plan on the bus not playing along, and soon he's in the bus rolling down the hill and out of control. Andrea and Rick follow by car, and the bus crashes. Rudy crawls out of the wreckage, and Rick tumbles down the ravine to help him. Isis arrives and commands the smoke to form a staircase so that Rick and Rudy can climb back up the hill that the bus crashed down. When Andrea rejoins them, she's appropriately skeptical of this supposed "stairway of smoke."

Moral: Making people laugh doesn't always make friends, and practical jokes can lead to someone getting hurt.

Again, Andrea winks at the camera in this one. This episode marks the last appearance of Dr. Barnes, though he is referenced in the next couple.

"The Cheerleader"
Production #82025
October 2, 1976
Written by Sid Morse; directed by Hollingsworth Morse.
Rennie is alone in Andrea's classroom typing up the answer sheet for a big upcoming chemistry exam, and guarding the place like Fort Knox. Cheerleader Ann Taylor lures Tut away from the classroom, then reports to Rennie that the bird has taken off. While Rennie is off searching, Ann gets into the classroom and copies down the answers for the exam. She's got to get her grades up; she wants the No. 1 spot on the cheer squad, and her prime competition is Wynn, the current lead. Tut, meanwhile, is roaming the canyon and being eyed by predators like a coyote. The bird gets caught in a thicket, and Isis arrives just in time. She stops the animal in its tracks and gathers up her birdie. Back in class, it's time for the exam, and Ann uses her cheat key, while Wynn thinks through the answers. Ann then talks to squad captain Tom about that top cheerleader spot. But Tom keeps Wynn where she is, invoking Ann's further ire. She frames Wynn by putting her own answer key into Wynn's book. Andrea is skeptical that Wynn cheated, though, and talks to Wynn herself. Wynn knows exactly who set her up. Ann is upset that her setup still didn't displace Wynn from the squad, so she charges off half-cocked in a car. Isis follows by air, and Tom and Wynn by car. Ann gets out of her car and heads down a hill, but the still-running car slides down the hill toward her (and, like every bad horror flick we've ever seen, she keeps running right in the straight-and-narrow path of the car!). Isis commands for her to be lifted up into the air, out of the car's way. Afterward, Ann gets suspended from the squad for her cheating and frame-up.

Moral: Being No. 1 might not be as important as you think, and deceit is no way to get there.

This episode reinforces the idea of Rennie being a student assistant to Andrea, as she's shown not only typing up the answer key outside of class hours, but also sitting with Andrea at her desk while the students are taking the exam. Colleen Camp, Wynn here, originated the role of Kristin Shepard on "Dallas" just a couple years after this episode, a role later taken over — and made so deliciously famous — by Mary Crosby.

Laurette Spang, who was 25 here as Ann, already had quite a few TV credits on her resume. She went on to acclaim as Cassiopeia on the original "Battlestar Galactica." Just a couple months after this "Isis" episode originally aired, Spang appeared in the well-known "Charlie's Angels" episode "Consenting Adults," where Farrah Fawcett (then with the "-Majors") took to her skateboard for a daring escape, as we mentioned in the "Wonder Woman" section of this book. (This author recalls highly anticipating that skateboard scene, such an avid Farrah fan!!! Why do you think I begged Mother for a skateboard of my own!!!! Which my bro promptly broke by running it into the garage wall, but that's another story ...) Spang went on to play Mindy Lou on the 1981 "Dukes of Hazzard" episode "The Fugitive."

"Year of the Dragon"
Production #82027
October 16, 1976
Written by Ann Udell; directed by Hollingsworth Morse.
Andrea, Rick and Rennie are doing some shopping in Chinatown when they run into Andrea's student Julie Chen. She seems to be ashamed of her Chinese heritage and her father's occupation, which she lies about. Back in class, it's announced that Julie won a contest, along with classmate Dave Parker, but Julie doesn't want her father to be invited to the awards celebration. And she definitely doesn't want to be identified by her heritage. "Why do people assume I know everything from Charlie Chan movies to chop suey!" she tells Dave. She runs off, hiding in a car at the junkyard. Wouldn't you know it — that car is the next one to be demolished. Isis comes to the rescue, commanding the machinery to stop and for Julie to be lifted from the hanging car to the ground. But Julie doesn't want any more help. Later, Rennie stops by the Chens' shop, and Julie tells her she doesn't want her father coming to the awards celebration for her. She thinks her father and his outdated language and dress would be out of place, and she thinks she's sparing him from ridicule. Rennie tries to convince her otherwise. Later, Mr. Chen calls Andrea because he hasn't seen Julie, who also didn't show up to school. Rennie gets on the phone and tells Julie's father how upset the girl was. Julie has wandered off by herself, and she gets caught in a covered well. Mr. Chen goes looking for her. He decides to go into the well to get her, but it puts him in danger, too. Once he manages to help her out of the well, he slips further into it. Isis arrives and commands the nearby broken ladder to restore itself, then has it lowered into the well. When her father is rescued, Julie is very proud of him.

Moral: It's what is inside a person that's important, not the way they speak or dress.

In this season, the door to Andrea's classroom is often shown, and it bears a sign saying it's Lab 4. BRBTV admires Andrea's fashion sense in this episode: She's wearing a sharp, red, three-piece pantsuit as the action opens.

"Now You See It ..."
Production #82028
October 23, 1976
Written by Arthur Nadel, Len Janson and Chuck Menville; directed by Arthur Nadel.
Second appearance of Captain Marvel.
Rick Mason — a thief? Say it ain't so! OK, it ain't so — it's a man disguised to look just like him, stealing some equipment from a project called Operation Weathermaker. Elsewhere, Rennie is photographing the Amazing Ranji — magician and musician — as he rehearses. She even joins him for a song as Andrea and Rick watch from the stands. The authorities arrive to arrest Rick for stealing the top-secret weather machine. Ranji and Rennie gather the troops — their friends Feather Robbins and C.J. Howe — to solve this case and free Mr. Mason. Andrea sees Rennie acting funny and decides she better go to the government research center where Rick was working on the weather project to investigate. Security guard Kenny Gunderson at the facility sees the teen sleuths breaking in. As the kids run off, Feather falls on the rocky area outside the facility and encounters a snake. Isis freezes time to remove the snake from the scene, then has stern words for the sleuthing Feather, C.J. and Ranji. The teens jump right back into the fray, though, this time with Rennie snapping some photos of workers outside the research center. They spot the man who posed as Mr. Mason. They see him and a cohort abduct Andrea and Rick, and they follow in their van. The crooks want a demo of the weather machine, which they have in the trunk of their vehicle. The machine causes a bit of chaos, though, and Andrea scurries off to change to Isis. She sends Tut from the lab to fly off and retrieve Captain Marvel for a little backup. Cap arrives and helps Isis save the sleuths from the thieves' runaway car, which is about to crash into their van. But the bad guys have gotten away with the machine, and the weather of the state (or is it the state of the weather?) is in danger.

Yes, that was a real snake Isis picked up in that one scene! The actress has said in interviews that she doesn't have a problem with snakes and even once brought a cobra back from Africa.

Ronalda Douglas Lombardo, who got a chance to sing in this two-part episode as Rennie, is a singer in California these days. Though we only see security guard Gunderson's first initial, K, on his uniform, the script gives him the first name Kenny. Another fill-in detail from the script: The outdoor stage where Ranji and Rennie are singing for rehearsal is named as Busch Gardens' "Flying Eagle" theatre, and Lombardo mentions this Busch Gardens filming in her interview for the DVD.

"... And Now You Don't"
Production #82029
October 23, 1976
Written by Arthur Nadel, Len Janson and Chuck Menville; directed by Arthur Nadel.
Third appearance of Captain Marvel.
Turns out, the mastermind behind the weather machine's theft is the rival professor whose design was rejected for Rick's. Rick, Andrea and the SuperSleuths are celebrating Rick's being cleared of the crime. But the kids aren't done with this case; they're plotting how to catch the crooks. The rumor circulates that the kids have the machine's plans, which the Professor needs. Andrea and Rick overhear the teens communicating their plans on CB. They go to their warehouse meeting location. Rick finds the kids being terrorized by electric bolts inside, after an accident, and Isis arrives to tame the danger. Later, in Andrea's classroom, Inspector Bryce is thinking he could actually use the help of the kids — and Rick — to bring in these crooks. A meeting is set up, but Rick is uneasy. The thieves hijack Ranji's van, with Ranji and Rick in it. Ranji is able to hit the CB radio, sending their audio over so that Andrea can pick it up in Rick's car. It helps determine their location, then Andrea changes to Isis and calls for Captain Marvel by asking the mighty winds to lift her voice high into the sky. The abducted Rick is reunited with his evil rival, who wants the plans for the machine from him. Isis and Captain Marvel fly side by side to the location, then Cap grabs the helicopter in which the professor is attempting to flee. Isis shows Ranji some of her own magic as the other crooks try to escape, duplicating herself to surround them.

BEHIND THE SCENES: RESEDA HIGH SCHOOL

The "Isis" DVD extras say that Reseda High School was used as Andrea Thomas' school. Wikipedia affirms that the school was used on the show, but gives the name of Andrea's school as Larkspur (see the synopsis for "No Drums, No Trumpets" for a clarification). Nevertheless, the school, established in 1955 and located in the Reseda section of the San Fernando Valley region of Los Angeles, has been used in a lot of other filming over the years. This includes the movies "Grosse Pointe Blank" and "Boogie Nights" as well as TV shows "Buffy the Vampire Slayer" and "My Name is Earl."

Reseda High School. Photo from Wikipedia, licensed under the Creative Commons Attribution-Share Alike 3.0 Unported license.

Moral: Accept defeat responsibly — don't let a rivalry drive you into the wrong actions.

This two-part episode was designed as a pilot for a series focusing on the SuperSleuths, though it never materialized. Surprising, as the producers had assembled what seemed to be an ideal assortment appealing to kids: the Eastern Ranji with his magic, the Asian C.J. with his karate skills, and the white, street-smart, hoops-shooting Feather — plus, perhaps, the help of smart Rennie to round out the melting pot for color and gender.

"Shazam!"

Episodes of the companion "Shazam!" series featuring Isis, with Michael Gray as Billy Batson, John Davey as Captain Marvel and Les Tremayne as Mentor.

"The Odd Couple"
October 18, 1975
Written by Sid Morse; directed by Hollingsworth Morse.
Don and Susie are about to take a little trip in an airplane; Don just got his license. He's a little annoyed by Susie's tape player, though, as he fires up the engine and calls the control tower. At the beach, Billy and Mentor are playing checkers when the Elders call. This time, they talk to Billy about pride, which can blind a man to common sense, and say that sometimes even Captain Marvel can need help. Back up in the airplane, the readings on the dial are worrying Don a bit, but he doesn't want to call for help. Billy and Mentor turn to fishing, one of their favorite activities. (Mentor snags a tire!) Then the plane runs out of gas, spotted by the nearby Billy and Mentor. Captain Marvel intervenes, supporting the plane to a safe landing. Don and Susie realize her tape player messed up the plane's compass. Cap and Mentor are dismayed that Don wouldn't send out a mayday. Later, Don and Susie are taking a hike. Billy and Mentor are driving along in the RV when Billy smells smoke then spots a forest fire. Billy transforms with a "Shazam!" again, rushing to the fire as Captain Marvel and realizing he needs some help — this is a big one. And guess who's caught in it? Don and Susie. The former falls and gets injured. Mentor, meanwhile, calls the Elders and is advised to contact Andrea Thomas / Isis. He tracks Andrea down at her classroom, and she makes her own transformation to rush to the fire. Cap reaches the kids and ushers them into the stream, then Isis calls on the elements to cause it to rain and stop the fire.

Moral: We all need each other.

This episode sort of "introduces" Isis to Captain Marvel, as Mentor goes to Andrea's classroom to find her, though the "Isis" series had been airing for a few weeks by that point. Isis tells Cap, as she lands at the stream, that she's very glad to finally meet him, and he issues an open invite to help her whenever needed. Captain Marvel would appear in his first "Isis" episode about a month later.

"Finders Keepers "
October 2, 1976
Written by Susan Dworski; directed by Hollingsworth Morse.
Billy and Mentor are at the beach when they encounter Sister Mary Catherine, who's keeping her eye on two of her girls, Laura and Kate, who are metal-detecting on the beach. Andrea's bird Tut is spending the day with the wheelchair-using Sister Mary Catherine. Laura and Kate unearth a metal box of money, which they suspect is from a robbery publicized last week. They decide to give the cash to the Sister. The elders then clue in Billy on who he's going to meet. The robbers return to the beach and find their buried cash box empty. The girls witness this scene and panic, fleeing by boat. But there's a shark in these waters, and the girls freak. Sister is back on the beach with the rest of her class, and she spots Laura and Kate out on the boat. She alerts Mentor and Billy, who transforms to Captain Marvel. He pushes them to safety on shore. The girls then secretly try to retrieve the money they left behind. They encounter the thieves, then Mentor gets ensnared with them. Tut sees all and not only tells Billy but also flies off to get Isis. She catches up with Billy then uses her amulet to see into the past and what happened to Mentor and the two girls. The two heroes find where the captives have been taken and "smoke" out the enemy.

Moral: A dishonest act can't be covered up by a good deed.

This episode keeps good continuity between the two shows: When Billy sees Tut, he says he recognizes him from when the bird came looking for Captain Marvel once when Isis needed help. That's a reference to the "Isis" episode "Funny Gal," airing in November 1975, nearly a year before this episode, which in turn precedes Captain Marvel's second "Isis" appearance by three weeks.

"Out of Focus"
October 16, 1976
Written by Paolo Orsini; directed by Hollingsworth Morse.
Just after the Elders caution Billy that "winning isn't everything," he's called into action as Captain Marvel: A girl named Kathy runs up to the RV and explains that her friend Jim is in trouble with a couple guys who want to steal the documentary film he's been making — they think he's recorded their dirty theft of hi-fi equipment. But when Captain Marvel arrives, Jim says there wasn't really a problem. Later, Andrea runs into

BY THE NUMBERS

22 **Episodes** (15 in Season 1; 7 in Season 2)

Two-parter *(series finale)* **1**

43 **Chants of "Oh, mighty Isis"** *(including on "Shazam!")*

Chants of "Oh, zephyr winds ..." **20**

48 **Other incantations** *(including on "Shazam!")*

Uses of amulet *to see things hidden or in the past* **8**

7 **Assists by Tut** *(including on "Shazam!")*

Mentor and Billy, who are checking out a film contest. Jim and Kathy realize their film might have captured the hi-fi theft, but they're skittish about turning in the film to the authorities. Jim gives Billy a different film instead, because he wants to use the real film to win the contest. The other guys, Len and Marty, are still after Jim for the film. Kathy tells all to Billy, who transforms again to Captain Marvel. Jim flees to a dangerous canyon, and Len and Marty are there, too, when there's a rockslide. Len and Marty get trapped in a cave. Andrea watches Captain Marvel try to move the boulders, then gives him the idea to drill into the cave from the top. No go. He then uses super-friction to make a magnifying glass from the sand and rock, and then uses the sun to burn a hole in the side of the cave. But storm clouds move in, so Andrea must change to Isis to command a change in weather.

Moral: Don't be tempted to be dishonest just to win a contest.

Andrew Stevens, who was Casey Denault on "Dallas," stars as Jim.

"Tarzan and the Super 7 — The Freedom Force"

"The Freedom Force" was an animated segment series produced by Filmation and airing on CBS as part of the 1978-80 TV show "Tarzan and the Super 7." In it, our hero Isis has gathered together a team of heroes to fight evil: Hercules, Super Samurai, Merlin and Sinbad. Lasting just five episodes, "The Freedom Force" featured Diane Pershing as the voice of Isis. Pershing would be known years later as the voice of Poison Ivy on the 1990s "Batman: The Animated Series."

"The Dragon Riders"

Toshi is flying a kite, when suddenly the kite is struck by a firebolt. Isis flies up to rescue a boy who was riding his pet flying dragon. Turns out, the boy is the son of the leader of the Dragon Riders, El Hanouri. His father has gotten into a disagreement with his chief scientist, Aguro, and the two are now at war. Isis speaks to El Hanouri, who's angry and determined to fight his enemy. Isis then learns that Hercules has been captured by Aguro. The scientist has gone into the future to steal key tech secrets. Toshi, meanwhile, helps the boy train his dragon Zark to be a good flying warrior. El Hanouri leads his fellow Dragon Riders into war against Aguro, and Isis flies off to intervene. Toshi changes into Super Samurai to bust into Aguro's fortress and rescue Hercules, while Isis counsels the two enemies to patch up their differences.

Isis' mantras are a bit different in these animated segments. For instance, her recitation for flight: "Mighty winds that blow on high, help me fly up to the sky."

"The Scarlet Samurai"

Sinbad is sculpting a statue of Isis as Merlin is sensing an invisible evil force nearby. Toshi happens upon a young lad, Kyoto, practicing archery, and the two get into a match. Kyoto then challenges Toshi to race him into the forbidden valley. There, they see wild animals charging each other, and Toshi changes to Super Samurai to break it up. Kyoto is amazed — and jealous. He later inquires of his father if there is some magic that will make him big and strong, too. During the night he's enticed by an evil force to read a spell, which ends up freeing this evil force. Kyoto says "Scarlet Samurai!" and is able to transform into another being that is powerful just like Super Samurai. With this newfound power, he again challenges Toshi, who reluctantly battles him. The evil one, Caliostro, meanwhile, menaces

"The Freedom Force" series was released to DVD in 2006 on this "Space Sentinels" set, from BCI Eclipse LLC (under license from Entertainment Rights).

Kyoto's father, Ishito. Kyoto receives a message that his father is in danger, as does Merlin. Both Samurais rush to help, but Caliostro seizes Kyoto's power. Isis, Hercules and Merlin arrive, too, and Isis' powers are more effective against this evil force. Kyoto learns that jealousy is not right.

"The Plant Soldiers"
Isis is playing tag with Toshi. She splits into three versions of herself, then merges again. They then discover that the Necklace of Osiris has been stolen. Isis heads out with Hercules to scout the area. The two use their powers to stop a huge stone platform from flattening some Egyptian pyramid workers. They meet a king, who shows them that the Nile has dried up. They suspect the Necklace of Osiris is behind it, then realize the river has been "stolen" and diverted. The threesome encounters some sinister killer plants, and through them Isis tracks the missing necklace. It's Toth, lord of the Plant Soldiers, who plans to harvest his "crop" of soldiers with the diverted river. He imprisons Isis. Hercules and the king, meanwhile, are trying to find Isis and come upon Toth's palace. They break her free, then Isis commands for the river to be returned to its former course. Toth gets washed away, and the necklace is returned.

"Morgana's Revenge" *(sometimes listed as "Pegasus' Odyssey")*
BRBTV was unable to review this one as of presstime; see a synopsis at TV.com.

"The Robot"
BRBTV was unable to review this one as of presstime; see a synopsis at TV.com.

Inside an issue of Bluewater Productions' comic-book take on Isis.

“ The Filmation people were nice to me. I didn't expect a lot. I just thought it was going to be a two-week shoot one summer. Literally! I thought, 'This sounds fun! Okay, I can fit it in!' ”
— *Joanna Cameron, in a 2002-2003 interview, "The Unofficial Isis Appreciation Page," http://www.angelfire.com/tv2/isis/cameron2.html*

CREDITS

Giving credit where credit is due

Producer	**Arthur H. Nadel**
Executive producers	**Norm Prescott, Dick Rosenbloom, Lou Scheimer**
Directors	**Earl Bellamy, Arnold Laven, Hollingsworth Morse, Arthur H. Nadel**
Assistant directors	**Henry J. Lange Jr., Lee Rainer, Ken Swor**
Writers	**Kathleen Barnes, Russell Bates, Norman Cameron, Henry Colman, Peter L. Dixon, Sarah Dixon, David Dworski, Susan Dworski, Len Janson, Robert F. Joseph, Chuck Menville, Sid Morse, Arthur H. Nadel, J. Michael Reaves, Marc Richards, James Schmerer, Ann Udell, David Wise**
Music	**"Yvette Blais," "Jeff Michael" (Marc Ellis, Ray Ellis)**
Director of photography	**Robert F. Sparks**
Film editors	**James Gross, James Potter, Dick Reilly, A. Ray Williford**

Casting	**Fran F. Bascom, Ross Brown, Meryl O'Loughlin**
Makeup department	**John Norin, Maurice Stein**
Property masters	**Eugene Booth, Fred Westcott**
Sound	**Bill Randall, Harlan Riggs**
Camera and electrical	**Bill Kahlo** (key grip), **Drain M. Marshall** (gaffer), **Bob Stevens** (camera operator)
Costume and wardrobe	**Thalia Phillips**
Editorial supervisor	**Bill Moore**
Location / transportation	**Dale Henry**
Educational advisors	**Gordon L. Berry, Mary Wale Brown, Nina Byers, Norma Feshbach, James R. Sackett**
Script supervisors	**Cleo Anton, Frank Tudisco, Marshall J. Wolins**
Creative director	**Don Christensen**
Film coordinator	**June Gilham**
Production executive	**Richard Briggs**
Production coordinator	**Steve Nicolaides**
Developed by	**Marc Richards**
Electronic special effects	**Sonex International**
Music and sound effects	**Horta-Mahana Corp.**
Music publisher	**Shermley Music Co.**

A COMIC COMPARISON

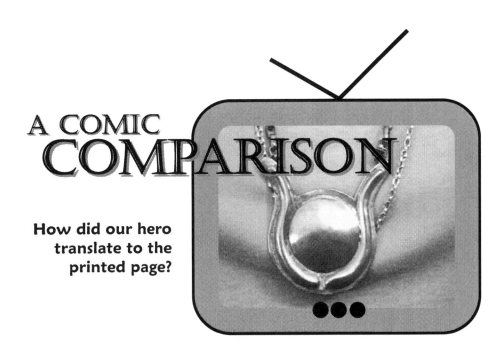

How did our hero translate to the printed page?

One way our two Superchicks differ is that in the case of Isis, her comics followed her screen debut. With that, it's worth drawing a comparison between the hero of the TV show and the hero of the comics panel.

When you take away the newer incarnations of Isis in the comics, such as Image's 2002 "Legend of Isis," Bluewater Productions' later version, and Adrianna Tomaz of DC's 52 series, the original series of Isis comics based on the TV show numbered only eight. This series, produced by DC, ran for two years, basically following behind the TV show, but only publishing every couple months or every quarter or so. As mentioned earlier, though, the character made her true comics debut in issue 25 of "Shazam!" from September-October 1976.

So how well does the core eight-issue comic-book series stick with the TV series? Here are some ways the comics stayed true:
- Isis' costume and look are the same, right down to the glam eyeshadow.
- She recites "Oh, mighty Isis" to transform.
- She recites rhyming incantations to release her powers.

The comics reflected higher stakes than the limited-budget TV show — Isis battled biggies like Set in issue 3.

- Her powers are the same — nature, the elements, etc.
- Andrea Thomas is a high school science teacher, and her colleague is Rick Mason, while her assistant is Cindy Lee.
- Cindy is adventurous and often gets into trouble.

Some ways in which the comics stray from the TV version:
- The stakes are higher with the freedom of the printed page: Without the worry over costly special effects, Isis battles big villains like Set and Serpenotep, who rampage around town and cause a lot of damage!
- Cindy hits on Rick Mason.
- You get a little more of Isis' origin and her discovery of the amulet in Egypt.
- There's no Rennie Carol.
- The idea that Isis is a goddess is emphasized.

- In issue 3, Dr. Barnes is a white man (he was black in earlier issues — no lie!).
- It's explained that the magic that transforms Andrea into Isis keeps everyone from recognizing her. (So hey — go easy on poor Rick!)
- Andrea and Isis are more of two distinct people, rather than one being the alter-ego of the other.
- Andrea's mother is shown.
- Isis actually gives up her Andrea identity later in the eight issues as she struggles with the issue of who she really is.

It's interesting to make note of the letters column in issue 2, where writer / story editor Denny O'Neil shares how he first learned the show would be produced, along with an invite to prospective members of the "Isis TV Show Fan Club," directing them to "Drawer 988" in Reseda, California. So sweet.

Here's a look at each of the eight issues:

No. 1, October-November 1976 (on sale in July)
Story: Denny O'Neil; art: Ric Estrada, Wally Wood.
"Scarab: The Man Who Would Destroy": An authentic ancient Egyptian pyramid is brought to town — along with the powerful evil magician who has been imprisoned in it, Scarab. After causing some havoc, he makes his way to the White House to take over this new land he finds himself in.

No. 2, December 1976-January 1977
Story: Denny O'Neil, Steve Skeates; art: Mike Vosburg, Vince Colletta.
"The Creature from Dimension X": When students Gini and Roger stay late at school to work on their science project, they unwittingly release a strange phenomenon — an other-dimension creature made of electricity. In a second, shorter story, Isis rescues Cindy, who's gone out on a scavenger hunt in a storm.

No. 3, February-March 1977
Story: Denny O'Neil, Steve Skeates; art: Mike Vosburg, Vince Colletta, Liz Berube.
"The Wrath of Set": With a hailstorm comes Set, an evil ancient god who wants the people of this modern time to worship him as he thinks they worship Isis. In the second story, Isis rescues a foolish birdwatcher then must save the day after a mysterious laryngitis affects the crowd at a political event.

No. 4, April-May 1977
Story: Denny O'Neil, Jack C. Harris; art: Mike Vosburg, Vince Colletta.
"Treasure of Lost Lake": Isis faces an ancient Indian legend of a lake monster that has come true — the ghost and monster are on the rampage. In the second story, Isis must teach a lesson to a hunter who inadvertently causes an avalanche.

No. 5, June-July 1977
Story: Denny O'Neil, Jack C. Harris; art: Mike Vosburg, Vince Colletta.
"Perilous Pyramid Power": An ancient, all-powerful space god seeks to destroy as Isis battles Aten, God of the Sun. She also gets a new headquarters in this issue, and Isis takes a turn in Andrea's classroom.

No. 6, August-September 1977
Story: Denny O'Neil, Jack C. Harris; art: Mike Vosburg, Vince Colletta.
"The Ominous Ooze": Isis and Rick are attacked by the slimy "Ooze" creature. In this one, Isis decides to leave her Andrea Thomas identity and become fully Isis.

No. 7, October-November 1977
Story: Jack C. Harris; art: Mike Vosburg, Frank Chiarmonte.
"Feel the Fangs of the Serpent King": Rick has gotten increasingly suspicious of Isis, thinking she might have done something to Andrea, since his fellow schoolteacher has now disappeared. He does some research at the museum on the original, ancient Isis. In the course of that, he finds himself innocently reciting some ancient words — which inhabit his body with Serpenotep, the evil being once defeated by the original Isis who's holding a bit of a grudge.

No. 8, December 1977-January 1978
Story: Jack C. Harris; art: Mike Vosburg, Frank Chiarmonte.
"Darkly Through the Mutant's Eyes": Isis has realized after last issue that maybe there is room in her life for Andrea Thomas, after all. What she hasn't realized, however, is that when she discovered Rick Mason at the museum after defeating Serpenotep, that Rick was actually still inhabited by the evil ancient beast! So now, Serpenotep sets his sights on a new foreign exchange student at the school, who develops some surprising powers.

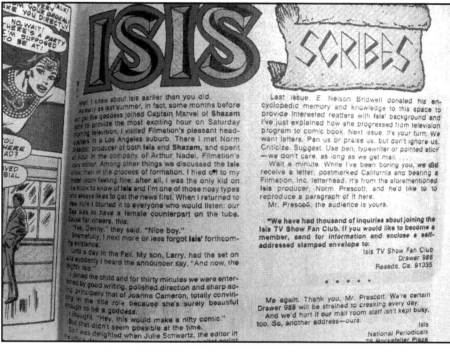

While the first issue of the eight-issue run featured a background story on the real ancient Isis written by E. Nelson Bridwell, writer Denny O'Neil, serving as the story editor for this series, explained in the back of issue 2 the story of his visit to Filmation's headquarters in L.A. There, he learned that Captain Marvel would be joined by a female counterpart on Saturday morning television. As he watched the series himself, he thought it would make a nifty comic, but it didn't seem possible until Julius Schwartz asked him to write a pilot script. On this letters page you can also see the call for fan-club members, directing them to Drawer 988.

AND NOW A WORD FROM...

Behind the scenes — and the DVDs!

Brian Cutler:
Nowadays, this teacher ... well, teaches!

As schoolteachers go, he was pretty heckin' hunky. But was Rick Mason the brightest bulb in the pack? *Well* ... not only was there the Lois Lane quality about him, he also had the audacity to tell Andrea he'd love a gal that cooks like her ... but looks like Isis. *Ouch*. We're quite sure, after chatting with Cutler via phone in March 2011, that the actor himself is much wiser. These days, he lives in Kansas City, Missouri, and runs an actor's studio, mentoring aspiring actors.

How did you learn about the role of "Isis"?
"They were casting the show. A whole bunch of guys auditioned for it. Norm Prescott and Lou Scheimer liked me. I was the first person cast for the show, and then I was there for the rest of the casting. It was the normal audition process. I was cast, and then we went from there."

What was the audition like?
"They had some sides from the script. You know, some pages of dialogue. I just had to cold-read them with Norm and Lou. They were very hands-on because they'd been in animation for a long time, and this was their second attempt at live action.

"I get emails from all over the world from people. I got an email from an Asian gentleman who's very big on the New York Stock Exchange, and he had to tell me how important the series had been for him, because in the neighborhood he grew up in, all the kids he knew were either dead or in jail. It's amazing the impact the show had on people."

Rick Mason is really an easygoing, kindhearted, stand-up sort of guy. How much of a character description of him did you get, before you began the role?
"They always give you a general breakdown of what the character is like, and then you bring your own stuff to it."

What aspects of Brian Cutler do we see in Rick Mason?
"Gosh, I don't know. The only acting coach I ever studied with was Charles Edward Conrad. We became very good friends. Charles' whole thing was to be in the moment all the time. So whatever happens, just go with it. Learn the words and hit your mark and go where it goes. So I guess there's always a little bit of who you are in the character. ... I always kid that I'm the Lois Lane of 'Isis,' because Lois never knew Isis." (Laughs.) "Didn't look like the same person at all!"

Who was the one you got along with the greatest on the set?
"Joanna Pang. I just love her. It was so wonderful, we were the guests at Comic-Con when the DVD series came out. Joanna flew in with her husband and her son, and some of the guys from the other series were there. Sid Haig was there. Craig Littler was there. I hadn't seen any of those guys in many years. We just hit it off, had a wonderful time. But Joanna and I just had a special thing. We've stayed friends ever since we've been on the show, so to see her at Comic-Con was a special treat."

Were there any bloopers from the "Isis" set that we'll perhaps never see?
"Oh, I'm sure there were. I don't know that I can remember any in

particular. There are two episodes where I'm wearing sunglasses. I never wore sunglasses in any other episode. Right between the eyes I had been stung by a bee or wasp, and it showed. But we had to keep shooting, so I said just give me some sunglasses, and we went right on shooting."

Do you have any keepsakes from your days on the "Isis" set?
"No. But I do have, years ago they made those ... it was a cardboard thing, and it had a piece of plastic on it. And you draw on it, then lift up the plastic, and it erases. I have one of those from the show. A fan in Virginia, he still had one of those View-Masters. You know those View-Masters? Well, they put 'Isis' on the View-Master. I think I mentioned in my DVD interview that I had never gotten one of those, and this guy in Virginia sent me his. Kinda fun. So now I have one of the boards that you can write on, then I have the View-Master and several of the discs. I did keep all of my scripts for years, but then in moving from coast to coast, they just sorta got lost somewhere. They could be in storage somewhere, for all I know."

How about the clothes? Any of those still in your closet?
"Oh, God, no. No, no, no. They're all gone. They're gone to another universe, I think. Where they belong."

As you mentioned before, and you commented in your DVD interview, there was a sort of "Lois Lane" quality in Rick Mason. At one point did you realize there would be this suspension of disbelief, and was it difficult for you, as an actor?
"No. It wasn't hard at all. You just live the moment. It was kinda fun, actually."

What kind of fan mail do you get these days, regarding your role as Rick Mason?
"Tons. It's amazing. I can't believe, of course, now with the wonderful world of electronics. I get several emails a month, and I have for years. Especially since the DVD came out. I get them from everywhere. The show is big in South America. A fan there called me ... He's a young artist, his name is Pierre, and he lives in Sao Paulo, Brazil, and he loves the show. He has done artist's renderings of the show. He started sending them to me. I've taken them all and had them printed, and I have them at my Actors Studio, and have them framed. It's really a treat. ... I hear how it changed their lives, how thrilled these adults are right

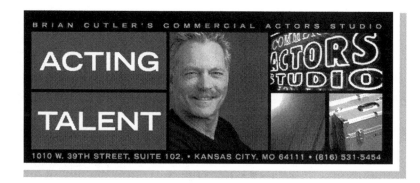

now, that they can sit down and watch the series with their sons and daughters."

Do you get recognized when you go out?
"Nah. I did for years. But it's been a long time."

What do you think now, years after "Isis" went off the air, is the most important message of the show?
"To be good to your fellow man. To understand each other. To listen. To not judge. It covered all those things, you know. In every episode they covered a piece of all of that."

I see you started up the Commercial Actors Studio in 1994. What made you decide to do it?
"Well, let's see. ... Most of the time people say what am I doing in Kansas City. But my wife, who was born and raised here, wants to move to L.A. Which may be in the works; we'll see.

"I came to Missouri to do 'The Unsinkable Molly Brown.' The woman who started the Missouri Repertory Theatre came to see the show and came backstage after the show and said, 'I really love your work. Would you be interested in working in the Missouri Repertory Theatre?' I said sure. Because what does an actor want to do? An actor wants to act. I was going through a difficult time. I thought this would be a nice change. That contract, which was a two-year contract with the Missouri Repertory Theatre, turned into a 14-year contract."

"Theatre and film are two totally different areas. I thought I would see if there was any interest in the area in film, and I saw that there was. We're known as one of the best acting studios in the country.

"There are a lot of people that say they were trained by Charles Conrad, but Charles was a very reclusive man. I can say that I was close friends with him, and he would help a lot of people become big stars, and somehow they would say that they made it on their own. They would forget Charles. So I wanted to carry on his legacy. I wanted him to have someone he knew and trusted carrying on his legacy.

"We've done three feature films in the past few years. 'My One and Only,' 'Ambrose Bierce: Civil War Stories,' 'Hope.' 'Hope' is a story about a family in crisis that is against stem cell research, and it turns out stem cell research is the only way they can save someone they love. We stay busy, production-wise. I like directing. I like coaching. My wife is the unit production manager. We get very involved in what we do; we have a great team that we work with."

What's the last production you were involved with?
"The last stage production was 'A Christmas Carol' at the Missouri Repertory Theatre, which is now called the Kansas City Repertory Theatre." (laughs) "I'm not sure why it was renamed — maybe because it's in Kansas City. I played Jacob Marley and Joe the Beetler. The beetler was the person that when graverobbers stole from the grave, he bought the things they stole."

What does a typical day in your life look like these days?
"I still do a lot of voiceover work for different companies in the area. I'm doing a big photo shoot next week at sunset for a big chemical company. I do things like that. On a daily basis, I usually get up, work out, go into the studio about 3 o'clock.

"There are very few places in the country that teach voiceover, so it's a very good thing to have in your bag of tricks. So I trained a student to teach that on Thursday night.

"Saturday mornings I teach a master's class.

"Wednesday is sort of a catch-up day."

"Thursday and Friday ... I do work privately ... Joe Goldman, attorney who became a mystery writer. He became interested in voiceover, and I work privately with him one day a week. There's another gentleman in town who's a very successful restaurateur, and he decided he wanted to do voiceover, so he works privately with me one or two days a week."

So there's a lot of voiceover work in Kansas City?
"What's happened is because of the Internet, you can work anywhere. They just patch you into a recording studio. I have students who have recording studios in their basement, and they'll be recording in the basement in Kansas City and working with someone in New York, Los Angeles and Florida at the same time.

"Hallmark's based here. Sprint Nextel's based here. There are a lot of big companies that are in the Midwest because it's centrally located."

Any chance of making a return to the small (or big) screen?
"I don't know. I was up for a role ... George Clooney was here shooting a movie last year, and I was up for a role. Periodically I'll audition for things, if it's something I really want to do. It would have to be something that I really really wanted to do, because I'm busy with the studio. I was offered a couple of sci-fi movies last year, and it's not that I don't like sci-fi, I do like sci-fi, I enjoy it immensely. It seems that if you look back at people who were stars in the '70s and '80s, it seems that in 2011 they're all doing really bad sci-fi movies now. I don't mean to put that down. They're working."

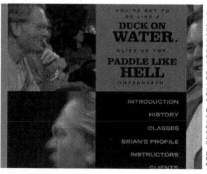

Joanna Pang Atkins:
For this positive gal, life dances on

Joanna Pang Atkins is not at all bitter that she only got to stick around for one season of "The Secrets of Isis." Quite the contrary — she's happy for the blessings in her life and the career that followed. BRBTV had the opportunity to chat with Atkins via email in January 2011.

You said in your interview for the "Isis" DVD set that when you got the call about this show, you had done some other work for CBS. What was that?
"Other CBS shows ... 'Patchwork Family' (Saturday morning children's show), 'CBS Festival of the Lively Arts,' 'The Return of Phoenix,' an ancient Peking Opera, 'CBS Daytime 90 special.'"

Where are you originally from? And in what state are you based now?
"I am originally from California and I moved to N.Y. to pursue more work in the theatre. I ended up having a lot more work in television. Now I live in N.J."

This was certainly a TV show that spoke to the idea of female empowerment, not only in the Isis character, but also in Cindy Lee, particularly in the episode "Fool's Dare." Were there any of your own experiences, growing up, that helped inform your portrayal as the girl who could do anything those silly boys could do?!
"'Shazam!,' with Captain Marvel, was an appealing superhero that many boys admired. 'The Secrets of Isis' was created so that girls could have a superhero to look up to. The first season was called 'The Shazam / Isis' Hour.' I did like that Cindy Lee was always interested and trying to do things — including what the boys did — even if not always making the smartest decisions ... but how else would she need Isis to come to the rescue?!

"My mother instilled a lot of confidence in my brother and me. I think we both believed that we could do anything we set our minds to."

How much of Joanna Pang did we see in Cindy Lee?
"Cindy Lee was always positive, active and enthusiastic. She always wanted to help others and be involved. It was easy for me to play Cindy

Lee because I had many of those same traits."

You've said that you were able to have a little influence on the definition of Cindy Lee through her clothing, that you could shop for her wardrobe, but that in the matter of hairstyle, they wouldn't let you change the pigtails. Were there other ways in which you felt you were able to influence the producers in the portrayal of Cindy?
"I was just concentrating on doing my job — learning my lines and being prepared. I trusted the writers, directors and producers to keep the character on track. I wanted to perform as best I could. Different actors approach the job differently."

Is there anything you would have changed about her character, if you could have?
"I was wishing Cindy would have a superpower, too, and she could be the sidekick to Isis. So I love your next question! That way I could've stayed out of trouble situations."

If Cindy were a superhero, too, what powers would she have?
"I think Cindy would want to fly, because she admired Isis, and then she could keep up!"

The show was ahead of its time where diversity was concerned, putting front and center a school leader who was African-American and a key student who was Asian. How aware were you of this, at the time? And did you get fan mail commenting on that?
"All the actors were just happy to be working, and I don't know that we were thinking so much in terms of diversity then (at least among the actors). My fan mail was from boys and girls that loved the show. Most of the letters asked for an autographed picture. Some of the girls would tell me they wore their hair in pigtails like Cindy, and one young fan asked me to marry him and he sent me a ring. I think he told me it was his grandmother's, so of course I had to send it back!"

Have you ever read the Isis comic books that were released at the time of the show? They did feature Cindy! In fact, in the comics, she comes on to Rick Mason — any comment on that? ;)
"I have some of the Isis comic books, but I haven't read all of them! I didn't know that in one of the stories Cindy came on to Rick Mason.

Often a young girl will have a crush on her teacher. I think it would be up to the adult to handle that situation appropriately. Maybe in the comic books Cindy has grown up!"

Were there any female superheroes you looked up to when you were a little girl?
"I wasn't really aware of any female superheroes when I was young. I liked Superman."

Who from the show are you still in contact with these days?
"Brian Cutler and I became good friends while we worked on 'Isis.' He was like a big brother to me. I hadn't seen him in many years, and then a few years ago we were in San Diego at Comic-Con to help promote the 'Isis' DVD. Our friendship was renewed, and it felt just like in the 'Isis' days."

Tell me a little about your work in teaching dance to children. What do you find most fulfilling about that?
"I am very involved in arts education. I am a teaching artist that is placed in schools for multicultural dance residencies. The residencies are very rewarding because I see children blossom and become more confident. I also want them to learn about the culture and traditions of other countries and become more accepting of differences between people and places. I've just put up a new website with lots of that information at www.JoannaPangAtkins.com."

What's your preferred style of dance?
"I enjoy all styles of dance. I started in ballet when I was very young, and with that training and technique, you can move more easily into other

areas of dance. I toured the world with an Asian dance company, which eventually led to my world dance residencies. Recently I started taking Nia classes. Nia is a class that combines movements and concepts from yoga, Tai-Chi, Tae Kwon Do, Aikido, jazz and modern dance."

Your story on the "Isis" DVD of not being asked back to the show for the second season is such a downer — and you explained what must have been an incredible disappointment in such a respectful, professional way. Any chance you'll make a return to acting?
"I started performing when I was very young. You go to hundreds of auditions, and sometimes you get the job and sometimes you don't. When you don't get the job, you just have to move on to the next one. As an actress your fate is decided by casting people, producers, directors and often network executives, so you don't have a lot of control as to whether or not you get the job. You have to go to auditions and do the best that you can, and have a thick skin about it. Of course I was disappointed that I was not asked back for the second season of 'Isis.' I'd had a lot of great jobs and opportunities before 'Isis,' so I had to be ready to move forward to the next great jobs after 'Isis'!

"I really enjoy the teaching, so I haven't thought about acting in a while. But my husband, Dick Atkins, is a producer, so maybe he'll cast me in something!"

Andy Mangels:
Bringing it all together for future generations

Andy Mangels has done this kind of thing before, producing DVD sets, so don't be surprised that you see a quality product in the "Isis" DVDs. He told BRBTV a little more about what went into it via email in February 2011. (And he's the *premier* Wonder Woman fan, by the way!)

You've done a whole lot of production work on some great entertainment icons: "Star Trek," "Wonder Woman," "Roswell." How did you get this gig to produce the "Isis" DVD set?
"In November 2002, my book 'Animation on DVD: The Ultimate Guide' was released, reviewing over 1,600 animated DVDs that had been released to that point from various companies. One company only had a single title which I reviewed, BCI Eclipse, but one of their managers contacted me as they were licensing the Filmation 'He-Man and the Masters of the Universe' DVD set for review. They flew me down to California for a consultation meeting to discuss what might be good to put on the sets, and I walked out of there with the job of producing all the special features for the DVD sets.

"When 'He-Man' was released in the summer of 2005 and was a huge hit (and won a prestigious DVD award), BCI licensed the rest of the Filmation library for DVD release, and I was put in charge of all the special features for the line. Although I had enjoyed most of the Filmation line over the years, my top favorite show of theirs was 'The Secrets of Isis,' so it was the show I was most excited to work on."

Were you a big fan of the show when it originally aired?
"I was a fan of both 'Shazam!' (which predated 'Isis' by a year) and 'Isis.' I grew up in a small town in Montana, and we only got one channel on our black-and-white TV (KCFW, an NBC channel from Kalispell). However, if you moved the antennas just right, you could get signals for the ABC and CBS stations from Spokane, Washington. 'Shazam!' aired on CBS and I loved it, and in September 1975, they debuted the new 'The Shazam! / Isis Hour,' with a female heroine. I had always loved Wonder Woman in the comics and animated on ABC's 'Super Friends,' but the Lynda Carter TV series wouldn't debut until November 1975, so Isis became a new live-action favorite."

"I loved the rhyming verses that she did to cast her magical spells, and actually used to have a big piece of butcher paper that I would write the spells on as quickly as possible so I could remember them. Then, when I was outside playing, I would use Isis' spells in my 'pretend time.' When 'Wonder Woman,' 'Isis,' and then 'Bionic Woman' were on the air in 1976, I was in heaven. I loved superheroes of any type, but particularly enjoyed the super-heroines. Not so much Batgirl, as I rarely got to see the Batman reruns, but the trio above."

I have to say that this DVD set really has the most diverse and expansive set of extras I've seen for a TV show — with not only interviews and photos and other goodies, but the scripts of the episodes, no less! What kinds of priorities came into play, when you set about putting it together?
"Knowing that this was likely to be the only DVD set the series would ever have, I wanted to put as much on the set as possible. The only real issues that came up were space and budget. Every time you put something onto a DVD, even if it's as simple as a PDF of a script, it costs the company money, so I had to justify every choice.

"I would have liked to have the isolated music and effects tracks for more episodes, but since the music was really repetitive anyhow, it would have mostly ended up sounding the same. I did make sure, though, that we did that with the 'Shazam!' cross-over episodes, so that we could get all of his themes put in."

Was there anything you planned to include but weren't able to?
"I wanted to put in the original series bible and some other material that was used in the development of the show, but it just wasn't feasible. I also wish that we had gotten all of the morals and better versions of the bumpers and alternate credits, but we went with the material we could get. A lot of that material just doesn't exist any longer. When Filmation was sold in 1989, to L'Oreal and later Hallmark, much of the material that wasn't useful for syndication markets was just thrown out. The original film and music, any bloopers, etc., were all just gone! Thankfully, series co-star Joanna Pang had a video collection she had put together, and I had some older materials, and between the two of us, we were able to get as much rare footage as possible.

"I wish that Bob Kline had been able to find his original presentation and opening credits art that he had created for Isis, but alas, he wasn't able to.

We discussed having some packed-in exclusive comic art postcards in the set, similar to those we did for 'He-Man,' 'She-Ra,' 'Flash Gordon,' and 'Defenders of the Earth.' We were going to go with Alex Ross and Matt Haley, both of whom are Isis fans, but those didn't work for the budget.

"We discussed doing an 'on-pack exclusive' for Best Buy or another retailer which would have included a sculpted version of the Isis amulet, and even provided reference for a sculptor, but the costs were deemed too high, and the retailer exclusive market was too small to justify the expense.

"We also talked about having a live model as Isis for Comic-Con 2007, and were talking with a costumer about that, but it didn't happen. We did give out temporary tattoos of the logo, and had some Isis T-shirts printed for Comic-Con, though!"

How did you choose who would be interviewed for the extras?
"It came down to availability and interest. Brian Cutler and Joanna Pang (Atkins) were relatively easy to find, as I had contacted them for interviews in the past that never happened. Because we had such a small budget, we couldn't fly out to interview them, or fly them in, so we used Craigslist postings to find local film crews who shot their interviews. Brian's was shot in his acting studio, and Joanna's was shot at her home.

"Ronalda Douglas was very difficult to find, but I eventually found her through a church, as I recall. She was interviewed by our regular DVD crew, at her home. All three of those interviews were done by me, using a speakerphone to ask questions. So, I didn't see the footage until it was sent to me! These days, I might use Skype if I were in a similar situation.

"I wanted to have an interview with John Davey for the Captain Marvel cross-overs, as I knew it would be quite a long time before Warner would ever do the 'Shazam!' sets, but he wasn't really interested.

"The others that were interviewed, producers Lou Scheimer and Richard M. Rosenbloom, writers David Dworski, Michael Reaves and David Wise, designer Bob Kline and assistant director Henry J. Lange Jr., were people who were coming in for our mammoth one-week session down in Burbank where we brought in dozens of Filmation people to interview about dozens of shows and record commentary tracks all at once. It was madness trying to coordinate all of them! Henry Lange was great, because he's now fairly successful, but he's young enough that he remembered a lot of information from one of his earliest jobs."

Why wasn't Joanna Cameron among the interviewees on the DVD set?
"I pursued Joanna fervently for quite some time. The status in Hollywood is that 99 percent of DVD companies do NOT pay anyone for interviews or commentary tracks, and most stars and production personnel are fine with that. They consider it a part of PR, or furthering their legacy, or a gift to their fans. Joanna lives in Hawaii now and works at a hotel. We offered to fly her to Los Angeles for two to three days, and put her up at a nice hotel, and give her a reasonable fee for coming in; we also talked to her about appearing at Comic-Con. She would have filmed all of her material in about a two- to three-hour time, and then been able to enjoy L.A. on the company.

"Unfortunately, Joanna felt that our offer was not enough. I begged the company to do more, and we made a second offer, which was also rebuffed. Then, using the idea I had from the interviews with Brian Cutler and Joanna Pang, I went on Craigslist for Hawaii. I found a film crew there who were very close to Joanna. The woman who ran it was an award-winning documentary director, and, it turned out, was an Isis fan. They were willing to go to Joanna's house or the hotel she worked at, at her convenience, to do the interview by speakerphone, as I had done the others. Additionally, we did offer Joanna a fee to do this."

So, for a few hours' work, she'd get a good fee, did not have to leave home, got to work with a female-run crew, and got a chance to speak to her fans. Joanna chose not to do it. It's her choice, but it's the biggest regret that I have with the DVD set. I know how much Lynda Carter and Lindsay Wagner have appreciated their fans, and both of them appeared on their DVD sets. It would have been wonderful for Joanna to do the same. Unfortunately, she chose not to, so we have to respect that."

Did your level of involvement come down to actually scripting the interview questions? (I have to ask that one, because I was very glad, for one thing, to hear Joanna Pang Atkins so respectfully and carefully explain why she wasn't back for the second season.)
"Yes, as explained, I did the interviews by speakerphone. I had a generalized list of questions, which I think I provided to the actors beforehand, and then we went with the flow from there. I've been interviewing people for 25 years, so a "live" interview is second nature for me. And they, of course, were quite used to being on-camera.

"The issue of Joanna Pang not appearing on the second season was really a touchy subject, and one which what you see on film from Joanna and Ronalda and Lou Scheimer is about what we know. The actual reasons have been lost in time to the people who are no longer living. I was very nervous about that line of questioning, but everyone was very nice about it.

"It was quite interesting for Joanna and Ronalda to meet each other for the first time ever, at Comic-Con in 2007! They and Brian Cutler and their spouses all came out for the Con and signed and met their fans. I got to do dinner with them all, and they were wonderful!"

What do you feel is the most important message of "The Secrets of Isis," in the '70s and now?
"I think that Andrea Thomas being a schoolteacher was an integral part of the character, and made it a much stronger show than if she had investigated crimes, as the original concept would have been. In both identities, Andrea and Isis were strong, caring, and independent, qualities that were amazing to see on television at the time. She really was a feminist heroine, and like Wonder Woman, someone you'd want as a big sister to protect you if you were a kid. And the morals and messages of the show were very important, not just to the producers, but to the viewers themselves."

I should note that, like 'Wonder Woman,' 'The Secrets of Isis' had its share of teenage boy and adult male viewers (and probably lesbian teens and women as well) because of Joanna Cameron's striking looks, short skirt, and beautiful legs."

If the show would've aired for more seasons, and you would've been one of the producers, what kinds of things would you have added or explored on-screen for this iconic character?
"I would have added more comic book elements to it as special effects improved, and perhaps explored more of the Egyptian background of the character. Today, the super-stunts on 'Isis' seem positively tame, and perhaps even a little lame, but given the low budget and state of special effects back then, and that this was a show that was aimed at children first and foremost, it holds up amazingly well.

"But it would have been great to see some actual supervillains as well, and to have Isis address the public a bit more. Both her and Captain Marvel were always 'known' by people when they appeared, but you never saw them being interviewed or appearing on TV. They were superheroes, but I would have liked to see them explored more as 'role models' if the shows had progressed more."

Why aren't the morals actually attached to the episodes on the DVDs?
"When the shows went into syndication, especially in the British market, the morals were removed from the episodes. Since the digital prints we were provided by Entertainment Rights (now Classic Media), the current owners of the Filmation library, were for the British runs, the morals had not been digitized. Whether those film elements even still exist in a warehouse somewhere in Europe is unknown, but we found as many as we could, in the best quality that we could, and put them on the discs."

I find the tie-in with Bluewater's comic interesting, since Bluewater's Isis incarnation is not very similar to the TV show. How did that tie-in happen?
"That was something that BCI did on their own, in exchange for PR in the Bluewater comic line. It wasn't a decision I made, but it was an interesting choice. Clearly the Bluewater series is influenced by the Filmation version, as is DC's newest incarnation of Isis."

The DVD set's nice-looking booklet includes some of the episodes' airdates and shooting dates, but not all. How did you go about digging up that information, and why was some of it missing?
"Not all of that information was available. I got most of it from Joanna Pang's notes, although I've since gotten a few more dates and information from digging around files at Lou Scheimer's house as we've been working on his autobiography, 'Lou Scheimer: Creating the Filmation Generation.' Look for an updated list of dates in that book."

I see that your book with Lou Scheimer is due out for the San Diego con this year — will the two of you be there signing?
"The hope is that Lou will be able to be at Comic-Con this year with me for the debut of his book. It will probably be Lou's last appearance at Comic-Con if so, and he would love to see fans there!"

A 1979 TV Guide story about Joanna Cameron by Ellen Torgerson. Photo from eBay.

As noted in the masterful coffeetable book, "Mego 8" Super-Heroes: World's Greatest Toys!" by Benjamin Holcomb, the Isis Mego was originally a Montgomery Ward catalog exclusive for Christmas 1976. It's not an easy one to nab on eBay these days.

BIRTHDAYS

A sprinkling of special days of key cast and crew

Albert Reed   January 28, 1910
  (died May 31, 1986)
Norm Prescott   January 31, 1927
  (died July 2, 2005)
Arnold Laven   February 23, 1922
  (died September 13, 2009)
Earl Bellamy   March 11, 1917
  (died November 30, 2003)
Craig Wasson   March 15, 1954
Chuck Menville   April 17, 1940
  (died June 15, 1992)
Arthur H. Nadel   April 25, 1921
  (died February 22, 1990)
Laurette Spang   May 16, 1951
Brian Cutler   May 18, 1945
Sidney Morse   May 29, 1920
  (died November 30, 2003)
Leigh McCloskey   June 21, 1955
David Dworski   June 29, 1937

Ben Frank September 2, 1934
   (died September 11, 1990)
Joanna Cameron September 20, 1951
Christopher Norris October 7, 1953
Ronalda Douglas October 12, 1952
Lou Scheimer October 19, 1928
Jerry Douglas November 12, 1932
Marc Richards November 21, 2006
Hollingsworth Morse December 16, 1910
   (died January 23, 1988)

Above, a closeup of part of Colleen Corrigan's Isis costume, which we told you about in the intro section. And at right, Colleen lets BRB take the trim pieces for a test drive! More of an "Evil Isis" look, don'tcha think? Hmmm ...

And yes, we're going to talk Colleen into wearing her costume to a comic con sometime! We've told her she'll get photographed nonstop!

Photo courtesy of James R. Green Jr.

MERCHANDISE

There's not much, so it's a real treasure!

"The Secrets of Isis" was not exactly the most merchandised superhero show out there. We've done some digging, and here's what we've found.

- Mego figure
- Halloween costume
- Golden Book
- Magic Slate
- Comic books
- Coloring books
- Sticker set / "Sticker Fun" book
- View-Master reels
- Boxed puzzle
- Frame tray puzzles
- Magazines

The truly glorious Isis Mego in her box, front and back. Photos courtesy of MegoMuseum.com.

A precious Golden Book featuring our beloved hero, on display at Geppi's Entertainment Museum in Baltimore.

The "Sticker Fun" book, at bottom, and one of the jigsaw puzzles, left. Photos from eBay.

The Image version of "Legend of Isis" from 2002, later transformed into Bluewater Productions' Isis comics.

DC Direct's Isis figure from the 52 series, sculpted by Karen Palinko and released in 2007. Photos from eBay.

We just love what pops up on eBay. This June 2012 auction was for a replica of the Isis necklace seen in the series. "This is completely screen accurate to the prop," the description said. "The necklace is resin. The chain is metal and is about 32 inches long. I will have the tiara with the amber gem up for auction soon."

The View-Master set. Photo from eBay.

Acknowledgments

BRBTV issues heartfelt thanks to the following for their kind assistance with this book:

Alan Brennert
Andy Mangels
Anne Collins-Ludwick
Brian Cutler
Brian Heiler and MegoMuseum.com
Chuck Gregory and his family
Colleen Corrigan
Dale Cuthbertson — *thanks for the usage of your magnificent art!!!*
Jason Waggoner
Jeannie Epper
James R. Green Jr.
Joan Van Ark
Joanna Cameron
Joanna Pang Atkins
Lisa Everetts
Los Angeles County Arboretum & Botanic Garden
Mia Cruz and Wonderland-site.com
Michael Netzer
Mike Serrico
Nicolas Coster
Paul Davison
Peter Mark Richman
Robert Gillis
Robert Washburn
Ron Ely
S. Pearl Sharp

Special thanks to my "ChickTrip" pal Tracy Davis for gifting me with the "Wonder Woman" DVDs and starting off this whole project!

And thanks to my buddy Big Dee for all those "WW" posts on my Facebook wall, and for his support in general.

Bibliography of Supplemental Sources

Like the other books in the BRBTV fact book series, "Superchicks" was compiled and written, first and foremost, from BRB's own viewing and love of these two TV series (the episode synopses, for instance, are her own original content). BRBTV would like to acknowledge, however, the following supplemental sources, often attributed within the text, for extra fun facts and tidbits on the show:

- "The Complete Directory to Prime Time Network and Cable TV Shows, 1946 to Present," Tim Brooks and Earle Marsh, Ballantine Books, 2003.
- TV Guide magazine
- Internet Movie Database (IMDb)
- MyComicShop.com
- Seeing-Stars.com
- TV.com
- YouTube
- Wikipedia
- Wonderland-site.com
- WonderWomanMuseum.com
- WonderWoman-online.com for some good videos and print articles

> There's something about that goddess within, that secret part that resides in every woman that is a wonder woman. That yearns for that independence and strength. I've had more letters and stories retold to me of how 'Wonder Woman,' what it meant to them in their lives. And it always surprises me. And I'm so grateful to have had a role that is enduring.
> — Lynda Carter, "Wonder Woman" DVD interviews

Made in the USA
Lexington, KY
27 April 2013